To Write English

To Write English

A Step-by-Step Approach for ESL

Janet Ross
BALL STATE UNIVERSITY

Gladys Doty
UNIVERSITY OF COLORADO

HARPER & ROW, PUBLISHERS, New York
Cambridge, Philadelphia, San Francisco,
London, Mexico City, São Paulo, Singapore, Sydney

1817

Sponsoring Editor: Phillip Leininger
Project Editor: Ronni Strell
Text Design: Helen Iranyi
Cover Design: Caliber Design Planning, Inc.
Text Art: Fine Line, Inc.
Production: Delia Tedoff
Compositor: ComCom Division of Haddon Craftsmen, Inc.

Printer and Binder: The Murray Printing Company

To Write ENGLISH: A Step-by-Step Approach for ESL
Copyright © 1985 by Gladys G. Doty and Janet Ross
The previous edition of this book was entitled Writing English: A
Composition Text in English as a Foreign Language, Second Edition.

Library of Congress Cataloging in Publication Data

Ross, Janet.
  To write English.

  Bibliography: p.
  1. English language—Text-books for foreign speakers.
I. Doty, Gladys G.   II. Title.
PE1128.R689 1985   808'.042   84–10881
ISBN 0–06–045593–4
85 86 87 88 9 8 7 6 5 4 3 2 1

Contents

Lesson 1   **ESTABLISHING STEPS
IN THE WRITING PROCESS**   *4*

Rhetorical Principles: Limiting the subject; Topic
and thesis sentences; Developing an idea by details,
examples, and illustrations

Grammatical Patterns: Recognizing a sentence—
complete verbs, subordinate clauses; Present tense
for customary actions; Subject-verb agreement and
inclusion of unstressed words

Student Composition: Modern Marriage
in Japan   *17*

Lesson 2   **DEVELOPING GENERALIZATIONS AND
CONCLUSIONS**   *28*

Rhetorical Principles: Limiting the subject;
Awareness of the reader; Developing an idea by
facts, figures, citation of authority, comparison and
contrast

Grammatical Patterns: Present tense and present
continuous; Use and omission of articles; Commas
between items in a series and after long introductory
elements; Positions of adverbs; Avoiding
run-together or incomplete sentences; Punctuation of
sentences

conclusions; Using outside sources—taking notes, writing summaries; Writing essay examinations

Grammatical Patterns: Parallel structure; Reported speech; Sentence connectors; Subordinators

review of grammatical patterns; Spelling and
punctuation

Student Composition: A Solution to the Problem of
Littering in Curaçao   *223*

HANDBOOK

Preface

To Write English is designed to improve the written composition skills of intermediate or advanced students in classes of English as a foreign language. Such classes, in our experience, are composed of students who come from various countries, who have different levels of competence, and who have diverse ideas as to what "good" writing is. This text is designed to cope with problems presented by such a heterogeneous group and to provide each student with the writing skills that university professors in the United States expect of their students. More specifically, the purposes of the activities in this book are to show students how to round up a flock of ideas and present them in the most effective way, to cultivate respect for grammatical forms and conventions in writing that make the written word understandable to the reader, to provide activities that contribute to fluency, and to help students realize that written communication of ideas, though not easy, offers a great deal of satisfaction.

The following philosophy underlies the training provided here.

1. The period before the actual writing begins is an important dimension in the writing process. It is at this time that the student chooses the topic, clarifies his or her thoughts about it, and establishes the writing procedures that suit him or her best. Classroom discussion of possible topics for an assignment helps students get ideas and choose an angle from which to write.

2. Students write with more fluency when their writing involves them personally. The pressure of time in class assignments, in examinations, and in deadlines for term papers makes fluency in writing important.

3. Content and organization are of primary importance in writing. Rewriting is often a process of making changes in the content (adding, cutting out, or rearranging).

4. People write best when there are no premature and rigid attempts to correct their work. Editing is a last stage.

5. Writers should cultivate the habit of looking at what they are

writing from the reader's point of view. They need to consider the reader's possible interests, knowledge, and attitudes.

Each of the 10 lessons focuses on a different writing problem and presents rhetorical principles that might be used in the particular writing task. These principles are learned through reading and analysis of writing samples and discussion of student writing: how the writer worded the thesis sentence, developed his or her ideas, and—for longer compositions later in the course—organized the writing effectively. In the early lessons—until students gain confidence in writing—the assignments are kept simple and suggested topics accommodate students of varying proficiency in English. Students proceed from writing about what they know at first hand to writing about subjects that demand the use of material from outside sources. In other words, the assignments proceed from personal essays to academic writing required in college courses.

Because teachers find that almost every student of English as a foreign language needs some instruction in grammar, grammar exercises constitute roughly half of each lesson. Points introduced relate as far as possible to structures students may need to use for the writing assignment for that lesson. The use of these exercises is flexible. Some may be class activities and others assigned to individual students as needed. Still others may be omitted.

Because the authors believe that classroom procedures should be interesting to students and to the instructors as well, each lesson provides a variety of activities. Hence there are group exercises and class discussions as well as individual exercises in paraphrasing, summarizing, sentence building, modification of paragraphs, writing from dictation, and student speeches.

Procedures for the written composition in each lesson have evolved from long experimentation with various methods to find out which produce the best results. The lessons in this text were tried with classes in English composition for foreign students at the University of Colorado before the final version was written. The sequence of activities in each assignment begins with discussion of possible topics and the kinds of content needed to develop each. The students then choose a subject and in class begin jotting down ideas. Some may prefer to begin rapidly writing a rough draft and in the writing process generate ideas. With this procedure students have a chance to discover the composition process best suited to themselves and to their subject. They take the ideas home, think them over, and bring in a "first" draft of the composition for possible class discussion. This acquaints the instructor with student strengths and weaknesses in writing. It also provides an opportunity to give the students individual help. The students then complete and/or rewrite the first draft outside of class. In another class session, selected student compositions may be read and analyzed rhetorically for discussion of what is well done and what needs to be improved. After this, outside of class, the final draft is written. When the final draft is due, both drafts are handed in. In some cases more than two drafts beyond the rough version may be necessary to produce a final, excellent paper. The student should strive for the best possible formulation of the ideas and learn through writing what these will be. The instructor's written corrections on the first draft are optional. It is the authors' belief that all too often in composition classes too much time is spent correcting and grading papers rather than in helping the student in the process necessary to produce better papers. (At semester end, in answer to questionnaires about class procedures, students who used the materials on a trial basis consistently rated rewriting as the most valuable aspect of the course.)

In many ESL texts on writing, the handling of outside sources in research papers is presented in one or two chapters. We believe that such training must be introduced early and become a part of many lessons, because, for some students, lifting material from books and journals became routine in home countries and this practice presents problems in American classrooms. Demonstrations of paraphrasing ideas and summarizing the content of a paragraph or an essay are given a number of times throughout the text, as are explanations of footnoting and the manner in which credit can be given for the ideas of others.

Other features of the text designed to improve student writing are the use of examples of many kinds of writing of the type that students are expected to master and inclusion of student compositions both in early forms and in final refinement to show what is possible for students to accomplish. Included also is advice on how to write an evaluative essay or report, how to answer an essay question on an examination, how to write business letters in proper form, and procedures for term papers.

Following Lesson 10 is a Handbook containing numbered grammatical explanations to which students can be referred for individual study or which the instructor can use, if desired, in grading papers.

The Handbook as well as some of the grammar exercises and sample paragraphs in the text are taken from *Writing English,* second edition.

We thank the students from other countries in the composition classes at the University of Colorado who used the material for this book in trial form, and we thank Ruby Fulk for her typing of the manuscript.

Janet Ross
Gladys Doty

To Write English

WRITING AS A PROCESS

All writers of informational material, even professional ones, are faced with certain problems when approaching the writing task. They must ask themselves questions such as these: What can I say that my readers will want to know? How can I catch their interest? What do I say first? How do I begin the writing process? Do I take notes? Do I outline? Do I just start to write, putting down ideas as they occur to me and then sorting them out later? What means shall I use to develop the ideas and thus make them clear to my reader? Shall I use examples and illustrations? What details shall I include? Shall I restate or define? Shall I quote someone who is an authority in order to make my readers accept what I say? How do I arrange my ideas? The student whose native language is not English has additional problems. The means by which ideas are presented and clarified in formal writing in the native culture may be quite different from those that are expected in compositions in English. Vocabulary and grammar may also cause difficulties.

In creating the final version of an essay, no two writers go about their task in quite the same way. Yet they do proceed according to a plan, with some variations depending on the subject and purpose for writing. The emphasis throughout this text is on the process that goes into producing the final composition.

STEPS IN THE WRITING PROCESS.

Following are steps in the writing process that are used by many writers and that are presented in the lessons in this text.

Stage I. Prewriting
  Step 1. Brainstorming for ideas
  Step 2. Phrasing the thesis sentence
  Step 3. Jotting down ideas and refining a point of view

In this initial stage you select a subject, narrow it, and decide on the purpose and point of view. You may do the latter in part by jotting down things you want to say, perhaps in a list or perhaps by beginning to write a rough draft. Steps 2 and 3 may thus overlap, or in some cases, after working on them, you may go back to step 1 for a new subject.

Stage II. Giving Form to the Composition and Studying Techniques
  Step 4. Writing a first draft
  Step 5. Studying rhetorical principles

After your ideas are down on paper, you will study selected rhetorical devices that may make the final draft of your composition more effective.

Stage III. Critiquing and Revising
  Step 6. Analyzing and revising the first draft
  Step 7. Writing the final draft

In this stage you will analyze what you have written and apply what you learned in step 5 in a final version of the composition. As you critique the first draft, you will see how the subject can be developed and the ideas arranged more effectively. You will have an opportunity to get suggestions from your instructor and classmates. You will also check your final paper for accuracy in grammar and mechanics of writing.

INTRODUCTORY IN-CLASS EXERCISE.

In order to help your instructor understand your writing needs, to help you make the most of your abilities, and to help you understand some of the principles of sentence structure, write in complete sentences the answer to each of the following questions.

1. What is your native country and your native language?
2. What is your major subject and what year of school are you in? Are you a graduate or an undergraduate?
3. What kinds of compositions did you write in your own

language in school? (essays, poems, answers to essay
examination questions)
4. How many years have you studied English? Were your
teachers native speakers of English?
5. What kind of writing have you done in English?
6. In what way can writing easily in English help you in your
present activities? If you are in school, does your major subject
of study require reports, answers to questions in examinations,
term papers, a thesis or dissertation?
7. Will you need to write in English after you leave school? In
your profession? In your social life?

ESTABLISHING STEPS IN THE WRITING PROCESS

Rhetorical Principles*	Grammatical Patterns*

Limiting the subject
Topic and thesis sentences
Developing an idea by
   details, examples,
   and illustrations
	Recognizing a sentence:
	   Complete verbs
	   Subordinate clauses
	Present tense for customary
	   actions
	Subject-verb agreement and
	   inclusion of unstressed
	   words

Writing a Composition

Assignment: You come from countries with differing cultures and where different customs prevail. In an essay of 250 to 350 words acquaint your classmates and your instructor with some aspect of the culture of your country that might be different from theirs.

*The rhetorical principles and grammatical patterns listed at the beginning of each lesson are the topics covered in the lesson.

Stage I. Prewriting

STEP 1. BRAINSTORMING FOR IDEAS

EXERCISE 1.

Here are some aspects of the culture of your country about which you might exchange information with your fellow students and some questions about each that you might like answered. Read them quickly. The class will then pick three that they would like to discuss. You may suggest others that are not listed.

1. *Man-woman relationships*

Are schools coeducational? How does a person find a husband or wife? Where and how do they meet? How well do they know each other before marriage? In a household, who handles the finances and makes decisions about how money will be spent? Are certain duties expected of a husband and of a wife? What are they? Is it possible to exchange roles—with the husband or wife doing what is expected of a person of the opposite sex—without community criticism? Do women work outside the home? Are certain jobs traditionally held by men or by women? Do men and women workers receive equal pay for the same kind of work? Do men and women in general have the same level of education? Is there a double standard of conduct (men being allowed to do certain things without public censure that a woman would be censured for or vice versa)?

2. *Parent-child relationships*

Which parent usually makes day-to-day decisions about the child? Are small children generally allowed to do as they please or are they expected to obey parents? Are children brought up by their parents, or do children feel closer to a nursemaid who looks after them? Are children punished for misbehavior? If so, how? Does the child consider that a parent is a friend who is very close to the youngster, or is the parent one to be respected but hardly to be loved? In what ways is a child expected to show respect to the parents? At what age does a young man or woman "leave the nest"? Is there a "generation gap"? Do young people do things today that their parents do not approve of? Do children feel that their parents do not understand them?

3. *Differing customs in educated and uneducated families*

Is there more quarreling in less educated families? Are there lower or higher (or merely different) moral standards? Is the wife in a lower-class family considered more as a servant, the wife in the upper-class family more as someone to be cherished and respected? What is the attitude of lower-class to upper-class people and vice versa?

4. *Old people in society*

At what age is a person considered old? Is there an emphasis on youth in your culture and do older people try to look and act young? Are old people generally respected? In what ways do people show respect for them? Does the old person live with the children in the last years of life or in a retirement home? Does the government provide financially for old people? Do young people and old people dress differently? Do they like different kinds of entertainment? Do they engage in different activities? Are people required to retire at a certain age? Are benefits provided? Does one consult the family patriarch or matriarch before taking any important action?

5. *The role of religion*

Is there a predominant religion in your country? What other religions do some people believe in? Does religion prescribe certain customs? Does it forbid others? Do people mainly socialize with people of their own religion? Do people of different religions marry? How widespread is this? Are people of any religion discriminated against? How?

6. *Family treasures that reveal personality and character*

What sorts of things are considered treasures in your family? Are they cherished because they are expensive or because of the associations connected with them? What treasures of your family were handed down from a preceding generation? What do the treasures that your family has collected show about their interests? What treasures have you acquired, and why are they treasures? Do you collect any special thing? What is it? Do you expect to take home treasures from foreign travel? If so, what sorts of things?

7. *An event that changed the lives of my present family, my ancestors, or myself*

Did some historical event (such as a conquest, a migration, a change of government, a daring deed, meeting with a famous person) greatly affect your ancestors? How? What event changed the course of your parents' lives and thus yours (a new job, a revolution or war, a typhoon or tornado, a fire, an accident or illness, an unexpected opportunity)? Has any experience you have had changed the course of your life but not that of your family?

8. *Attitude toward ancestors*

Are pictures of ancestors displayed in your home? Are stories about ancestors handed down from generation to generation? Are certain ceremonies or customs regularly observed to honor ancestors? What is the attitude toward the family "black sheep"? Are there clubs or organizations in your country whose members are descended from a certain prestigious group? Are certain people honored in your society because they are descended from a famous person?

9. *Respected professions*

What professions in your country are most respected? Are these the professions that demand intellectual effort or some particular skill? Are they the ones with the highest monetary rewards? Can anyone from any class in society aspire to these professions? Does society limit the number of people who can go into these professions? Do sons generally follow the profession of their father? Are the rewards of prestigious professions sufficient to compensate for the effort to enter the profession? Is a person's status in society determined by profession? What are the least respected ways of earning a living? How are people in these occupatiosn treated?

10. *A typical family*

How big is the family? Is it an extended family or just the husband, wife, and children? What are means of family cohesion? (Do members of the family eat their meals together, play games together, engage in common tasks, exchange ideas, and value each others' opinions?) How important is the family as an institution in your country? How common is the single-parent family? Are there different types of families in your country (single-parent families, families of unrelated people, or families made up of several generations, and so on)? How common is the "live-in" arrangement of unmarried couples? Does the wife take the husband's name? Are children named for relatives? Does the family as an institution seem to be declining in your country?

11. *Characteristics of modern society*

What features make modern society in your country different from the society of the past? Is it a difference in values? In technology? In social structure and family relationships? Is there some value or point of view that is particularly important? What is it? Would you prefer to live in a more simple society, or are you eagerly anticipating future developments?

EXERCISE 2.

After class discussion, choose for your composition a general aspect of the culture of your country that you believe your classmates would like to hear about. It may be one of the topics that have been suggested, or you may prefer to write on another aspect of your culture.

STEP 2. PHRASING THE THESIS SENTENCE

It is impossible to write in an essay of limited length everything that can be said about a general topic. You cannot, for example, tell everything about parent-child relationships or about professions in your society in 250 to 350 words. You must narrow the subject by choosing some aspect of it to be discussed. You can do this by making a generalization or assertion or stating a conclusion about it that you will then expand and develop. A sentence that states the central idea of a paragraph is called a *topic sentence.* A sentence that states the central idea of an entire composition is the *thesis sentence.* Such sentences indicate the purpose of the writing or take a point of view toward it.

The following indicate how two of the topics suggested for this assignment may be narrowed and a topic sentence formulated:

Topic 1. Man-woman relationships
        Marriage customs
        Arranged marriages in my country

In my country, Japan, the custom of going through *omiai,* an arranged ceremonial first meeting, is an important part of the marriage process.

Topic 11. A characteristic of modern society
A value that is important in modern society

Measurement of time is extremely important in a modern technical society.

While you have a purpose in mind and may have formulated the thesis sentence before writing, you may modify it later as writing reveals what you want to say.

EXERCISE 3.

Read the following topic sentences for the subjects suggested in the assignment for this lesson. Then members of the class will suggest other topic sentences that might be used.

1. Man-woman relationships

The man should be the dominant member of the household.

2. Parent-child relationships

The "generation gap" exists in my culture.

3. Differing customs in educated and uneducated families

In my culture the women in educated families are more protected than those in uneducated families.

4. Old people in society

Treatment of the elderly in *(country)* reveals society's attitudes toward old people.

5. The role of religion

Religion prescribes social behavior in my country.

6. Family treasures

My family's treasures reveal their interest in travel.

7. An event that changed the life of my family

My search for my father during the last war changed my attitude toward America.

8. **Attitude toward ancestors**

Even in France where ancestor worship is not a custom, people are proud of their ancestors.

9. **Respected professions**

There are good reasons why parents in *(country)* want their sons to be lawyers, doctors, or teachers.

10. **A typical family**

Certain attitudes and behavior of my family make it typical of my country.

11. **Characteristics of modern society**

In my country certain traditions have been abandoned.

EXERCISE 4.

Formulate a tentative thesis sentence for the composition you will write.

STEP 3. JOTTING DOWN IDEAS AND REFINING A POINT OF VIEW

After you have narrowed your subject and tentatively formulated your thesis sentence, you begin to write down ideas that will go into your composition. This writing may be in the form of lists or notes, or you may generate ideas by beginning to write quickly as ideas occur to you. Following are examples of each method. After you have thought about your subject or started writing, you may find that what you want to say requires a somewhat different thesis sentence.

The Importance of Accurate Time in Modern Society

Need to measure fine degrees of time
Old methods : hour glass
* shadows (cave men) } not adequate now*
* falling water (Chinese)*
Present needs : mining - dynamite
* rockets - "blast off" time*
* giving medicine*
* getting to work and to appointments*

Arranged Marriages in Japan

In past - marriages arranged by nakodo - customary
W.W.II - change
Some Japanese wanted to be western
Ren'ai kekkon - became popular
But not all
    Many parents like nakodo system
        Good points - social status, economic background,
                girl and man's interests
     Old way - girl and man had to marry after omiai
     Today - Can reject, until it's a love match
Combination of omiai and choice - working out well

EXERCISE 5.

Jot down ideas that you will use in your composition.

Stage II. Giving Form to the Composition and Studying Techniques

STEP 4. WRITING A FIRST DRAFT

EXERCISE 6.

Write a first draft of your composition to bring to class for critiquing by your classmates and instructor. Try to pick a time for writing when there will be minimal distractions.

As you write, concentrate on communicating ideas. Be constantly aware of your readers' interests, knowledge, or lack of knowledge.

Try to group ideas that belong together and present them in a sequence that is easy to follow.

You may want to read sections aloud to see what you should add or delete or rearrange. Some writers find it helpful to read the whole composition to someone else. The listener may offer suggestions, and as you read, you may see where improvements can be made.

Matters of grammar and vocabulary can be taken care of later.

STEP 5. STUDYING RHETORICAL PRINCIPLES: DEVELOPING AN IDEA

It is not enough merely to state a conclusion or make an assertion. The reader is constantly asking three questions:

- What do you mean exactly?
- How do you know?
- Why do you think that?

Three ways to answer the question "What do you mean?" are by use of (1) specific details, (2) examples, and (3) illustration. Others will be presented in later lessons.

Development by Specific Details

In the following passage note how details support the conclusion that "In the oases of the Arab world, Arab men and women weave the distinctive fabric of their life."

LIFE IN AN ARAB OASIS*

In the oases [of the Arab world], large and small, Arab men and women weave the distinctive fabric of their life. New factories are breaking the monopoly of pyramids; new habits clash with old; yet within it all there is a fusion and a unity.

The fabric is visible in multitudinous details. A bearded old man, white turban wound tightly around his red fez, punctures the cold hours before dawn with his age-old cry: "Prayer is better than sleep!" A jet streaks through the pale sky as donkeys patter through village lanes. In government offices and in the bazaars, there is the rattle of spoons in glasses of mint tea. There is the hum of gossip as bolts of vivid cloth are unrolled before dark-eyed women. In coffee shops, the radio . . . blares the news of the day. In curbside stalls boys fan charcoal as meat is grilled. A scent of spice makes an ordinary street mysterious, and when the day ends, the night, identified in Arab poetry with the lover, brings magic under the sapphire stars. From the desert, beyond the minarets and palm trees, come the howls of jackals.

*Desmond Stewart and the editors of *Life, The Arab World* (New York: Time Incorporated, 1962), 10. Reprinted by permission.

EXERCISE 7.

Answer these questions about the passage you have just read.

1. What verbs show how the Arab men and women *weave* the distinctive fabric of their lives? Put appropriate verbs in the following blanks.

   A. New factories _____ the monopoly of the pyramids.
   B. The old man _____ the dawn with his cry.
   C. The jet _____ ; donkeys _____ .
   D. Boys _____ charcoal.
   E. The jackals _____ .

2. Note how the details focus on activities to explain what the verb *weave* means here. What details appeal to each of the following?

   A. sight _____
   B. hearing _____
   C. taste _____
   D. smell _____

Development by Examples

Note the use of several examples to support a conclusion in the following composition.

THE IMPORTANCE OF TIME IN MODERN CULTURE

(1) If one were asked to name items that are absolutely necessary for life in a modern technological culture, one of the things that would have to be mentioned are items that tell time. Clocks and watches that indicate not only hours but minutes and seconds are constantly needed.

(2) How would modern men and women in such cultures cope with the daily demands on their time if they had no more than shadows, such as those the cavemen used, to let them know how the day was progressing? How would an hourglass help to time competitors in Olympic races? Could the ancient Chinese clock of falling drops of water be carried around by today's

university students to keep track of time for classes? Or would they prefer to carry burning candles measured to indicate time?

(3) In every advanced culture today, knowing the exact time is certainly important. Processes in factories are often timed, not just to the hour but to the second. Miners have to know just how many minutes it will be before a blast of dynamite goes off. Aerospace rockets depend upon split-second timing for successful launches and other maneuvers. Bank vaults depend upon time clocks for opening. Nurses and anaesthetists often depend on minute and second hands to time the dispensing of drugs.

(4) However, it is not just industry and special businesses that are time oriented in our culture. The average worker uses an alarm clock or watch to wake up on time. At breakfast the three-minute soft-boiled egg must be timed. The family turns on the radio at an exact time to get the morning news, keeping an eye on the clock so that those who work outside the home will leave the house in time to avoid being late for work. A person may be somewhat bored with his or her job and ready to quit the moment the watch indicates that it is time for the midmorning coffee break. One's doctor's appointment after work is also at a specific hour and minute. After dinner, members of the family collapse in easy chairs and consult the TV schedule to find out what channels carry the best programs and at what time. The clock also tells them when to go to bed.

(5) What would we do without watches and clocks?

EXERCISE 8.

Answer these questions about the thesis sentence and the means of development used in the selection you have just read.

1. What is the thesis sentence? Is it stated in exactly the same way as it was in the example in step 2, p. 9? Why do you think the author changed it?

2. In step 3, p. 10, you saw some of the notes that the author used in planning the composition. Did she use all the examples of methods of telling time in the past that were in her notes? What did she add to these examples?
3. What examples of the importance of time in modern society do you find? List them.
4. Are the examples nouns or verbs?
5. What examples or details would you use to develop the following statements?

   a. It's a beautiful day.
   b. Good writing demands hard work.
   c. Some food requires long, slow cooking.
   d. Some students are unprepared for college.
   e. Preparing for a ski competition takes a long time.

Development by Illustration

Study the following passage and note that illustration is example in extended form. One illustration or one example needs other facts, figures, or testimony from an authority to support a conclusion, for one illustration might not be typical.

THE WISDOM OF THE MUD DAUBER WASP

Man can only marvel at the miracle of instinct--
at how various animals and insects, in order to
perpetuate their species, unerringly complete
a complicated process which no one taught them.
Take the case of the mud dauber wasp, so common
in the barns and attics in the United States.
The mother constructs a mud nest composed of
hundreds of tiny mud cells. After she fashions
each cell, she stings a spider (not killing it,
only anaesthetizing it), puts it in the cell,
and lays an egg upon it. Then she seals the cell
with mud and begins to construct another cell,
repeating the process of providing food for her
newborn and then laying the egg. The mother dies
before the young are hatched, but the young wasp
has been provided with vital fresh food enough
to last him until he can forage for himself.
When the new female wasp gets to be an adult, she

too will know, without being shown, exactly how
to do this.

EXERCISE 9.

Answer these questions about the use of illustration.

1. Which contains narrative—example or illustration?
2. Which of the following statements would you develop by
   example and which by illustration?

   a. The symptoms of the common cold are most annoying.
   b. You have to experience a disappointment before you can
      understand another person who is suffering from
      disappointment.
   c. Many great men were not appreciated when they were
      alive.
   d. I can never forget my embarrassment when I ate my first
      meal on an airplane.

State III. Critiquing and Revising

STEP 6. ANALYZING AND REVISING THE FIRST DRAFT

EXERCISE 10.

Check your first draft for the following rhetorical points:

1. What is the central idea? Is it stated clearly in a sentence?
   Does it say what you want to say? If not, restate it.
2. Are the ideas that you present sufficiently developed so that
   the reader clearly understands what you mean? If not, add
   details, examples, or illustrations that might make your ideas
   more effective.
3. As a result of your writing and thinking about your subject
   and on the basis of class discussion, are there other ideas that
   should be included to make a more effective composition? Is
   there material that should be omitted? Should the material be
   rearranged to make the relationship between ideas clearer?

   Study the following composition written for the assignment in
this lesson and be prepared to comment on how it was developed
through steps 1 to 6.

MODERN MARRIAGE IN JAPAN
Tomiko Sato, Japan

(1) Before World War II, when a young woman in Japan reached her early twenties, the customary age for marriage, the parents called in the nakodo, the marriage arranger. The nakodo was generally an elderly woman who was acquainted with all the families in the vicinity and knew their social and economic status and what their interests were. Probably she had known the young people since they were children. Thus she could judge who would make a good pair. After she selected a mate for the young woman, the families of the two planned an omiai, a ceremonial first meeting. This generally took place in a restaurant. After introductions, the young couple were left alone for a time to get to know each other. They were expected to marry, since their parents, with the help of the nakodo, had selected them for each other.

(2) Today many young people consider an omiai kekkon, or arranged marriage, old-fashioned. They want to be like their counterparts in Western culture and have a ren'ai kekkon, a love marriage. My friend Kyoko is such a person. On her return from study in the United States, her parents thought it was time for her to marry, but she said she would never consent to going through an omiai. She had a good job as a translator and secretary in a business firm and would find a husband for herself. Like most Japanese, she is a practical person and knew the advantage of having a mate of the same general background, whose personality would be congenial and who would share her interests. Unfortunately, however, she did not meet such a person. Her job was demanding, she worked long hours, and she did not have much time for social activities. She came to realize that such an important matter as marriage should not be left to chance. Like many young girls today, she reluctantly agreed to an omiai.

(3) An omiai of today is not quite like an omiai

of the past, however. If the couple who meet are not attracted to each other, they are not obliged to marry. They may, instead, go through another <u>omiai</u>. Or they may avoid the <u>omiai</u> and consult a computer marriage service, which matches the characteristics of the young man and young woman. There are about 500 such computer services in Japan today.

(4) Kyoko chose to try the <u>omiai</u>. Of the first man she met that way, she said, "He was a real bore. He just wanted to give me a lot of statistics about his job and didn't want to listen to anything I had to say." She rejected the second one because he was the eldest son and would have the major responsibility of looking after his parents. Finally, on the fifth <u>omiai</u>, she and the young man were immediately attracted to each other. Contrary to custom in the past, they dated for several months before marriage. They are now on a honeymoon in Hawaii and are very happy.

(5) About 40 percent of the girls in Japan nowadays will admit that theirs was an <u>omiai kekkon</u>. Most will say they married for love. Yet, as the example of Kyoko illustrates, an <u>omiai kekkon</u> can be a <u>ren'ai kekkon</u> too.

EXERCISE 11.

Answer these questions about the sample composition.

1. What is the central idea? Where is it stated? How has it changed since the limitation stated in step 2, p. 9?
2. List some details that the author uses.
3. Do you find any use of examples?
4. What illustration does the author use?
5. How did the author expand the material beyond the rough draft written in step 3, p. 11?

STEP 7. WRITING THE FINAL DRAFT

EXERCISE 12.

After you have analyzed your first draft for the points mentioned in exercise 11 and made changes, read it carefully, perhaps aloud, to check for wording. You may wish to make a second draft before preparing the final one. Before you make the final copy check the composition carefully for the following grammatical points.

1. Is each sentence complete (with a subject and complete verb)?
2. Are clauses with subordinating words, such as *although, if, since, because, when,* or *so that,* preceded or followed by a main clause in the same sentence?
3. Are the adverbs in the correct place in the sentence (not between the verb and the object)?
4. When using the present tense, have you included the *-s* on the end of the verb when the subject is singular?
5. Have you included needed articles and prepositions?

If you have questions on these points, check the grammar exercises at the end of this lesson.

Check your paper also for spelling and punctuation. Copy it neatly and turn it in in the form required by your instructor. Hand in the first draft along with the final one.

Reviewing Grammatical Patterns

These exercises are designed for use at the discretion of your instructor. A given exercise may be assigned to one student or to a few students who have the same problem. If a certain problem is common to sufficient numbers in the class, the exercise on it may be used in class.

RECOGNIZING A SENTENCE

Study sections A1a and A1b in the Handbook. These sections will acquaint you with the components of a sentence and show you various types of sentences that are common in English. Such knowledge is basic to writing.

GRAMMAR EXERCISE 1.

In the following sentences, draw one line under the subjects and two under the verbs and complements (predicates). Note that a sentence may contain more than one subject, verb, or complement.

1. Even professional writers think that writing is not easy.
2. Everyone needs to discover his best time to write and the conditions under which he writes best.
3. Ernest Hemingway liked to write before others were awake.
4. Leon Uris considered himself a twilight writer.
5. Uris considered four to seven in the late afternoon better than any other period of the day for writing.
6. Victor Hugo always wore a robe when he wrote.
7. His valet took away his clothing and would not return it until the time that Hugo expected to be through with his day's writing.
8. Joseph Conrad prayed about his writing.
9. Françoise Sagan sometimes walked around her typewriter and screamed at it.
10. A student must not conclude that he is the only one who has trouble getting started.

GRAMMAR EXERCISE 2.

Which of the sentences in the preceding exercise contain more than one subject-predicate pattern (clause)? Explain.

Complete Verbs

Study section A1d in the Handbook to review the difference between participles and full verbs.

GRAMMAR EXERCISE 3.

Put a check mark before each of the following that are not complete verbs. Discuss with your instructor verb forms that are not complete without an auxiliary.

do	went	speaking
written	recited	am
are speaking	was talking	had gone
am speaking	had spoken	will go
are going	goes	ought to go
am talking	have gone	shall go
taking	wrote	can go
have spoken	talk	going
go		

GRAMMAR EXERCISE 4.

Some of the following word groups with verbals are complete sentences. Some are not. Put a check mark in front of those that are sentences, and punctuate them correctly. Using the preceding patterns as a guide, complete those that are not and punctuate them correctly. Note that some of the word groups may be completed in more than one way.

1. The water dripping from the roofs _____.
2. The speaker interested me in his subject _____.
3. The lecture interesting to those who want jobs _____.
4. The table covered with a yellow cloth _____.
5. A yellow cloth covered the table _____.
6. My friend seeing all of those exhibits _____.
7. The helicopter is hovering over us _____.
8. An item listed in the paper _____.
9. A professor giving a lecture _____.
10. The professor given a good lecture _____.
11. The work begun none too soon _____.
12. The work has been done excellently _____.
13. That man listening to me _____.
14. That fellow to go to the farm with me _____.
15. They were known as good fellows _____.

Subordinate Clauses

Study "Combining Sentences with Subordinators," section A2b in the Handbook and "Uses of Subordinators," section H23.

GRAMMAR EXERCISE 5.

Combine each group of words that is not a complete sentence with another group of words to form a complete, meaningful sentence. Use periods and capitalization appropriately. You may need to add or delete words when ideas are combined.

while they write
some students like to listen to music or munch nuts.

Some students like to listen to music or munch nuts while they write.

1. writing is not easy
2. even if you are a professional writer

3. Ernest Hemingway wrote best in the morning
4. before others were awake
5. Victor Hugo's valet took the writer's clothes away from him
6. otherwise Hugo might not have stuck to his writing
7. when she was frustrated with her writing
8. Françoise Sagan screamed at her typewriter
9. Joseph Conrad wrote in English
10. although his native language was Polish
11. since Conrad could write in whatever language he chose
12. his frustration must not have been simply because he wrote in a foreign language

GRAMMAR EXERCISE 6.

Without referring to material in previous exercises, complete the following sentences in your own words.

1. Even if a person is not a professional writer _____ .
2. Since _____ , students may expect to spend time and energy in writing.
3. When she became frustrated in writing, Françoise Sagan _____ .
4. It is comforting to know that even great writers _____ .
5. Because _____ , I feel that I am something like Joseph Conrad.
6. I am not like Victor Hugo because _____ .
7. Before I write, I _____ .
8. Whenever I have to write a term paper, _____ .
9. I wonder if the day will ever come when I can write in English _____ .
10. I study writing in English so that _____ .

GRAMMAR EXERCISE 7.

Underline the adverbial elements in the sentences of the preceding exercise. Tell where adverbial clauses occur in a sentence.

PRESENT TENSE FOR CUSTOMARY ACTIONS

The present tense of verbs is used for customary actions.

GRAMMAR EXERCISE 8.

Supply the correct verb form in the following sentences about wedding customs in the United States. Remember that the third-person singular of verbs (except certain auxiliary verbs) ends in -s.

1. The bride's parents _____ (pay) the expenses of the wedding.
2. The groom's parents _____ (host) the wedding party (the bride and groom, the attendants, and parents) at a dinner on the evening before the wedding.
3. There is a tradition that on the day of the wedding a bridegroom _____ (not) _____ (see) the bride before the ceremony.
4. The bride usually _____ (wear) white.
5. At the wedding ceremony the bride who _____ (follow) tradition _____ (wear) something old, something new, something borrowed, and something blue.
6. A betrothal party _____ (be) not a usual occurrence. However, sometimes one of the parents _____ (send) an announcement to the local newspaper.
7. One feature of the wedding _____ (be) the reception afterward.
8. Receptions _____ (be) often simple, with a wedding cake and punch served in the church dining room.
9. Sometimes a reception _____ (be) elaborate, with a buffet supper, an orchestra, and dancing.
10. At the end of the reception the bride and groom _____ (leave) for a honeymoon.
11. Since traveling on a honeymoon _____ (be) often by automobile, friends often _____ (play) pranks on the couple by tying a string of tin cans to the back of the car, painting the car with the sign "Just married," decorating the car with crepe paper, or stuffing the inside of the car full of crumpled newspaper.
12. To avoid such pranks, a wise groom _____ (hide) his car during the wedding ceremony.

SUBJECT-VERB AGREEMENT AND INCLUSION OF UNSTRESSED WORDS

GRAMMAR EXERCISE 9.

Your instructor will read aloud the following paragraph once in its entirety at a normal rate of speed and with normal reduction of vowels in unstressed words. Then he or she will dictate it, pausing at intervals marked by the slash marks (/). Do not look at the paragraph before you write. After you have finished, compare your writing with what was dictated.

Students with little background in English may wish to copy the selection first, then write from dictation without looking at the copy.

HOW A WRITER SPENDS HIS DAY

My friend Paul is a writer./ He likes to get up early in the morning/ before anyone else has gotten up./ When he gets up/ he makes a pot of coffee/ and then works for two hours before breakfast./ He says that he thinks better/ at this time of day./ After breakfast he usually goes for a walk/ and then returns and works for two hours before lunch./ In the afternoons he sometimes plays tennis/ and then revises what he has written in the morning./ Some people dislike getting up early./ They groan when the alarm goes off./ They say they can't think before ten o'clock./ They love to stay up at night, however,/ and they do their best work then.

Check the verbs in the paragraph you have written. When did you put a final -*s* on a verb? Why? Check your writing with the paragraph in the textbook. Were you correct in your use of final -*s* on verbs? Did you omit any of the small function words (articles, prepositions, conjunctions)?

Unstressed Words—*a, an, the*

GRAMMAR EXERCISE 10.

If your native language does not contain articles *(a, an,* and *the)*, you may have difficulty in knowing when and when not to use them. The following exercises are designed to give you training in awareness of articles in the speech of native speakers of English.

After your instructor says each of the following words or word groups (with the rate and with the vowel reduction of normal speech), tell him whether he said one, two, or three words. He or she will repeat word groups in which you have not heard the unstressed words.

friend	a talk	an eraser
a friend	for a talk	a piece
of a friend	floor	of chalk
to a friend	student	of a talk
on the table	examination	talk
to the table	an examination	the theme
job	the table	to an examination
for a job	table	hamburger
a shoe	from the table	a hamburger
the shoe		

Now your instructor will dictate these words and phrases to you. When you have completed the exercise, check what you wrote with the preceding list, and tell your instructor how many words and phrases you heard correctly.

GRAMMAR EXERCISE 11.

Repeat each of the following sentences after your instructor. He or she will make normal use of /ə/ in unstressed syllables. Then tell whether *a* or *the* is used in the sentence.

1. I see a pencil.
   /ə/

2. The pencil is lying on the desk.
   /ðə/

3. There is a chalkboard here.
   /ə/

4. It's at the front of the room.
   /ət/ðə/   /əv/ðə/

5. It's behind the instructor's desk.
   /ðə/

/ðə/
6. The students sit in chairs.

/ðə/
7. Their books are on the floor.

/ə/
8. I know a student from Greece.

/ən/
9. He lives in an apartment.

/ðə/
10. The apartment is below mine.

/əv/ðə/
11. We take some of the same courses.

Unstressed Words—Prepositions

GRAMMAR EXERCISE 12.

After your instructor says each of the following sentences, tell what preposition was used in the sentence. Again, your instructor will use unstressing as in normal speech. (Prepositions that will be used are *of, to, at, from, but,* and *for.*)

/tə ðə/
1. Last night I went to the movies.

/ət/
2. The show began at seven o'clock.

/wəz frəm/
3. My companion was from India.

/əv ðə/   /wəz ə/
4. Outside of the theater was a long line.

/n/
5. We got in line.

/wəz/   /n ðə/
6. But it was unpleasant out in the cold.

/tə ðə/
7. Once inside, we went over to the counter.

/səm/ /ən/ /ə/
8. We got some popcorn and paid a lot for it.

/n ðə/ /əv ðə/
9. We sat in the back of the theater.

/əv/
10. Alongside of us were two people who talked constantly.

/tə/
11. We moved to another spot.

END NOTES

1. Keep a list of words that you misspell. Review the correct spelling each time before you write a new composition.
2. Do not capitalize subjects studied in school unless they refer to a country or geographical area (German, Japanese, Middle Eastern affairs, but geometry, chemistry, geography).
3. Capitalize the first word of every sentence and use appropriate end punctuation.
4. Write out numbers to 10 (one, two, three), except with ages, measurements, and percentages. Use figures for numbers 10 and over.
5. *Few—a few. Few* stresses the small number.

   He has few (almost no) friends.
   He has a few (some) faults, but I like him just the same.

DEVELOPING
GENERALIZATIONS
AND CONCLUSIONS

Rhetorical Principles

Limiting the subject
Awareness of the reader
Developing an idea by
facts, figures, citation
of authority, comparison
and contrast

Grammatical Patterns

Present tense and present
continuous
Use and omission of articles
Commas between items in a
series and after long
introductory elements
Positions of adverbs
Avoiding run-together or
incomplete sentences
Punctuation of sentences

Writing a Composition

Assignment: To write a composition (of 300 to 500 words) informing your classmates about some aspect of your hometown or your country, developing it by means of facts, figures, citations from authority, comparison, contrast, example, illustration, or details.

Stage I. Prewriting

STEP 1. BRAINSTORMING FOR IDEAS

EXERCISE 1.

Your hometown (home country) is the general subject for this composition. Quickly look over the suggested topics that follow and choose three that appeal to you for class discussion. Your instructor will find which subjects are the most popular and conduct discussion of probable details that could be used for these topics. The discussion will inform each writer about the probable interests of potential readers.

1. *Tourist attractions*
What attracts tourists to your country? To your hometown? Is it the beauty of certain places? The climate? Recreational facilities? Museums, cathedrals, palaces? Historical significance? What do travel folders say about the country? To what degree do you think they paint a true picture? What places are not especially famous but you believe are worth seeing? If tourists want to get acquainted with people in your country, where should they go? What language(s) do people in your country speak?

2. *Customs a visitor needs to understand*
How do some of the customs in your country differ from those you have found here? Are there customs in introductions that are important? What types of clothing are approved or disapproved of? When guests are invited to dinner, are they supposed to arrive at an exact time? How long should they stay? Is a dinner guest expected to bring a gift? Can anyone attend services in your places of worship? Is certain dress required in your places of worship? When should you tip in your country and how much? What advice can you give the visitor who rents a car for travel in your country?

3. *Misconceptions*
Do people think there isn't much to see there, that it is too hot (or too cold) for a pleasant vacation? Do people think that people in your country are antagonistic to tourists? Do they think travel is too difficult there? Do people think that there are no souvenirs to be had

there? Do people think you dress in native costume and spend most of your time in festivals? Do people think it is dangerous to travel in your country when it really is not? Do people fail to realize the industrial development that has taken place in your country?

4. *Historical background*

When was your town built? By whom? Was the town built because of a strategic location, because it was the home of remarkable people, or because it was the site of an important industry? Or was it the crossroads for trade? How has your town changed through the years, and what historical events have changed it? What historical events are commemorated by monuments or statues? Explain. Do the facial characteristics, the stature, the clothing, the speech, and/or the names of people reveal different ethnic backgrounds? Do people of certain ethnic backgrounds tend to live in certain sections of the city? What brought these people to your hometown? How does the size of the town compare with the size 100 or 200 years ago? What caused the increase or decrease? What changes have resulted from the change in size?

5. *Appearance*

Is the town located in the mountains, on a plain, on the ocean front, on a river bank? What do the surroundings look like? (Is the area arid, lush with vegetation?) If there are many plants in and around the town, are they tropical, grown in temperate zones, or grown in the arctic? What style of architecture is found in the homes and public buildings? Are there parks and public gardens, and if so, what do they look like? Are the streets wide or narrow, beautified by shrubs and flowers, paved in some way? What does the typical home look like? Is there a garden around it? Do people mostly live in apartments? What kinds of vehicles are on the streets? What kinds of activities do you see? How do people dress?

6. *The place in my country that I enjoy most*

What is it? Where is it? Why do you enjoy it? Is it more enjoyable in some seasons than in others? Do you have to pay to see it? Do many people go there? Is it a place that tourists might visit? Do you go there only occasionally or often? Do you go alone or with someone else? Can one get there easily?

7. *An important industry*

How has it influenced the daily life of the people who work there? Where is it located (in many towns, in the country, in one town, in a large city)? How is life different now from the way it was before the industry was introduced? (Give some figures or statistics that show the importance of the industry as compared with others.) What is the future of the industry in the life of your country? What kinds of skill does the industry call for? Is it done in a factory or by individuals in their homes? If you have worked in the industry, describe the process.

8. *Shopping tips*

What products are famous in your country? Where can the products generally be purchased? Are there places where one can get them more cheaply than in prestigious shops? Are some products characteristic of certain parts of the country? Explain. Are they sold in shops, from homes, in central markets or bazaars? Is bargaining common? How can the visitor gauge what the value is by the beginning price named by the seller? For the person who does not know anything about the product, where can one get reliable information? Do you have advice about how to judge quality items? By what means can items be paid for (checks, traveler's checks, credit cards)?

EXERCISE 2.

Choose some general aspect of your hometown or country for the subject of your composition. There may be some other limited aspect that you would prefer to write about and that would be of interest to your reader. Feel free to do so.

STEP 2. PHRASING THE THESIS SENTENCE

EXERCISE 3.

Here are possible thesis sentences for the suggested topics. Study them, and then suggest others that might be used.

1. Tourist attractions

Though *(country)* is not as famous for its tourist spots as some other countries are, there is still much in it that will be of interest to a visitor.

2. Customs a visitor needs to understand

Knowledge of certain customs in *(country)* will help the visitor enjoy his stay.

3. Misconceptions

I am constantly puzzled by the odd misconceptions that people have about the industrial development in *(country)*.

4. Historical background

The history of my home town is reflected in the architecture, the monuments, and the faces of the people.

5. Appearance

My hometown is beautiful (is typical of towns in my country, is not beautiful but is an interesting one).

6. The place in my country that I enjoy most

There is one spot in my country that I enjoy above all others.

7. An important industry

People who enjoy Iranian dates often do not know about the careful tending that date trees require.

8. Shopping tips

Visitors to *(city, country)* will do well to learn certain facts about shopping there.

EXERCISE 4.

Formulate a thesis sentence for the composition you will write.

STEP 3. JOTTING DOWN IDEAS AND REFINING A POINT OF VIEW

EXERCISE 5.

Jot down ideas that will help you to develop your topic (or start writing a first draft if ideas flow better by doing that).

You may want to read the example composition, page 41–42. Here are notes the author made before writing it.

Burgos - Las Huelgas Museum - unusual
Tombs of nobility -{ buried 700 years ago
{ opened after Civil War - 1930's
Clothes show something about life of Spanish people of
*   Middle Ages.*
Moorish influence on Christians
*   Queen Eleanor - describe clothes, pillow*
*   Marriage*
*   Ferdinand de la Cerda - describe clothes*
Made history seem human.
Thesis sentence: Las Huelgas Museum is a place that
*   would be interesting for tourists to visit.*

Stage II. Giving Form to the Composition and Studying Techniques

STEP 4. WRITING A FIRST DRAFT

EXERCISE 6.

As you write, use techniques you found valuable in writing the composition for the first lesson. Here, briefly, are procedures some writers find helpful.

- Write as quickly as possible, focusing on ideas.

- Try to make your points clear and interesting to the reader.

- Group ideas that belong together and present them in a sequence that is easy to follow.

- Read the first draft aloud. You may have a listener or imagine that you have one.

- Revise as needed. Good writing involves revision.

- Check grammar, spelling, and punctuation later.

STEP 5. STUDYING RHETORICAL PRINCIPLES

Limiting the Subject

As we discussed earlier in this lesson and in Lesson 1, you must limit your subject so that it can be discussed adequately within the scope of your paper.

Awareness of the Reader

You must be aware of how knowledgeable your readers are about your subject and of how much interest they have in it. If the readers know little about the topic, you may have to offer more facts or compare or contrast what you are discussing with something that is familiar. If the readers are likely not to be interested, you may have to spark interest in your introduction by showing how the subject relates to them or by explaining how you became interested in it.

Developing an Idea

In Lesson 1 you saw how an assertion, a generalization, or a conclusion can be developed by details, examples, or illustration to make the idea clear to the reader. Other methods of development are facts, figures, quotations from authority, comparison, and contrast. Study the following examples of these methods and decide which ones can be used to advantage in your present composition.

Development by facts. A fact is a statement that can be verified by someone, or that could have been verified by someone in the past, as being the truth. In the following paragraph note the facts about porcelain that help prove the statement in the topic (subject) sentence of the paragraph (the second sentence in the paragraph).

WHY PORCELAIN IS EXPENSIVE

My country, France, is known for its fine porcelain. Pieces of pottery and chinaware made out of porcelain are more expensive than objects made out of other kinds of clay, and they are well worth the difference in price. Porcelain products are more translucent than other pottery, and white porcelain is also whiter. Porcelain is also harder than other materials and thus is less likely to be broken. There are two reasons for this. When shaped and decorated, porcelain is fired in a kiln at a temperature of 1,300° to 1,500°C. Therefore, if one pours hot liquids into porcelain cups and bowls, they do not break. Also porcelain is a good conductor of heat and does not expand as rapidly as glass or inferior clay.

EXERCISE 7.

Answer these questions on the preceding paragraph.

1. How would the content of the paragraph be changed if the first sentence were the subject sentence?
2. Which of the statements made in the subject sentence does the paragraph develop?
3. How many facts can you list that the author uses to support the main point?

Development by figures or statistics. Figures often make a point perfectly convincing. We may say that automobile accidents are increasing, but if we give the number of automobile accidents last year as compared with the number 10 years ago, our reader can see the problem more clearly. In quoting figures, remember the following:

- Use only reliable sources for figures
- Quote the figures accurately
- Make sure the figures are up-to-date
- Present the figures in some kind of rememberable form. Use "round" numbers (*nearly 1 million* instead of *998,986*) or percentages and fractions.

Statistics are figures that are inferred from scientifically selected instances. Polls such as the Gallup poll may report that 35 percent of the people in the United States are in favor of a certain governmental policy, but this does not mean that every voter in the United States was queried in order to arrive at that figure. A scientifically determined sample of people from high-income, low-income, and middle-income groups, a certain number of Republicans and Democrats, and so on, are interviewed. From the figures obtained by interviewing sample numbers of Americans, the pollsters make predictions about the whole population. In using statistics, a writer must make sure of the following:

1. The *source* of the statistics must be a reliable one and must be made known to the reader.
2. The date when the statistics were gathered must be relevant to what is being said. If you are writing about current matters, the statistics must be recent.
3. The statistics must be *representative.* They must be scientifically

classified. If you write that women are better drivers than men because women drivers had fewer accidents than men had last year, the reader will want to know whether women had fewer accidents because there were fewer women driving cars. Handle statistics with care.

The following paragraph illustrates the use of figures to develop a point.

ICE: A LUCKY PHENOMENON

Ice, which causes water pipes in houses to burst and radiators in cars to crack, may be a lucky phenomenon. Imagine a winter world in which the creeks, rivers, and lakes in temperate zones are ice from top to bottom and where oceans are solid ice for many feet down. Ships could not be used for many months of the year, and, for some cities, drinking water would be difficult to get. Such a catastrophe does not happen because of a strange phenomenon of nature. All substances, except one, shrink when they freeze, thus becoming heavier. Water expands when it becomes frozen, so that 11 cubic feet of water becomes 12 cubic feet of ice. The 12 cubic feet of ice weighs only 56.9 pounds, while the water weighs 62.5 pounds. Since ice is lighter than water, it floats, and a river or ocean does not become solid ice from the bottom up. Because of this, commerce by ship is often still possible in the winter, and drinking water is available. This characteristic of ice is thus helpful to man.

EXERCISE 8.

Answer these questions about the preceding paragraph.

1. What is the subject sentence of the paragraph?
2. What use of figures do you find?
3. What other means of development are used? Give examples.

Development by citation of authority. In order to support a point, we sometimes need to cite an authority whose judgment our readers respect. When we do this, we must be sure that the one we quote is really an authority and that our readers will recognize the person as such. If they may not know him or her, we give information to indicate the person's competence. Here is an example of citing an authority to support a point.

FLYING SAUCERS: ARE THEY REAL?

(1) "I saw this thing coming up right over the top of the canning factory last night," said Mrs. John J. Smith of Jasonville, Michigan. "It seemed to be coming from the field behind the building. It was sort of flat and round like a plate and made quite a bright light. It kind of stayed there a minute just over the building and then went off to the right somewhere." The account of another strange light given by Mr. and Mrs. Phillip Doe of Losantville, California, is even more vivid. "We were driving home about 11 o'clock," Mrs. Doe said, "and this bright thing seemed to land in the middle of the road. Then it moved over into the trees. Two figures got out but they ran back into the space ship as we drove forward."

(2) Did these people really see "flying saucers," objects from outer space? What do scientists say about unidentified flying objects? Recently a two-year study of UFOs, funded by the U.S. Air Force and headed by a former director of the National Bureau of Standards, concluded that there was no evidence of manmade objects from outer space invading the earth. However, when Peter Sturrock, an astrophysicist and director of the Institute for Plasma Research at Stanford University, read the report, he felt that the conclusions did not follow from the case histories. "This is not the way science usually works," he said. A poll of his own professional association, the American Astronomical Society, revealed that nearly one in every five members had seen something he could not explain. Sturrock recently organized a new society, called the Society for Scientific Exploration, to provide a forum for the scientist who wishes to

investigate UFOs and other phenomena outside
the normal description.[1]

(3) All this does not prove that extraterrestrial beings are sending spaceships to the
earth. According to a pilot and atmospheric
scientist at the Massachusetts Institute of
Technology, "The whole matter could be settled
in two years. Air-traffic- control radar and
military radar blanket almost the entire
country. If UFOs are solid objects, they will
register. All that is needed is a mandate to the
Federal Aviation Administration and the
military to pay attention to anomalous blips."[2]
As yet, however, the unidentified flying
objects that people claim they see remain
largely unidentified.

[1]John P. Wiley, Jr., "Phenomena, Comments,
and Notes," *Smithsonian* 13 (August 1982): 27.
[2]Ibid., 28.

EXERCISE 9.

Answer these questions on the preceding selection.

1. Which authority is more convincing: the eye witnesses, the
   named scientist, the unnamed pilot? Why are all three quoted?
2. Is there any indirect quotation from authority?
3. Do any of the citations prove the existence of unidentified
   flying objects?
4. Do any prove that they come from extraterrestrial beings in
   outer space?
5. What is the central idea of the selection? Where is it stated?

Development by comparison. Comparison is often used effectively
to explain a complex point in terms of something that the reader
knows. If readers can picture what they do not understand in terms
of what they do understand, it helps them see the new process or
situation more clearly. Of course, it is important that the things being
compared are actually comparable. It would be of little use (as well
as impossible) to explain the organization of a government by comparing it to a gasoline engine. Note the things that are compared in
the paragraph that follows.

HOW NEURONS "FIRE"*

The neurons, or nerve cells in your brain, function to pass information from one part of the body to another. Each nerve cell contains a certain amount of stored up electrical energy that it can discharge in short bursts very much like the firing of a gun. . . . Whenever a wave of electrical energy passes from the fibers of one cell to those of another, we say that the nerve has fired, because the action involved is much like the firing of a gun. There is a great deal of potential energy stored in the chemical gunpowder in a bullet. When you pull the trigger on a gun, you translate this potential chemical energy to the mechanical energy of an explosion, and the bullet is propelled down the barrel of the gun. And when a neuron fires, it translates its resting potential into a burst of electrochemical energy.

Every time you move a muscle or think a thought, or experience an emotion you do so in part because one group of nerve cells in your brain <u>fires off</u> messages like a machine gun to your muscles, glands, or other groups of neurons.

EXERCISE 10.

Answer these questions about the preceding passage.

1. The preceding selection is part of a chapter in a book. As we have said, not every paragraph in longer expository writing contains a subject sentence, but it does have a central idea which the reader grasps easily. What is the central idea that is not expressed in this selection?
2. What is the basic comparison that is used?
3. Do you think the comparison is effective in helping the reader understand the subject? Why or why not?

Development by contrast. Comparison is a means of pointing out similarities; contrast emphasizes differences. Both comparison and

*Adapted from James V. McConnell, *Understanding Human Behavior*, 3d ed. (New York: Holt, Rinehart and Winston, 1974), 40–41.

contrast can be used effectively to make a point clear. In describing one country we sometimes need to contrast conditions in a different country, as is done in the following passage about the American frontier.

THE AMERICAN FRONTIER*

To Americans the word <u>frontier</u> has a meaning quite different from its use in Europe. There the frontier is a stopping place, a place patrolled by guards, where one must show his papers before passing through. But the American frontier has meant freedom, opportunity, room to expand in. It is not a stopping place but an open door, not a place where you must identify yourself, but a place where you can escape identification if you wish, a place where civilization has not established its rigid pattern, where spaces are wide and men can make their own laws.

The feeling that the frontier was there, to the west, even if a man did not choose to go there, has always been a conditioning factor in the American temperament. The frontier, in American thought, was a place beyond civilization where nature took over from man and where the evils concocted by human duplicity were washed away by great rivers, the wide sky, the brisk, clean air.

EXERCISE 11.

Answer these questions about the preceding selection.

1. What is the subject sentence of the selection?
2. What two things are contrasted?
3. What words or phrases in the selection itself emphasize the contrast?

Stage III. Critiquing and Revising

STEP 6. ANALYZING AND REVISING THE FIRST DRAFT

EXERCISE 12.

Check your first draft for these points about content.

*From Bradford Smith, *Why We Behave Like Americans* (New York: J. B. Lippincott Company, 1957). Reprinted by permission.

1. Have you narrowed the subject sufficiently? Do you need to restate the central idea?
2. Have you been aware of what the reader already knows and what will be new and of interest? Are there ideas you wish to add or delete?
3. Have you taken advantage of the best ways to develop your ideas? Have you created interest by using more than one form of development?

_____

Read the following student composition and answer the questions that follow it.

THE MUSEUM OF LAS HUELGAS
Carlos Balaquer, Spain

(1) Tourists in Madrid of course see the palace and the armory, go to the Prado, attend a bullfight, and go to a nightclub to watch flamenco dancers. I recommend a longer stay that would include a one-day trip to Burgos with its noted cathedral and the nearby convent, Las Huelgas. The convent means much to me, and I think others would find it interesting--for a very unusual reason.

(2) The reason is the things that are displayed there. The museum is different from any other in Europe, I am told. Some of the exhibits are people who were buried 700 years ago. You may think that you would not like to see such things. I would not either if they were in bad condition. However, they are not, and what stories they have to tell!

(3) During the Middle Ages this convent admitted only noble ladies, and people have always been interested in the wealth that has been buried with titled people. Some of the caskets were opened during the Napoleonic invasion. Others were opened only after the Civil War ended in the 1930s, when Franco's government gave permission for the tombs to be opened, probably for historic reasons. What the workers discovered was astounding. The bodies are in a marvelous state of preservation, even some that had not been embalmed. The clothes, though a little faded, tell the observer a great

deal about Spanish people of the Middle Ages.
The guide who was showing my group through the
convent made a comment that especially caught
my attention. We were looking at the display of
Queen Eleanor, wife of Alfonso VIII. The guide
asked us to notice the dainty muslin--almost as
thin as chiffon--worn by the queen, her fancy
headdress 12 feet long, her Arab shoes, and the
pillows in the coffin (one of tapestry and one
with woven stripes of gold thread). "The
Christian nobles," the guide said, "hated the
religion of the infidels, but they loved to buy
Moorish cloth and eat delicacies such as
oranges, olives, pomegranates, and so forth,
which the Arabs introduced into Spain."

(4) I noticed with great interest the silk
garments of Ferdinand de la Cerda--a sleeved
tunic and short trousers under a knee-length
coat. They were embroidered all over with the
shields of Castile and Leon with a background of
pearls. All this work was done by Arabs 250
years before Columbus sailed for America, and
the sight of these clothes made me aware that
the Moorish culture added greatly to what
Spain used to be--and probably to what Spain
is today.

(5) The guide also said something that showed
me the human side of history and sent me to
reading my history books more carefully. Of
Eleanor she said, "She was only 8 years old when
Henry II of England and his wife Eleanor of
Aquitaine sent her to Spain to be married to
12-year-old Alfonso VIII in a magnificent
ceremony." I wondered whether marriage at such
an early age was common, looked in my history
books, and found that such early marriages were
the rule when politically minded fathers saw
marriage as an easy way to avoid war.

(6) I have only seen Las Huelgas once, but I
can never erase from my mind what I saw and can
testify that it taught me much. That is why I
recommend it to others.

EXERCISE 13.

Answer these questions on the student composition you have just read.

1. What shows that the author is aware of the readers?
2. What is the central idea?
3. What details at the beginning arouse the reader's curiosity?
4. Why did the author find the museum of Las Huelgas interesting?
5. Where does the writer use each of the following:

facts	comparison or contrast
figures	examples
quotation from authority	illustration

6. Which of the following does the conclusion accomplish?

   a. tell a story that illustrates the central idea?
   b. use a quotation that embodies the central idea?
   c. restate the central idea?

STEP 7. WRITING THE FINAL DRAFT

EXERCISE 14.

Make revisions of the first draft as determined in step 6. Read the composition carefully, rewording ineffective sentences and looking up words you are not sure of. You may need to write more than one draft before the final one.

Check the composition for the following things:

1. avoidance of run-together or incomplete sentences
2. correct punctuation at the ends of sentences
3. correct spelling
4. correct use of present and present continuous verb forms
5. correct use of *a* and *the* before nouns
6. correct use of commas between items in a series and after long introductory elements
7. correct position of adverbs

Prepare a neat copy of your final draft. Fold and sign it as your instructor requests. Hand in your first draft along with the final one.

Review the corrections in the composition that you wrote for Lesson 1 to avoid making the same mistakes.

Reviewing Grammatical Patterns

PRESENT TENSE AND PRESENT CONTINOUS

Study the uses of the present tense and the present continuous in sections D8a and D8b in the Handbook.

GRAMMAR EXERCISE 1.

In the following groups of sentences, the present tense and present continuous are used correctly. Tell why each of the italicized verbs is in the present or present continuous. Could the other verb form be used?

1. I *live* in a suburban area at the edge of a city.
2. The city *provides* bus service for people who *work* a long distance from their homes. I *ride* to work on the bus every day.
3. My suburb is very beautiful. A river *flows* through it, and in the spring and summer flowers *bloom* in the gardens.
4. Today is a beautiful spring day. The sun *is shining,* birds *are singing,* and flowers *are blooming* everywhere.
5. My parents used to live in the city. Now they *are living* in a small town. They *live* near a city, however, and *go* to the city often. They *like* to attend plays and movies there.
6. I seldom *go* to movies. I *like* to stay home in the evenings. I *visit* with members of my family, *read* a book, or *watch* a program on TV. Tonight, however, a good movie *is showing* at a theater near me, and I *am planning* to attend.

GRAMMAR EXERCISE 2.

Supply the present or present continuous form of the indicated verb in the spaces provided. Then discuss with your classmates which form is more appropriate.

1. Every year many visitors _____ (come) to Bavaria. Some _____ (enjoy) our winter sports. Others _____ (visit) our castles and old villages. More visitors _____ (come) every year.

2. Right now I _____ (sit) in the library. I like to watch the people I see there. A girl near me _____ (try) to study, but her boyfriend _____ (interrupt) her all the time. She keeps telling him to keep quiet. Another student _____ (write) a paper. Another _____ (sleep).

3. My hometown used to be quiet and peaceful. Now the population _____ (increase). This _____ (bring) more traffic. The cars _____ (pollute) the atmosphere, and the noise of traffic _____ (keep) people awake at night.

4. My grandmother does not like the machine age. She says people _____ (hurry) about too much, cars _____ (pollute) the atmosphere, and children _____ (watch) television when they should _____ (study) arithmetic.

5. I usually _____ (study) about 40 hours a week, but now it is near the end of the semester. All my instructors _____ (give) examinations, so I _____ (study) more than usual.

USE AND OMISSION OF ARTICLES

In Lesson 1 you listened for the articles that students of English as a foreign language often omit before nouns if their native language does not use articles. Even if your language contains articles, it may use them in a way that is different from their use in English. Review the occasions when articles are omitted by reading sections B3a, B3b, and C7 on non-count nouns in the Handbook.

GRAMMAR EXERCISE 3.

With your books closed, number from 1 to 15 on a piece of paper. You will hear phrases, some of which include an article and some of which do not. Place a check mark after the number of the phrase in which an article is used. Your instructor will read the phrases with the articles unstressed, as in normal speech. Listen carefully.

/ðə/

1. on the table

2. on time

3. after lunch

4. in seconds

/ə/
5. in a minute

11. too many parties

/ə/
6. under a tree

/tə/
12. to study history

7. after long study

/ðə/ /əv/
13. the history of England

8. I ordered coffee

/ðə/
14. read the books

/ðə/
9. the coffee that I ordered

/tə/
15. books to read

/ə/
10. go to a party

After you have listened to all the phrases, check your paper with the text. Discuss why an article is used or omitted in each case.

COMMAS BETWEEN ITEMS IN A SERIES AND AFTER LONG INTRODUCTORY ELEMENTS

In the chapter "Conventions in the Mechanics of Writing" in the Handbook, study section A3, on uses of the comma. Note the use of commas in this lesson as illustrated here.

Commas are used between words, phrases, or clauses used in a series. (commas between elements in a series)

Not every paragraph in longer expository writing contains a subject sentence, but it does have a central idea that the reader grasps easily. (commas between clauses joined by conjunctions *and, but, or, for*)

Comparison points out similarities and contrast points out differences. (no comma because the clauses are short)

As we have said, check your compositions carefully so that you do not make the same mistake a second time. (comma after an introductory element)

In the winter we like to ski. (no comma because the introductory element is short and the sentence will not be misread without the comma)

GRAMMAR EXERCISE 4.

Put necessary commas in these sentences.

1. Imagine a winter world in which the streams lakes and rivers were frozen from top to bottom.

2. Such ice might be good for skaters but drinking water would be difficult to get.
3. If oceans froze solid ships could not navigate in winter.
4. Fortunately ice is lighter than water and for this reason it floats.
5. Because of this commerce by ship is still possible in the winter and it is possible to obtain water to drink.
6. If you have never been to Minnesota you may think that Minnesota is frozen solid in the winter and that everyone in the state lives like an Eskimo.
7. Minnesota is not located on an ocean but it is on the shores of one of the Great Lakes and there are reported to be 10,000 smaller lakes in Minnesota.
8. Sometimes the harbors on Lake Superior freeze for some distance from the shore but they are not frozen solid all the way to the bottom.
9. When they freeze shipping is disrupted.
10. In such cases large ships called icebreakers go out to clear a path through the ice.

POSITIONS OF ADVERBS

Study the rules for positions of adverbs, section H21, in the Handbook.

GRAMMAR EXERCISE 5.

Expand the sentences below by adding the requested information in appropriate places. Remember that (1) adverbs of time appear at the end or beginning of a sentence; (2) when a series of adverbial elements follows the verb, the order is generally location, manner, time; (3) adverbs telling why generally appear after other adverbs; (4) adverbs of frequency generally precede the verb; (5) modifiers of an entire sentence go at the beginning of the sentence.

1. I could not go. (When? Where? Why? Fortunately or unfortunately?)
2. He gave me the ticket. (Why? When?)
3. The jewel thieves spent the night. (What day of the week? Where? Why? Willingly or reluctantly?)
4. Can you come? (Where? When? With whom?)
5. Please send the information. (To whom? Give the recipient's location. How?)

6. They jog. (How often? When? Where? Why?)
7. The package came. (Where? When? Why? How?)
8. We plant trees. (How frequently? When? Where?)

AVOIDING RUN-TOGETHER OR INCOMPLETE SENTENCES

Review in the Handbook sections A1a, on complete sentences, A1d, on participles versus complete verbs, and A2b, on combining with subordinators.

GRAMMAR EXERCISE 6.

Some of the following word groups are complete sentences and some are only long adverbial elements. For each word group that is not a complete sentence, complete the sentence with as few words as possible and punctuate it correctly. For each word group that is a complete sentence, put in the appropriate punctuation.

1. once we agreed immediately upon a place to take our vacation
2. once we have decided upon a place to take our vacation
3. afterward we studied hard all semester and took our final examinations
4. after we have studied hard all semester and have taken our final examinations
5. now that we have gotten through the annoying red tape of registration
6. now we have learned how to get through the annoying red tape of registration
7. as soon as we can notify our parents
8. as soon as November we can notify our parents
9. while we were waiting Bill appeared at the corner
10. while we were waiting for Bill at the corner
11. for so long his family kept sending him a generous allowance
12. so long as his family keeps sending him a generous allowance
13. whenever possible I write my long term papers during vacation
14. whenever I write my long term papers during vacation
15. before he decided that law was the profession that most nearly suited him
16. before he came he had decided that law was the profession that suited him

Rewrite sentences 2, 4, 5, 7, and 10, putting the long adverbial element in regular order at the end of the sentence. How will the punctuation of the sentences in this rewriting differ from the punctuation used in your first writing?

GRAMMAR EXERCISE 7.

Some of the following should be written as one sentence. Some should be two sentences. Punctuate and capitalize correctly. Be able to justify the punctuation you have used. Some sentences may be correct as they are written.

1. I think of mountains when I think of home mountains rise up behind my village.
2. If I close my eyes I can picture mountains with white limestone summits and green foothills in front of them.
3. The mountains look different at different times of the year for example in winter when snow comes the foothills as well as the summits are white.
4. I love the mountains especially when the sun shines on them they are most beautiful then.
5. The mountains are favorite places for hiking in summer we go to the mountains in winter also.
6. The ski slopes in our mountains are famous so in winter many people come to our village.
7. Some people come when they have vacations they like to rest and enjoy the scenery.
8. Some people come in winter some come in summer.
9. Some come every year they like it so well they don't want to spend their holidays anywhere else.
10. Come to my village whenever you are in my country I will take you to the mountains.

USE AND OMISSION OF ARTICLES AND PUNCTUATION OF SENTENCES

GRAMMAR EXERCISE 8.

Your instructor will read the following paragraph aloud once in its entirety. Then he or she will dictate each sentence by phrases but at a normal rate of speed, leaving pauses for you to write. Listen carefully for the articles, which will be read with reduced vowel sounds (called *schwas*) as in ordinary speaking. Then you will hear it again at normal speed so that you may check your writing. Be careful to punctuate sentences correctly.

DIFFICULTIES IN WRITING

The writing of famous authors was not done easily. An author has to discover for himself or herself the best time and the best conditions in which to write. Conditions that suit one writer may not suit another. For example, early in the morning was Hemingway's preferred time. Late afternoon was the best time for Leon Uris. Some writers may prefer to use a pencil in order to think better. Others prefer to dictate what they want to say.

When you have finished writing, check the copy in your textbook to see whether you have omitted articles or other small unstressed words. Make sure that you have avoided run-together or incomplete sentences. If you have made mistakes in spelling, write the correct spelling on your paper.

END NOTES

1. Note the use of the plural in these expressions (see also Lesson 1):

   one of the book*s*   *many* of the exercise*s*
                                  (or *many* exercise*s*)
   a lot of student*s*   *most* of the citie*s*
                                  (or *most* citie*s*)
                                  all of the lesson*s*
                                  (or *all* lesson*s* or *all* the lesson*s*)

2. In giving directions or locations, note the correct use of these expressions:

   in the northern *part of* my country
      (*Not:* in the north of my country)
   on the western side of the mountains
   on the eastern border
   north of the border

EXPLAINING A POINT OF VIEW

Rhetorical Principles	Grammatical Patterns
Developing an idea by explanation	Modifiers of nouns
Unity and relevance	Relative clauses
Placement of the thesis sentence	Modifiers of verbs
Relating the subject to the reader	Modals
	The passive
	Articles with count and non-count nouns and with specific and nonspecific nouns

Writing a Composition

Assignment: In the composition assignment for this lesson, explain to your classmates and your instructor a point of view or opinion that you hold. It may or may not be one with which your readers are likely to agree. You may give reasons for your belief. However, your purpose is not to persuade but to inform.

Stage I. Prewriting

STEP 1. BRAINSTORMING FOR IDEAS

EXERCISE 1.

Following are some general areas in which you may have an opinion to express. Pick one you would like to discuss in class or possibly write about and be prepared to suggest a statement of opinion within the area that could be the subject of a paper. Also suggest topics that are not on the list. There will be an opportunity to exchange ideas on selected topics in class.

1. *Education*

   Examinations
   Grading systems
   Banning books
   The use of computers in education

   What schools should teach
   The value of an education
   How I believe schools should be reorganized
   Problems in education today

2. *Politics*

   The problems of holding public office
   My idea of a statesman

   Trade relations with other countries
   An ideal form of government
   Foreign aid to underdeveloped countries

3. *Sports*

   My favorite sport
   My opinion of American football
   The Olympic Games

   Jogging
   Fishing
   Exercise and health

4. *Science*

   Uses of nuclear power
   Flying saucers
   Superstitions about science

   Animal intelligence
   What sciences should be taught in schools

5. *Society*

   The position of women
   Marriage

   A practice that I think is morally wrong

My opinion of a tradition in my country	Prejudice

6. *Travel*

Why I enjoy travel My favorite mode of travel	The advantages (disadvantages) of travel My favorite vacation spot

EXERCISE 2.

Select a general topic on which to write.

STEP 2. PHRASING THE THESIS SENTENCE

EXERCISE 3.

The central idea of the composition for this lesson will be an *assertion* —a statement of opinion rather than a statement of fact. Which of the following sentences do *not* express an opinion and thus would not be satisfactory for the central idea of a composition for this assignment?

1. I believe that grades in the university should be abolished.
2. I have learned many things through travel.
3. Soccer is a better game than football.
4. *(Name)* is the hero of my country whom I admire the most.
5. The first settlers in North America endured many hardships.
6. Hitchhiking is the best way to see a country.

How might you reword those that are statements of fact to make them statements of opinion?

EXERCISE 4.

Here are some suggestions for topic sentences for this assignment. Read them; then in class suggest others in each area or in other areas. For at least one of them give suggestions about what one might say in explaining the idea expressed in the topic sentence.

1. Education

Examinations for admission to a university in my country are too difficult.

The most important things that one learns are learned through experience.

Grades are not a valid measure of what a person knows.

2. Politics

The problems associated with holding public office make it an undesirable occupation.

A federal system is (is not) the best form of government for a country such as mine.

Politicians are not to be trusted.

3. Sports

Tennis is a more interesting spectator sport than football.

The best way to relax after a difficult week of work is to go fishing.

Rules for the Olympic Games should be changed.

4. Science

Animal behavior may be explained by intelligence as well as by instinct.

The stars do (do not) determine our fate.

Flying saucers are (are not) sent by men from outer space.

5. Society

Women should (should not) work outside the home.

The happiest marriages are those arranged by wise parents.

Mankind's moral development has not kept pace with increased knowledge of science and technology.

My objections to certain traditional ways of doing things are justified.

6. Travel

Hawaii truly deserves the title "Paradise of the Pacific."

Travel by bus is better than driving.

(Place) offers some of the best scenery in the world.

No one country has a monopoly on the best ways of doing things.

EXERCISE 5.

Formulate a tentative topic sentence for your composition and present it to the class for comments. Your final thesis sentence may not be determined, however, until you have thought about your subject and written down some ideas.

STEP 3. JOTTING DOWN IDEAS AND REFINING A POINT OF VIEW

Following are some notes that a student wrote in preparing a composition expressing a point of view on the general subject *home*. Read them; then answer the questions that follow them.

Home – things I miss
  The house and its surroundings. The things in it.
                    Souvenirs
                    Wedding presents
Things my family did together
    Feasts – mother preparing the lamb
    Father – morning prayers
    Children – excitement of new clothes,
                anticipating the feast
Things my husband and I did together
    Nights in the garden together in the summer
    Driving to the Dead Sea by full moon
My baby
    Hands touching my face
    Playing together
Neighbors – types
    The neighbor difficult to please
    The noisy neighbor

EXERCISE 6.

Answer these questions about the notes you have just examined.

1. What point of view toward home do you think the writer had in mind when making the notes?
2. What possible thesis sentence might emerge from these notes?
3. What plan do you think the writer had in mind for grouping the materials? Is it consistent? Can you think of a better one?

EXERCISE 7.

Jot down notes for the composition you will write or, if you prefer, begin writing a rough draft. Keep in mind the point of view you are explaining.

Stage II. Giving Form to the Composition and Studying Techniques

STEP 4. WRITING A FIRST DRAFT

Write a first draft for your composition. State your point of view clearly and use material from your notes, grouping similar ideas. Include details that will help your readers understand the subject. Avoid irrelevant material. Revise while you write. Read your composition, possibly aloud, noting how you can improve wording or content.

STEP 5. STUDYING RHETORICAL PRINCIPLES

Developing an Idea by Explanation

Your entire composition for this assignment is an explanation. It may employ any of the methods of development we have studied—details, examples, illustrations, facts, figures, comparison and contrast, and citing of authority.

Explanation is also a means of developing one of a number of ideas in a composition. In an essay on magnanimity, C. P. Snow gives Sir Walter Scott and Turgenev as examples of magnanimous men. He realized, however, that his readers probably would not know the details of Turgenev's life, so he explained what action showed Turgenev to be magnanimous. Following is a paragraph from the essay.

MAGNANIMITY*

My next example [of a magnanimous man] is Turgenev. Turgenev had great literary success young, and in fact remained successful all his life. He was ten years older than Tolstoi, and when they first met, Turgenev was the most distinguished writer in Russia, and Tolstoi a beginner. Fairly soon that position changed. Tolstoi published War and Peace when he was in his late thirties, and was, with surprising speed, recognized as the first novelist not only of Russia, but of the world. Turgenev was

*C. P. Snow, "On Magnanimity," *Harper's Magazine* (July 1962). Reprinted by special permission.

not simply a fine writer. He was a man of acute
critical perception. He knew, and said, that
this estimate was just. It cannot have been
easy. Turgenev had lived for his art more than
most men--much more than Tolstoi had--and it
cost him great suffering to admit that he had
been surpassed. And yet his heart was large
enough. As he was dying, he wrote Tolstoi one of
the most moving letters in all literature,
begging him to return to writing novels,
calling him "greatest writer of the Russian
land."

EXERCISE 8.

Answer these questions about the preceding selection.

1. What facts does Snow present to show why he considers
   Turgenev an example of magnanimity?
2. How is contrast used as a method of development?
3. The first sentence contains an example. Does the rest of the
   paragraph make use of examples as a means of development,
   or does it use illustration?
4. Might this explanation also be considered a definition?

Unity and Relevance

Unity is a rhetorical term for sticking to the subject. Do not include
material in your writing that does not relate directly to your central
idea. In other words, include only material that is relevant.

EXERCISE 9.

Underline the subject sentence in each of the following selections.
Then cross out the sentence(s) that you consider irrelevant in developing the subject. Be able to defend your choice.

1. Lev Vygotsky, the late Russian linguist,
believed that it was harder to write than to
speak because writing requires double
symbolization. We all recognize that speech
consists of symbols. When we utter the sounds in
the word dog, those sounds only symbolize the
furry animal, and the sounds in the word run are

only symbols for what the animal does. But when
people write about dogs, they not only are
involved in the symbolization that constitutes
speech but are concerned with yet another set of
symbols, marks on paper, that substitute for
the sound symbols. Personally, I have found
that punctuation and capitalization are even
greater annoyances in writing. Spelling, too,
is a problem for writers of English, because the
spelling is unphonetic. For some people,
correct spelling comes naturally, but I am not
one of those people.

2. The living room was a pleasant one. It was
obviously occupied by a person of taste, Paul
decided. He saw Persian rugs, period French
furniture, an organ as well as a piano, and a
wall of windows overlooking a terrace. Beyond
the terrace was a meadow where cows were
grazing. The cows, being Holsteins, would of
course be part of a dairy herd, and Paul
wondered how much money the owner made from
them. On the walls were original oils of French
Impressionists and watercolors by artists whom
Paul recognized as being able to command high
prices for their works. All the furnishings
made Paul eager to meet the count.

3. Germany, on the morning of January 17,
1917, during World War I, had its problems.
German civilians were living on potatoes, and
15-year-old boys were being drafted into the
army. The recent offer to negotiate a peace had
been made only as a gesture to wring more
sacrifice from the army, the German people, and
the now unenthusiastic Austria. England had no
money and no ideas as to how to achieve a
victory.

EXERCISE 10.

Let us assume that you wrote the paragraphs in the preceding
exercise, and you think that all the information should be included
in the selections. Rephrase the subject sentences so they include the
material you marked irrelevant in Exercise 9. Explain how you would

rearrange the content of each selection to fit the new subject sentence. Tell also whether some ideas would need further development.

Do all three of the selections explain a point of view? Justify your answer. Do all give an explanation?

The two student compositions that follow illustrate different methods of arrangement and development for the same subject and different points of view.

WHAT HOME MEANS TO ME
Numati Nurredin, Jordan

(1) What does home mean to me? Is it the country that I came from? A particular house? The parents by whom I was loved and brought up? The man with whom my happiness is complete? The baby whose birth changed my outlook on life? Home is all the people and all the things that I miss while being away from home.

(2) Jordan, the heir to a rich historical and religious heritage, is my larger home. It extends from the temperate heights of the rugged purple-hued mountains of Moab to the gently rolling hills of Jerusalem; from the deep tropical Jordan Valley, with its luxuriant vegetation, to the Dead Sea, the lowest spot on earth; and from the spectacular sandstone cliffs of Wadi Run to the arid desert of the eastern plateau.

(3) On Jabal Amman, one of the nicest hills in the capital, stands a small red home surrounded by lemon and almond trees with their aroma filling the air. In this little house I started my married life with the man I dearly love. Though simply furnished, the house has all the necessary conveniences and a large collection of souvenirs and wedding presents that we received from our families and friends. The one present I like the most is a sheepskin carpet that I received from my parents. It is made of sixteen lambskins that my family collected from past feasts.

(4) The word <u>feast</u> reminds me of feasts at my parents' home where Mother stayed awake a whole

night stuffing and cooking a whole lamb for the
family to eat when they gathered on a feast day.
It reminds me of the children waking up before
dawn, waiting impatiently for the morning to
approach so that they could exhibit to their
friends in the neighborhood their new clothes
and shining shoes. Also, I can hear my father's
sweet voice in the early morning as he said the
morning prayers after the Imam called for them
from the minaret.

(5) To me, home is my husband, with whom I have
experienced happiness, love, and security. I
remember the hot summers when we spent most of
the nights out in the garden listening to music
or reading because of the intolerable heat
inside. I remember our shishkabob parties,
where friends would gather around a blazing
coal fire eating while more skewers of meat were
being broiled. Home reminds me of my husband and
me driving to the Dead Sea every month at full
moon. The moon reflected its beauty on the sea
just as a beautiful woman reflects her beauty in
a looking glass.

(6) More than anything else, the word <u>home</u>
takes me quickly to my dear baby, and I can hear
his cry for food and affection. I can feel his
little hands scratching my face as he started
developing his manual skills. It reminds me of
my play time with him when we both rolled over
the carpet and his laughter filled the house
with joy. It takes me back to the hard time I had
to keep him from soaking the kitten with him in
the tub as he was taking a bath.

(7) I also remember my neighbors as I say
<u>home</u>--the easy-going neighbor and the more
difficult to please; the quiet, calm neighbor
and the vigorous, outspoken one; the shy one and
the aggressive one. The neighbor I had the most
trouble with lived on the second floor, just
above us. She seemed to enjoy clicking over our
heads with a noisy pair of slippers that never
seemed to wear out.

(8) In a short Arabic poem, two doves from

Hijaz decided to migrate to Yemen, and while on
their way they stopped on a bush to rest and talk
about their trip. A passerby heard them
discussing their migration to Yemen and said,
"How lucky you are to live there. I wish I could
join you."

(9) Before he even finished, one of the doves
said to him, "Suppose Eden were not in Yemen;
home is still Eden to me."

EXERCISE 11.

Answer these questions about the composition "What Home Means
to Me."

1. What is the thesis sentence?
2. How does the author develop the idea?
3. Make a list of the things that the author misses while being
   away from home. Does this list develop the thesis sentence
   well? Explain.
4. In what way does the author "zoom in" on her subject?
5. By what word in each paragraph does the author achieve
   coherence and remind the reader of her subject?
6. How does the conclusion reflect the central idea?
7. What is the primary method of development used in the
   composition? Is it the only method used?

MY POINT OF VIEW TOWARD HOME
Mousa El Hafez, Saudi Arabia

(1) A great many people, when they speak of
home, tend to associate it with a certain
atmosphere, certain physical surroundings, and
certain emotional attitudes within themselves.
This sentimentality toward home is something
that has come down to us from the past. Many
modern people do not have it, and I think it is a
good thing that they do not.

(2) In the old days life was difficult.
Enemies could attack you and kill or rob you,
and you had little protection against them.
People did not live in well-built houses where
doors could be locked. They did not have the

protection of an organized police force and
telephones which could summon the police
instantly. How did this influence the way
people felt about home? Small family groups
clung tightly together for protection against
beasts and against other men. Only the bravest
went beyond the small family area. Even in the
Middle Ages only the most daring went to lands
beyond the sea. The human pursuit of security
conditioned men to love their homes, to feel
safe only in or near their homes. I am sure that
this feeling must have been very strong among
the early settlers of the United States who were
obliged, by famine and oppression, to take the
plunge and go to the new land where they knew no
one and where they were subject to Indian
attack. We can see this even today in the
attitudes of minority groups who, because of a
feeling of insecurity, still preserve cohesive
family ties.

(3) Today, thanks to modern transportation
and well-organized societies, thousands of
people willingly and eagerly leave the
surroundings where they were born, and the
oftener they do so the less sentiment they are
likely to have for those surroundings. I lived
in England for three years, and I noticed that
boys and girls left their parents' homes and
lived in dwellings of their own. There you could
just pick up the telephone and ask an agency to
provide you with a house or an apartment, and
that was your home. How has the meaning of this
word <u>home</u> been altered by such activity? What
does home mean to such people or to families who
move about living in first one hotel and then
another? I believe that for them home means a
place where you can have privacy.

(4) This idea of home as being a place of
privacy is emerging in my country, Saudi
Arabia, where the young are abandoning the
parents' homes to live their own kind of life.
As for me, the atmosphere and surroundings of
the place where my parents live has no

sentimental attachment for me. Home is where I can shut the door and be by myself. At the moment it is a room in Eaton Hall. When I left my parents several years ago, I was anxious to leave. You might call it unfeeling, but that is the way I felt. On the day of my departure for the United States, my grandmother sobbed and wept. My father, however, indicated that he understood how I felt. "Son," he said, "I am not sorry that you are leaving us. I only hope that you make the most of your time."

(5) Bedouins in my country, who are a nomadic people, always living in a changing atmosphere and making their homes where grass and water exist, have a proverb: "Water pushed by the current does not become stagnant."

EXERCISE 12.

Answer these questions about the composition "My Point of View Toward Home."

1. What is the writer's point of view toward home?
2. Is his purpose to instruct or to get the reader to accept his view? Explain.
3. A short outline of the selection would probably look like this:

   Thesis: It is desirable not to be sentimental about home.
       I. Ancient reasons for such intense loyalty are no longer valid.
      II. Modern transportation and well-organized societies do not require it.

What is the overall plan of organization?

4. The author uses the following line of reasoning as one means of support for his belief that close home ties are not as important as in ancient times. State the conclusion of his reasoning.

   Home ties used to be necessary for protection.
   People no longer need to band together closely for protection.
   Therefore _____ .

5. Does the material about families in the Middle Ages and young people in England and Saudi Arabia today contribute to

the author's line of reasoning, or is it irrelevant to his discussion of his own point of view toward home?
6. How does the quotation from the author's father help to support the thesis?
7. The description of the grandmother's actions is an example of what kind of support?
8. By what means does the author conclude the composition? Is it or is it not effective? Explain.
9. Does the author state his central idea clearly? What do you think it is?

Placement of the Thesis Sentence

In an essay the central idea is usually stated at the beginning but sometimes it is more effective to place it at the end—or even in the middle if you think it will be more understandable to the reader there. Sometimes the logical order of thought is not the order in which you present the material to the readers. If you explain a point of view to which the readers may be hostile or which they may not understand without explanation, it may be more effective to present it after you give the chain of reasoning that led you to the particular point of view.

EXERCISE 13.

Answer these questions about the two example compositions.

1. In the first composition is the thesis in the expected place?
2. What is the effect of the questions in the first paragraph of that composition?
3. In the second composition where does the author tell you his point of view toward home? Where does he give you his definitions?
4. Is his central purpose to tell you his definition of home as a place of privacy or to develop the idea that one should not be sentimental about home?
5. Would the second composition have been more effective if it were organized like the first? Explain.

Relating the Subject to the Reader

In writing an essay you are concerned not only with expressing your point of view but with appealing to the interests of the readers so that they will want to read what you have said and so that they will find it interesting. This is true whether or not you are trying to persuade your readers to accept your point of view. If you are presenting a point of view with which they may not agree, relating the subject to the readers is of particular importance. The following exercise reviews how this is done in the two example compositions you have just read.

EXERCISE 14.

Answer these questions about the two example compositions.

1. In composition 1 the author holds your interest, not by varying the type of supporting material, but by varying the type of details. What *sounds* remind her of home? What *sights?* What *people* remind her of home? What *things?* What *activities?*
2. Make a list of the types of things you learn about the culture in which the author grew up. Can a personal essay give information of general interest?
3. Do the details about the culture help the reader relate to the writer and share her feelings? How?
4. How does the author of composition 2 catch your interest in the first paragraph? Does he present an idea that is in accord with common belief? Is sentimentality toward home a point of view that the readers are likely to have? Explain.
5. What facts about life in Saudi Arabia does the author present that might be of interest to a person from another country?
6. What evidence does the author give that he is qualified to compare life in the past to life now?
7. What historical facts does he give that might appeal in particular to an American reader?

Stage III. Critiquing and Revising

STEP 6. ANALYZING AND REVISING THE FIRST DRAFT

EXERCISE 15.

Use the following questions to check the first draft of the composition you have written.

1. Is the central idea a statement of opinion rather than of fact?
2. Is the central idea stated clearly? If it is not stated at the

beginning of the essay, why is it more effective where you have placed it?

3. What types of development have you used? Is there other material that you might have included to make your explanation clearer?
4. Could you make your explanation clearer by rearranging your material?
5. Does each sentence follow logically from the preceding one?
6. What have you said to show that you have your reader in mind? Be prepared to read the composition to at least one of your classmates to make sure that he or she understands your explanation. Your instructor may divide the class into small groups for this purpose and classmates may ask questions or offer suggestions.

Later you will critique writing of your classmates. Evaluation of what others have written is a skill important for any writer. It helps you to judge what you yourself have written. Following is a composition that has much interesting material in it but that could be improved in several ways. Read it and critique it individually out of class. Discuss it later in class.

MY HITCHHIKING IN AMERICA
Yoshifumi Takaori, Japan

(1) At the start of every vacation I stand on the freeway with my guitar and sleeping bag and I stick out my thumb. It is the best way to see the United States.

(2) Before I get to the freeway, I have been awake for some time. When hitchhiking I always wake up at sunrise. I make a small fire and have tea and hard bread which I always carry in my backpack with some water. I then open my map and decide which direction to go in that day.

(3) I then work up to the freeway ramp and hold out my hand. At this moment I have no idea about what is going to happen. Hippy, junkie, housewife, businessman, gay—any of these might pick me up. I have never seen the same character twice. And I never know how long the ride is going to be. Some rides have been for only a few minutes, others for two or three days.

(4) As I stand there with my arm out, many cars pass me by, but eventually one slows down and stops. Each time a motorist does this, I have to deal with a driver whom I know nothing about. From this moment a new experience has started. I evaluate the character of the driver from the way he or she drives and from his or her unconscious movements and facial expressions. The way drivers control their voices as well as what they say also tells me what they are like. These actions help me to know how to communicate with each person, and this communication is important. Enjoying conversations is the key to the hitchhiker's success. It is a valuable way for me to learn about the country, and my response to what is said may keep me from being charged for the ride, or it may get me a dinner invitation, even free lodging for the night. By good conversation I get experience, long rides, make friends, and earn appreciation.

(5) When I arrive in a town or city, I sit down on some street and play classical guitar to get money to support my travel and also to get someone to start talking to me. Usually I get some money and some person tells me what the town is like, and sometimes the person offers me a place to stay. Not always, however. Rainy days are the time when it is easiest to get rides. (I guess people feel sorry for hitchhikers then.) On rainy days when I cannot get a ride out of town, I go to a freeway exit and find a spot under a crossover bridge. There is a dry place to sleep with the soft rain sound and also the heavy truck noise over my head.

(6) But sometimes I cannot find such a place to bed down. I had one such experience when I was in San Francisco and did not have any money. At night in big cities no one picks up hitchhikers. Since it is dangerous to sleep on the street or in the park, I hide from people, make no sound, and wait until morning. In San Francisco I slept in high-density bushes. In New York City I slept between big trash boxes with a lot of newspapers over me. From my experience the most dangerous

things are a street person in a big city and a rattlesnake in the desert.

(7) Although I sometimes get caught in a city at night, I generally try to be out of a city before night comes. I get out of the car in the middle of nowhere, work my way away from the freeway, and find a place to sleep. Sometimes it is in the woods, on a hill, or in the middle of a desert. I make a bed and make a small fire. By firelight I have some tea and some food, then write in my diary. I think back about the day and then dream in the starlight, firelight, and moonlight about tomorrow's road.

(8) Now you can see why I think hitchhiking is the best way to see America and to get to know its people.

EXERCISE 16.

Consider the following questions when you critique the preceding composition.

1. Did you find the material interesting? Why or why not?
2. In the first paragraph, the central idea seems to be "It [hitchhiking] is the best way to see the United States." Does the author prove that hitchhiking is better than traveling by bus, car, train, plane, or bicycle? What words could be substituted for "the best" to avoid having to make such a comparison?
3. What are the author's reasons for liking to hitchhike? List them.
4. Does the author explain more than just his reasons for enjoying hitchhiking?
5. Do you believe another thesis sentence is necessary for this composition? If not, why not? If so, write it.
6. The author might have developed his central idea by discussing things he learns about America through hitchhiking as follows:

    I. I learn about the types of people in America by the types of people who pick me up.
    II. I learn about the country through conversations with people.

III. _____.
IV. _____.
Complete points III and IV.

7. Do you believe that this is a better method of organization to explain the author's belief? Why or why not? Would you exclude any material if the composition were organized in this way? Is there material that you would add?

STEP 7. WRITING THE FINAL DRAFT

EXERCISE 17.

Make revisions in your composition as determined in Exercise 15. Read the composition aloud to check for wording and sentence structure. Check the following grammatical points:

1. Have you used articles before nouns when necessary?
2. Are relative clauses correctly formed?
3. Are modifiers of nouns properly placed to show the noun they modify?
4. Are adverbs and adverbial modifiers in the proper place in the sentence (*not* between the verb and direct object)?
5. Are there sentences in the passive that could be better stated in the active?
6. Are sentences correctly punctuated? Have you avoided incomplete sentences or two sentences run together as one?

Copy your paper neatly and hand it in in the form required by your instructor.

Reviewing Grammatical Patterns

MODIFIERS OF NOUNS

In describing her home, the author of "What Home Means to Me" has used various kinds of restrictive modifiers to limit or describe nouns and nonrestrictive modifiers to restate or to give further information.

Descriptive or limiting:

The parents *by whom I was loved and brought up* (relative clause to describe)

The one present *I like the most* (relative clause to limit; note omission of the relative pronoun)
The *temperate* heights of the *rugged, purple-hued* mountains (adjectives to describe)
A *small red* home *surrounded by lemon trees* (adjectives and past participle construction to describe)

Giving further information:

Jordan, *the heir to a rich historical and religious heritage* (appositive to give further information; note use of commas)
The deep tropical Jordan Valley, *with its luxuriant vegetation* (prepositional phrase to give further information; note use of commas)

GRAMMAR EXERCISE 1.

1. Find three more examples of modifiers used to describe or limit. Indicate what type of modifier is used—adjective, prepositional phrase, relative clause, verbal.
2. Find three more examples of modifiers used to give further information. These will be set off by commas.

GRAMMAR EXERCISE 2.

Read the selection that follows and then answer the questions about it.

The Qualities of a Leader

The man whom I would choose to lead my country should be a man of more than ordinary vision and judgment. He should be a man capable of guiding the nation wisely and firmly through difficult times, undaunted by the responsibilities of his position. He should be a man adept in dealing with people of diverse backgrounds, personalities, and interests, a man calm in difficult situations. He should have insight enough to anticipate a crisis and meet it with strength and determination, and the courage to act as his beliefs and conscience tell him. He should be a man unwilling to compromise his principles for personal gain. His office calls for a leader educated not only through reading but also through experience. Such men are described in John F. Kennedy's book <u>Profiles in Courage</u>.

1. List six different nouns and their following modifiers from the preceding selection.
2. Complete the following sentences by supplying a modifier. If you envision a woman leader, start each sentence with *she.*

    a. He should have the stability _____.
    b. He should have courage _____.
    c. He should have understanding of _____.
    d. He should have wisdom enough to _____.
    e. He should have the ability to _____.
    f. He should have the daring to _____.
    g. He should be a person dedicated to _____.

RELATIVE CLAUSES

Review the relative-clause patterns in sections A2c and J31 in the Handbook.

GRAMMAR EXERCISE 3.

Following are phrases containing relative clauses taken from "What Home Means to Me." Indicate whether the relative pronoun is the subject or object of the clause, an adverb, or the object of a preposition.

_____ 1. the country *that* I came from
_____ 2. the man with *whom* my happiness is complete
_____ 3. a collection of souvenirs and wedding presents *that* we received
_____ 4. the people by *whom* I was loved
_____ 5. feasts at my parents' home *where* mother stayed awake a whole night
_____ 6. the hot summer *when* we spent most of the nights in the garden
_____ 7. the neighbor I had the most trouble with (reword, using a relative pronoun)
_____ 8. a pair of slippers *that* never seemed to wear out

GRAMMAR EXERCISE 4.

Many students learning English write sentences such as these (the mistakes have been crossed out):

He is the cousin that I like ~~him~~ best.
This was the document that Churchill gave ~~it~~ to Roosevelt.

Modify each of the following nouns with a relative clause made from the statement in parentheses, using one of the following: *who, whom, that, which, where, when.*

the country (I came from the country.)
the country that I came from
or
the country from which I came
or
the country I came from

1. the woman   (I like to talk to her.)
2. the book   (My father gave me the book.)
3. the food   (I like this food best.)
4. a place   (I had never been there before.)
5. the time   (We went to Rome together.)
6. the assignment   (He gave the assignment last week.)
7. the feast   (We used to have them at my father's house.)

MODIFIERS OF VERBS

The author of "What Home Means to Me" has also used modifiers of verbs and of sentences effectively.

the things that I miss *while being away from home* (subordinator and verbal to indicate time)
It extends *from the temperate heights . . . to the gently rolling hills* (prepositional phrases to indicate location)
Mother stayed awake *a whole night stuffing and cooking a whole lamb* (adverbial to show time and participial construction to show purpose)

GRAMMAR EXERCISE 5.

Find four more different types of adverbials in the selection. Label each type: adverb, prepositional phrase, verbal construction, subordinate clause. Tell what the function of the modifier is—that is, does it tell time, location, manner, or purpose? Does each modify the verb or the sentence?

MODALS

Review the use of modal auxiliaries in section F14 in the Handbook.

GRAMMAR EXERCISE 6.

Without referring to the student compositions you have read in this lesson, complete the following sentences taken from them by inserting the appropriate modal auxiliary. You may use modals different from those the author used if they do not change the meaning.

1. In the old days life was difficult. Enemies _____ attack you. People did not live in houses where doors were locked.
2. I am sure that this need for security _____ have been very strong among the early settlers of the United States.
3. In England you _____ just pick up a telephone and ask an agency to supply you with a house or apartment.
4. You _____ call it unfeeling, but that is how I felt.
5. The children waited patiently for morning so that they _____ exhibit their new clothes and shining shoes.
6. I _____ hear my father's sweet voice.
7. I remember our shishkabob parties where friends _____ gather around a blazing fire.
8. I _____ feel the baby's little hands scratching my face.
9. A passerby said, "I wish I _____ join you in Yemen."

THE PASSIVE

Review the uses of the passive and *be* + past participle for description in sections E12 and E13 in the Handbook.

GRAMMAR EXERCISE 7.

Why was the passive used in the following sentences based on the example compositions in this lesson? Would the statements have been more effective in the active? Can each one be put into the active?

1. This composition *is concerned with* the meaning of the word *home*.
2. Does *home* mean the parents *by whom I was loved*?

3. The gifts *were given* to me by my friends.
4. My friends and I gathered around the fire eating while more meat *was being broiled.*
5. In the old days you *were not protected* from attack.
6. People did not live in well-built houses where doors *could be locked.*
7. The early settlers in the United States *were obliged* by famine to try their fortunes in a new land.
8. The meaning of the word *home has been altered* by the fact that people move about.

ARTICLES WITH COUNT AND NON-COUNT NOUNS AND WITH SPECIFIC AND NONSPECIFIC NOUNS

Study the summary of the uses of *a* and *the* with count and non-count nouns, section B3b in the Handbook, and the list of non-count nouns in section C7. Here are four principles of article use and meaning.

1. Sometimes the same word may be a count noun or a non-count noun, but the meaning of the two words is different.

   iron (the metal—non-count)   an iron (used for taking the wrinkles out of clothes—count)
   beauty (abstract term—   a beauty (a beautiful object—count)
   non-count)

2. The first time you mention a given count noun, it is preceded by *a* because it is unspecific. If you refer to the noun again, it is preceded by *the* because you are now talking about the specific thing you mentioned.

   A cat appeared at the door. (unspecific) *The* cat was a skinny little thing. (specific because it is the cat you just mentioned)

3. Sometimes the thing that makes the noun specific has not been recently mentioned but is understood. In the composition "What Home Means to Me," the writer tells us "In Amman, Jordan, is *a* small red house surrounded by lemon trees." She might have gone on to say, "This is *the* house in which I started my married life." In the second sentence the house is identified.

4. Note the meaning expressed by *a* and *the* in the following sentences:

He was *the* son of John Davis. (the only son)
He was *a* son of John Davis. (one of several)

GRAMMAR EXERCISE 8.

In complete sentences answer the following questions about the use of articles in the three selections in Exercise 9 of this lesson.

1. In selection 1, what is the effect of speaking of Lev Vygotsky as *"the* late Russian linguist" rather than *"a* late Russian linguist"?

2. In the second selection, we read that Paul "saw Persian rugs, period French furniture, an organ as well as a piano, and a wall of windows overlooking a terrace. Beyond the terrace was a meadow where cows were grazing." Explain *"a* terrace" and *"the* terrace."

3. In the last sentence of selection 2, why is *furnishings* preceded by *the?*

4. *Oil* is a non-count noun according to the list on page 251 of the Handbook. In the second selection, the author speaks of "original oils." Is this pluralization correct? Explain.

5. In selection 2, in the clause "Paul wondered how much money *the* owner made from them," why is *the* used before *owner* when the owner has not been mentioned before and there is nothing after *owner* to make the noun specific?

END NOTES

1. When several points of time are mentioned, name the most exact first and proceed toward the longest period.

on the morning of *July 2, 1979*
in the first half of the *nineteenth century*

2. When several single-word modifiers precede a noun, the one most permanently true stands nearest the noun.

a bearded old man (The man's age is more permanent than the beard.)

DEFINING A TERM

<table>
<tr><td>Rhetorical Principles</td><td>Grammatical Patterns</td></tr>
<tr><td>

Developing an idea by
definition
Developing an idea by
restatement
Definition of a paragraph
Achieving coherence in a
paragraph

</td><td>

Restrictive and
nonrestrictive clauses
and their punctuation
Modification by reduction
of relative clauses—
participles
and appositives
Positions of noun
modifiers
Punctuating interrupting
elements in a
sentence

</td></tr>
</table>

Writing a Composition

Assignment: In writing a paper for other classes or in explaining an idea to your friends or instructors, you often need to define exactly what you mean when you use a certain term. Two types of words need defining: (1) technical words (for example, *magnetic field*, *necrology*, *morpheme*) and (2) words that are used so frequently that they lose their specific meanings or mean different things to different people (for example, *good*, *education*, *justice*, *power*, *wrong*, *democracy*). In a 500-

word composition define a word of either of these types. It may be a technical term that you understand, perhaps because it is in your field of specialization or expertise, or a word in your language that cannot be translated exactly. If you define a more general term, select one that has some personal significance for you.

Sometimes a writer can make the meaning of a term clear in a word, phrase, or short sentence. Examples from the dictionary are *stray*—"to wander from a direct course"; *nursery*—"a place where children are temporarily cared for in their parents' absence"; *obese*—"excessively fat." These definitions can be expanded and made more precise by use of illustrations, examples, comparison, and contrast, or by restating them in some other way. A definition often includes an explanation. In writing your essay, do not simply offer a one-sentence definition such as is found in a dictionary. Develop and explain it in some way to make the meaning clear to your readers.

Stage I. Prewriting

STEP 1. BRAINSTORMING FOR IDEAS

EXERCISE 1.

Here are some suggested topics. Read them and, in class discussion, suggest others that you might like to write about. Ask for questions that the reader who wishes to understand the subject might ask.

1. *A term in your language (culture) that is difficult to translate into English.*
Is it a word that has no exact counterpart in English? What are some English words that have some similarity in meaning? How do they differ in meaning from the meaning of the word in your language? Is it a word that has no translation because of differences in the culture or habits of the two countries? If so, what are the differences?

2. *A technical term or a term used in a particular field of study with which you are familiar.* (Examples: *osmosis, hypnosis, morpheme, epic poem, mollusk, id, isotope, tort, proverbs*)
What are the particular characteristics that differentiate the term from other related ones? For example, the *id* is not the same thing as the *ego,* but the two are related. What are some examples of the

meaning of your term or of the things included in it? What illustration makes the meaning clearer?

3. *A general term that has particular meaning for you or has a specialized meaning in a certain field of study.* (Examples: *a good life, happiness, patriotism, creativity, a statesman, courage, honor, free speech*)

How does your definition of the term differ from the popular one? Relate a personal incident that shows what you mean by the term. What examples help clarify the meaning of your term? If your term describes a person, what characteristics must he or she have in order to illustrate the trait?

EXERCISE 2.

Choose a term to define for this composition.

STEP 2. PHRASING THE THESIS SENTENCE

The central idea of a piece of writing should be worded specifically, not vaguely. It should be a statement, not a question, although it should raise a question in the mind of the reader that the rest of the composition should answer. It may be a thesis reflecting the author's point of view toward the subject, or it may be a statement of purpose. In an essay defining a technical term, the central idea may be a statement of purpose. In an essay defining what a term means personally to the writer, it may be a statement of a point of view. As indicated in Lesson 3, often you realize what the central idea is only after you have thought about what you want to say and have jotted down some ideas. Then you decide how to word the idea and where to place it in the composition. A statement of purpose generally appears toward the beginning of an essay. Sometimes it is the opening sentence. More often it is stated at the end of the introductory paragraph. A statement of a point of view may appear at the end, after the writer has given evidence. Or you may decide, as the author of the selection on happiness did (p. 85–86), that the illustration speaks for itself without an explicit statement of a thesis.

EXERCISE 3.

Following are pairs of statements illustrating different ways of stating the thesis of a composition that defines a term. For each pair answer these questions:

1. Which is most specific?
2. Which do you think gives the reader a better idea of what the writer is going to say in the essay?
3. Which could be more adequately developed in an essay of about 500 words?
4. Which do you think would make a more interesting essay?
5. What are some means you might use to develop the topic sentence that you chose?

   a. For me culture means all the things that distinguish an educated man from an uneducated one.
   b. I am going to tell you what I mean by the term *culture*.

   a. People's ideas of honor differ.
   b. Since *honor* is such a vague term, I would like to explain what honor means to me.

   a. Freedom means different things in different contexts. The freedom I am going to discuss is political freedom.
   b. Freedom is liberty to do what you please as long as you do not harm others.

   a. History is what we learn about the past.
   b. History does not always tell what happened.

   a. A "good teacher" means something different to a child and to a college senior.
   b. A good teacher is not often found.

EXERCISE 4.

Decide tentatively on the purpose of your paper or the point of view you are going to take toward your subject.

STEP 3. JOTTING DOWN IDEAS AND REFINING A POINT OF VIEW

EXERCISE 5.

Here are some notes made by the writer of a paragraph defining the term *patriot*. As you read them decide what you think will be the central idea.

Patriotism
  Superficial signs – saluting flag
                    displaying flag on holidays
                    singing national anthem
                    taking part in public celebrations
  Inner qualities – loyalty to best ideals of government
                    trying to improve government by
                        active participation
                    holding up ideals of good government
                        in everyday life
                    obeying laws
                    (Quote Adlai Stevenson. Get
                    other quotations)

Read the selection on page 81 and see how the writer stated the central idea. Did you predict it correctly?

EXERCISE 6.

Write down some ideas for your composition. As you do so, refine or restate your thesis.

Stage II. Giving Form to the Composition and Studying Techniques

STEP 4. WRITING A FIRST DRAFT

EXERCISE 7.

Use your notes to write a first draft of your selection. As you write, revise, improving wording and adding and rearranging ideas. Think of types of developmental material that will make your definition more understandable (illustrations, examples, comparisons and contrasts, restatements, and the like). Keep your purpose clearly in mind and make sure it will be understood by your reader. Read your essay to another person, preferably one who knows less than you do about your subject, to make sure that you have made clear the term you are defining.

STEP 5. STUDYING RHETORICAL PRINCIPLES

Developing an Idea by Definition

Definition may be the purpose of a short essay or it may be a means of developing an idea in a longer composition. In Lesson 2

(p. 40) contrast was used to define the meaning of the term *frontier* in North America. Note the method of development used in the following essay defining the abstract term *patriot*.

A PATRIOT

(1) Many people think of a patriot as a person who stands at attention, hat off, when his country's flag goes by, who sings the national anthem with enthusiasm, and who celebrates national holidays. (2) These are only superficial signs of patriotism, however. (3) True patriotism consists of qualities of mind and spirit. (4) According to the nineteenth-century American novelist Mark Twain, "True patriotism is loyalty to the nation all the time, and loyalty to the government when it deserves it!" (5) This distinction between respect for the ideals of a government and respect for the actual government run by fallible men was voiced also by the twentieth-century French novelist Albert Camus, but with a slightly different point of view. (6) According to him, a patriot is one who gives his highest loyalty, not to his country as it is, but to his own conception of what it can and ought to be. (7) Camus saw patriotism as something that differs with each person because each person may have a different view of what the country ought to be. (8) Adlai Stevenson, the late American statesman, in his definition of a patriot adds another aspect. (9) He used to point out that the true patriot was not only willing to fight for principles but also to live up to them. (10) This stress on active participation in government and insistence that the principles of what makes a good society be reflected in every citizen's life shows an aspect of patriotism that many people would consider necessary in evaluating a given person as a patriot.

EXERCISE 8.

Answer these questions about the preceding paragraph of definition.

1. What is the purpose of the first sentence?
2. Why are the authorities quoted in the order in which they appear?
3. Which of the three men quoted do you believe would work the hardest for "good" government? Explain.
4. Where in this selection do you find explanation? Why is it used?
5. Is sentence 3 or sentence 10 the topic sentence? Explain.
6. Might the author have used examples and illustrations? Name patriots that could have been mentioned. Which ones would have required explanation?

Develop an Idea by Restatement

In defining, one often makes use of restatement. Restatement is not repetition. It is expressing the same idea in different words. Sometimes we do this for emphasis. More often we restate an idea because we realize that at first we did not express the idea as clearly as we should or that we used vocabulary that the reader probably would not understand. The example paragraph that follows gives still another reason for the need to rephrase an idea. Notice that the author uses restatement as a means of making clear why restatment is sometimes necessary.

UNDERSTANDING THE SPOKEN WORD*

(1) There is a time factor involved in understanding. (2) The clearest possible statement of a matter may not be grasped by the listener because his mind doesn't have time to develop it, unfold it, get a grip on it. (3) If he could have the statement before him in print so that he could reread it and study it, he might readily come to understand it. (4) And often the full import and implication of a statement is not grasped at once because the listener needs time to relate it and compare it with what he knows. (5) If a significant thought is thrown at him like a sudden dash of water, it may splash off without wetting the surface of

*W. M. Parrish, *Speaking in Public* (New York: Charles Scribner's Sons, 1947). Reprinted by permission.

his mind. (6) It takes time for some things to
soak in.

EXERCISE 9.

Answer these questions about the preceding paragraph.

1. What reason for the use of restatement does the author give?
2. The author is discussing the need for restatement in public
   speaking. What sentences tell you that?
3. Is restatement desirable in writing as well as in speaking? Why
   or why not?
4. Why might there be a difference in the amount or kind of
   restatement needed in the two media of communication?
5. In what sentences does the author use restatement to make the
   point clear?

Definition of a Paragraph

Why do writers indent from a margin (or change spacing) at certain places in their writing? Let us consider two types of paragraphs
and the purpose of each.

If we look through any book or magazine, we will find paragraphs
that consist of only one or two sentences—and sometimes only a
word or phrase. Such paragraphs are used (1) to introduce the reader
to the subject of the composition, (2) to relate what has preceded with
what will follow (transition paragraphs), or (3) to give dramatic force
to an idea. This last type of short paragraph occurs only occasionally.
Giving dramatic emphasis to an idea by putting it in a separate
paragraph is a device that cannot be used often without defeating its
purpose.

Longer paragraphs are more common. Single paragraphs are like
essays in miniature, centering around a unifying idea that may be
stated in a topic sentence. The rest of the paragraph develops the idea
by such means as examples, facts, and explanation. Adequate development of an idea is a feature of the writing of professionals. If a
longer paragraph is part of an essay, article, or chapter of a book, it
may start with a transitional sentence, one that relates what has been
said before to what will be said later. But no matter how the paragraph starts, the group of sentences comprising it has some unifying
idea.

Topic sentence refers to a statement that will be developed in a
paragraph. A *thesis sentence* is a statement of a central idea that will be

developed into a piece of writing that contains more than one paragraph.

EXERCISE 10.

Answer these questions about the selections you have read.

1. Why is the selection "A Patriot" written as one paragraph? What is the central idea?
2. In Lesson 3, why is the selection "Magnanimity" one paragraph?
3. In Lesson 3, the essay "What Home Means to Me" is in nine paragraphs, yet the whole essay has one controlling idea. Why do you think the author did not write it as one paragraph?
4. In the essay "What Home Means to Me" (pages 59–61) what is the purpose of paragraph 1? Of paragraph 2? Of paragraph 3?
5. Could paragraph 4 have been combined with paragraph 3, or is it more effective as a separate paragraph? Explain your answer.
6. What is the unifying idea of paragraph 5? Of paragraph 6? Of paragraph 7?
7. Paragraphs 8 and 9 are both part of a conclusion, but different speakers speak in each paragraph. How does this affect paragraphing?

Achieving Coherence in a Paragraph

In Lesson 3 we discussed unity in a paragraph or composition. Every statement that a writer includes should have some relevance to the central idea, and the thought in each sentence should develop from the thought in the preceding sentence. It is important, too, that the relation of each sentence to the preceding one or to the central idea of the paragraph should be clearly shown. Rhetoricians call this *coherence*, and it can be achieved by use of certain connectives, pronouns, word or phrase repetition, or parallel structure of words or phrases. In the following exercise you will discover examples of these various ways to achieve coherence in a paragraph.

EXERCISE 11.

Answer these questions about "A Patriot," page 81.

1. What pronoun in sentence 2 relates to ideas in sentence 1?
2. What words in sentence 3 contrast with the idea of "superficial signs of patriotism" in sentence 2?

3. What words in sentence 4 repeat wording in sentence 3?
4. How does the first word in sentence 5 relate to sentence 4?
5. In what way does "him" in sentence 6 refer to sentence 5?
6. Is sentence 7 related to sentence 6 by use of a pronoun or a repetition of words or phrases? Explain.
7. What are the words in sentence 8 that remind the reader of what has just been read in the previous sentences?
8. Is there more than one word in sentence 9 that contributes to coherence with what has been presented before? Be specific.
9. In sentence 10, what words contribute to the coherence of the selection?
10. Is sentence 6 related to sentence 5 or to sentence 1 or to both? How is the relationship shown?
11. Summarize devices for achieving coherence and give examples.

In the following composition the writer tells what an abstract term means to him.

HAPPINESS*

(1) Once upon a time . . . it seems as though it were yesterday and not away back in 1951 . . . I had a summer holiday with my two daughters. The older was six and the younger one four, and they just loved making trips with their father. This time we went to visit some romantic parts of Upper Hungary, and on a sunny day arrived at an old place named Hilvasvarad, where I had been planning to see a famous cave of primitive man. We had to set out early in the morning because the place was rather far--about four miles away--on the side of the mountain. My daughters were interested in everything--a butterfly or a nice flower was enough to interrupt our journey--but we finally got there about noon.

(2) The cave was not too interesting. Maybe it was my fault, because I am not too familiar with archaeology. But the magnificent surroundings of the place compensated for everything. Along

*The author, a scientist, was a Hungarian refugee in the United States whose wife and daughters had been detained in Hungary.

the valley that we walked up, there was a noisy
little brook running here and there over little
falls and hiding under ground and cropping up on
the other side of the rocks and spattering its
sparkly drops by making rainbows in the
sunshine. In some places in it there were small
ponds where trout flashed up and disappeared
again. We built a hut there from pine branches,
took a quick bath in the cold water, and played
some of those funny-stupid kids' games. Later
on I lit a fire and prepared a meal. It was
poor--only peas, onions, and bread, and some
half-ripe hazel nuts that we picked ourselves.
There was a real shortage of food in Hungary at
that time, and it was hard to find any food on
the market. No matter. We ate what we had with
good appetite.

(3) After the meal the girls got sleepy and
wanted to sleep in the hut with their father. I
made a bed of hay in it and we lay down, and with
a head on each of my shoulders, I watched my
daughters dream. That was true happiness, which
I have not known since.

EXERCISE 12.

Answer these questions about the example composition.

1. What is the central idea of the selection? Does the author state
   it in a thesis sentence?
2. When do you find out, other than through the title,
   that the selection will give a personal definition of
   happiness?
3. Is the way in which the central idea is made apparent to the
   reader effective? Why do you think it is or is not?
4. What is the primary means of development used in the
   selection?
5. What details contribute to the definition?
6. Why does the author not use a dictionary definition?

_____

The writer of the following composition attempts to make clear
to the reader the meaning of a term used in astronomy. As you read

it, note the difference in the method of development from that used
in the composition "Happiness."

STELLAR NOVAE

(1) Since ancient times star watchers and
astronomers scanning the sky with their
telescopes have come across new spots of
brightness that suddenly appear and gradually
fade away. Ancients regarded such phenomena
with superstitious awe as omens of important
events. These new stars, called <u>novae</u>, are
barely visible to the naked eye but bright
compared to most of the stars in our galaxy. Now
we know more about what they actually are.

(2) A <u>nova</u> is a nuclear explosion on the
surface of a star that has cooled until it
becomes a hard mass. Such a star is called a
<u>degenerate dwarf</u>. The explosion actually took
place many thousands of years ago and many light
years away. The light from it is only now
reaching us here on earth. A <u>nova</u> is born when
two stars about the size of our sun revolve
together. Such binary stars are common in our
universe. A star "burns" by consuming its
hydrogen, as does the sun. In this process it
flares for 200 million years or so into a huge
fireball like the sun. The hydrogen is
converted to helium. When the helium is
exhausted, the star contracts into a dwarf
about the size of the earth. This is what
happens to one of the stars in the pair.

(3) During the contraction, gravity squeezes
the star, converting it to carbon. The interior
becomes like a large diamond. As the dwarf and
its companion orbit together, the dwarf's
strong gravity pulls gas from the other star.
Its surface becomes wrapped in a spiral
rotating disk of gas called an <u>accretion disk</u>.
The action has been compared to that of water
swirling around a bathtub drain. The gas begins
to swirl at 5,000 kilometers per second,
heating to a temperature of 10 million

degrees.* Basically a new sun is created around the embers of a dead one. This mantle cannot shed its heat by expanding. Thus a nuclear explosion takes place. Astronomers believe that a nova releases as much energy in just one year as our sun does in a million.

(4) Each year some thirty dwarf stars in our galaxy become novae. Yet so completely are they hidden by interstellar dust that many are never seen. We actually learn about only 3 or 4 a year. It takes astronomers, many of them amateurs, constantly scanning the skies to discover them.

*Rick Gore, "The Once and Future Universe," National Geographic, 163 (June 1963): 722.

EXERCISE 13.

Answer these questions about the definition of stellar novae.

1. What is the purpose of the essay? In what sentence or sentences is it stated? Is the author taking a point of view toward the subject, or merely stating a purpose?
2. In defining a nova, the author explains how one is formed. Is this explanation necessary to understanding what a nova is? Why or why not?
3. Do you find any examples of the following types of development in the essay: details, examples, facts, comparison, contrast. What are they?
4. Why is the essay written in four paragraphs rather than one? What is the purpose of the first paragraph? Of the last? What is the controlling idea of the second paragraph? Of the third?
5. *Webster's Seventh New Collegiate Dictionary* defines a *nova* as "a star that suddenly increases its light output tremendously and then fades away to its former obscurity in a few months or years." What does the definition in the essay add to your understanding of a nova?

Stage III. Critiquing and Revising

STEP 6. ANALYZING AND REVISING THE FIRST DRAFT

EXERCISE 14.

Prepare the first draft of your essay of definition for critiquing with your classmates and instructor. (Your instructor may divide the class into small groups for discussion.) Check these points:

1. Is the purpose clearly stated?
2. Is there other information you should include to make your definition clearer?
3. Do you need to tell what the thing you are defining is *not* as well as what it is?
4. Should you make more use of the following methods of development: facts, figures and statistics, examples or illustrations, comparisons or contrasts, quotations from authority?
5. Are the sentences grammatically correct and worded clearly?
6. Would the material be more effective arranged differently?

STEP 7. WRITING THE FINAL DRAFT

EXERCISE 15.

Prepare the final draft of your composition, making use of the suggestions from the class and your own critiquing of the first draft. Check it carefully for wording and for the following grammatical points:

1. punctuation of nonrestrictive clauses and other interrupting elements
2. placement of modifiers
3. participles used as modifiers
4. complete sentences and sentences that are not run together

Copy the composition neatly and hand it in in the form required by your instructor.

Reviewing Grammatical Patterns

RESTRICTIVE AND NONRESTRICTIVE CLAUSES AND THEIR PUNCTUATION

Compare these two sentences:

A fellow who scored 80 points last season is our star basketball player.
Bill Clark, who scored 80 points last season, is our star basketball player.

In the first sentence, the clause identifies the person. It is thus necessary for the meaning of the main clause of the sentence. Such a relative clause is called a *restrictive* clause. In the second sentence, the clause gives additional information about a person who has already been identified. Such a clause is called a nonrestrictive clause. Commas precede and follow nonrestrictive clauses to indicate that they might be omitted.

GRAMMAR EXERCISE 1.

In the following passage, identify the relative clauses and tell why commas are or are not used to separate each one from the sentence in which it occurs.

HAWAII

In 1959 the territory of Hawaii, which consists of eight principal islands, became the fiftieth state of the United States. According to legend, the islands, which were visited in 1778 by Captain James Cook of the British navy, were settled many, many years ago by Polynesian people from Tahiti, who sailed across the Pacific in their large canoes. In the 1820s Protestant missionaries from New England, by whom the islands were Christianized, were followed by other Americans who came to develop businesses. Sugar and pineapple, which are the major industries of the island, formed the basis of fortunes for a number of these men. The Chinese and Japanese, who were also interested in jobs and in trade, also came in large numbers, and the islands have a mixed population of Asian, Polynesian, and European-American people. The beach of Waikiki, whose rolling surf attracts thousands of bathers, the sunny climate that shows little variation from day to day, and the beauty of the flowers that grow in profusion in the islands make Hawaii a place popular with vacationists, who believe the islands deserve the title "Paradise of the Pacific."

GRAMMAR EXERCISE 2.

Applying the principles that you have just learned, add any necessary punctuation to the following paragraph.

SOME ANIMAL AND INSECT TRAITS

A subject which is very interesting is the study of the peculiar traits of some animals and insects. A horned grebe which is a species of bird feeds her babies feathers. Koala bears eat eucalyptus leaves which furnish all the moisture that their bodies need; therefore the bears never drink. They are the only mammals that do not. A woodcock has a long bill that looks like a pencil and that can be inserted into the burrows of worms which the woodcock eats. The jaçana bird which is found in the tropics of America has spurs that unfold like a razor blade and that the jaçana uses to kill its enemies. The two-headed skink whose tail looks exactly like his head confuses his enemy. When a hawk that is pursuing him thinks that the skink is going to run one way he runs another. The May fly which has no mouth lives only one happy day. These are just a few of the many interesting creatures that live in the world around us.

MODIFICATION BY REDUCTION OF RELATIVE CLAUSES

Participles

Review section A2c, "Combining with Relative Clauses," and section J31, "Relative Clauses and Uses of Relative Pronouns," in the

Handbook. Then study section A2d, "Reductions of Relative Clauses," in preparation for the exercises that follow.

GRAMMAR EXERCISE 3.

Rewrite these sentences, reducing the italicized parts of the relative clauses to past participles.

1. Patriotism is a term *that is defined* by Albert Camus and Adlai Stevenson.
2. The definitions *that are given* by the two men have similarities.
3. The definition *that is given* by Camus emphasizes loyalty to a principle.
4. Men willing to live up to their principles are patriots in the sense *in which it is defined* by Stevenson.
5. George Washington was a man *who is admired* as a patriot by many of his fellow citizens.
6. He was a man *who is honored* as "the father of his country."

GRAMMAR EXERCISE 4.

Rewrite the sentences that follow, reducing the italicized part of the relative clause to a present or a past participle as appropriate.

1. I like to spend summer afternoons in a mountain valley *that is located* near my home.
2. In this valley there is a noisy little brook *that runs* over the rocks and *that makes* a pleasant splashing sound.
3. Beside its banks I often find people *who are fishing* in the water *that is flowing* over the rocks.
4. The water *that is flowing* sometimes makes people *who are listening* to it feel sleepy. (Which modifier goes before the noun?)
5. For me it is a place *that is designed* for an afternoon *that is spent* reading a good book.

GRAMMAR EXERCISE 5.

To test your understanding of the use of present participles ($v + $ *-ing*) and past participles ($v + $ *-ed, -en*) as modifiers of nouns, read the following sentences aloud, supplying the correct participial forms.

A girl who interests others is an interesting girl.
A girl who is interested by something is an interested girl.

1. A person who surprises others is a _____ person.
2. A person who is surprised by something is a _____ person.
3. A museum that intrigues someone is an _____ museum.
4. A lesson that confuses someone is a _____ lesson.
5. A noise that disturbs someone is a _____ noise.
6. Milk that someone spills is _____ milk.
7. A worker who is exhausted by a job is an _____ worker.

GRAMMAR EXERCISE 6.

Change the following sentences into phrases consisting of a noun with a verbal (present or part participle) as modifier. Then write a sentence using the phrase.

> The platform was draped with a flag.
> *a flag-draped platform*
> *The speakers sat on a flag-draped platform.*

1. The job pays modestly. a _____ job.

   _____ .

2. The steak was well done. a _____ steak

   _____ .

3. The coat was worn very much. a _____ coat

   _____ .

4. Her eyes were filled with tears. her _____ eyes

   _____ .

5. The car was moving fast. the _____ car

   _____ .

Appositives

Study section A2e, "Combining Sentences with Appositives and Nonrestrictive Clauses," in the Handbook. Reductions of nonrestrictive clauses or sentences are called *appositives*.

GRAMMAR EXERCISE 3.

Change the following italicized nonrestrictive clauses to appositives.

> C. P. Snow discusses Turgenev, *who was a Russian writer.*
> C. P. Snow discusses Turgenev, *a Russian writer.*

1. Do you know my friend Mary, *who is a physics major?*
2. My friend, *who is a good student,* always gets good grades.
3. She likes to study in the library late at night, *which is a time when it is quiet.*
4. She is writing a paper about neutrons. *It is a paper that she hopes to publish.*
5. The "London Scientific Journal" has expressed an interest in her paper. *It is a journal that specializes in such subjects.* (Can you make a further reduction in the italicized sentence?)

POSITIONS OF NOUN MODIFIERS

Study sections J29 and J30 in the Handbook for forms of adjectives and types of modifiers of nouns. Note their positions before or after the noun.

GRAMMAR EXERCISE 8.

Reread the passage "Life in an Arab Oasis" in Lesson 1, page 12. The selection illustrates different types of modifiers of nouns. From the italicized examples in the following list of modifiers taken from the selection, find an example of each of the following: a prepositional phrase, a single-word modifier of a noun, a relative clause, a present participle, a past participle, two single-word modifiers, and another noun.

1. the oases, *large and small*
2. the monopoly *of pyramids*
3. a *bearded old* man, *white* turban *wound tightly around his red fez*
4. the *distinctive* fabric *of their life*
5. *dark-eyed* women
6. the people *who live in the Arab world*
7. donkeys *pattering down the street*
8. the *blaring* radio
9. the *noonday* sun
10. the scene *the author described*

What conclusions can you draw about the types of modifiers that precede the noun? About the types of modifiers that follow the noun?

GRAMMAR EXERCISE 9.

Following is a subject, a verb, and an object for sentences. Write sentences modifying the nouns and the verb by adding details as directed. Modifiers of verbs are placed at the end or the beginning of a sentence. Modifiers expressing indefinite time *(sometimes, often, usually, never)* are placed before the verb.

1. man eats dinner   Identify the man by the color of his suit. (Use a prepositional phrase)
Tell where he is sitting. (Use a verbal construction.)
Is the man big or little?
Tell where he eats dinner.
Tell how often he eats dinner there.

2. Carl holds fork   Tell that Carl is your friend and that you will meet Carl soon.. (Use an appositive)
He uses his left hand to hold his fork. (Use a prepositional phrase.)
How often does he do this?

3. girl told story   Where was the girl from?
Was she smiling or frowning?
What kind of a story was it?
To whom did she tell it?

4. man sent box   Tell what his nationality is.
Tell when he sent it.
Tell whom he sent it to.
Identify the person in some way. (Use a relative clause)
Tell what the box is made of.

GRAMMAR EXERCISE 10.

Write a paragraph describing the highlights of the fabric of life in your culture or of some place you have visited and observed. Model your description on the passage "Life in an Arab Oasis" in Lesson 1. Include details that appeal to the senses—sound, sight, touch, smell, taste—as the author of the description of life in the Arab world has done. Note the topic sentence of that passage: "Within it all there is a fusion and a unity." In your description include a sentence that characterizes what you are describing.

PUNCTUATING INTERRUPTING ELEMENTS IN A SENTENCE

In Lesson 2 you studied punctuation of elements in a series and introductory modifiers in a sentence. In Lesson 3 you learned how nonrestrictive clauses (interrupting elements that give further information but that do not identify) are set off from the rest of the sentence. In the Handbook, review uses of commas, section A3, and of dashes, section A6, in "Conventions in the Mechanics of Writing."

GRAMMAR EXERCISE 11.

Punctuate the following selection.

WEATHERMAKING*

(1) Ever since the dawn no doubt the cloudy dawn of time man has been trying to change the weather. (2) For a long while he relied on magic and prayer later he switched to what we can loosely call science.

(3) Until quite recently all such efforts failed. (4) Only within the last fifteen years since a young scientist hit upon the technique called cloud seeding have we made any real progress. (5) And even the first experiments with that method after raising excited hopes proved disappointing.

(6) Cloud seeding . . . has touched off one of the most baffling controversies in meteorological history. (7) It has been blamed for or credited with practically all kinds of weather. (8) Some scientists claim seeding can produce floods or hail. (9) Others insist it has no effect at all. (10) The battle is far from over but at least one clear conclusion is beginning to emerge man can change the weather and he is getting better at it.

*William C. Vergara, "Weathermaking, a Dream That May Come True," *Harper's Magazine* (January 1962): 56.

END NOTES

1. The first sentence of an essay should be clear in itself. It should not depend on the title of the essay for its meaning.

   Incorrect:
   Title: "Tennis"
   Opening sentence: It is a very difficult game to play well.
   Correct:
   Title: "Tennis"
   Opening sentence: Tennis is a very difficult game to play well.

2. Do not use contractions in formal writing.

   Incorrect: It's difficult to play tennis well.
   Correct: It is difficult to play tennis well.

3. Divide words only between syllables. If you are not sure of correct syllabication, consult the dictionary. Don't divide one-syllable words at the end of a line or carry over only one letter to the next line.

4. Indent for paragraphs. If the second (or any succeeding) page of a composition does not begin at the beginning of a paragraph, do not indent.

5. Note these uses of *some* and *any:*
   Some is generally used in affirmative statements.

   There are *some* books on the floor.
   I need to do *some* work this afternoon.

   Some is sometimes used in questions.

   Do you have *some* money? (The emphasis is on the presence of the money.)

   Any is used in negatives.

   There aren't *any* books on the floor.

   or

   There are *no* books on the floor.

   Any is commonly used in questions.

   Do you have *any* money? (The emphasis is on the lack of money.)

Lesson 5

TECHNIQUES FOR WRITING TERM PAPERS AND ESSAY EXAMINATIONS

Rhetorical Principles

Organizational patterns,
  an overview
Outlining
Transitions, introductions,
  and conclusions
Using outside sources
  Taking notes
  Writing summaries
Writing essay
  examinations

Grammatical Patterns

Parallel structure
Reported speech
Sentence connectors
Subordinators

Writing Term Papers and Essay Examinations

Assignment: In this lesson, rather than writing a composition, you will study techniques for writing term papers and essay examinations that you will need in other courses you may be taking. Then you will practice these techniques in short exercises.

Writing a Composition Using Outside Sources

When you write a composition based on information you have gained through reading or by consulting people who have first-hand knowledge of the subject, you may be writing a paper a number of pages in length because you will be considering several aspects of the subject, not just one. Each of these aspects works with others to support a thesis. We refer to these major assertions as *main points*. This more complex writing requires the writer to consider the pattern of organization or arrangement that the main points should follow. Another important aspect of such writing is crediting the ideas and words of another person and incorporating them into a composition of your own. Problems of organization and of using outside sources will be considered in this lesson.

ORGANIZATIONAL PATTERNS, AN OVERVIEW

Organized writing follows an expected sequence of thinking so that the reader can follow the writer's line of thought and understand what is written. Like the thesis, the main points should be clearly stated and should clearly relate to the thesis sentence and to the other points.

Common patterns of organization are the following:

1. Time (forward, backward). This type of arrangement is used in narrative and when tracing the history of something.
2. Space (from east to west, top to bottom, and so on). This arrangement is commonly used in description.
3. Topic (physical, mental, moral; day laborers, blue-collar workers, professional men; and so on). This is a method of analysis or classification. It is the most common type of organization.
4. Cause-effect or effect to cause.
5. Problem-solution.

Such patterns of organization may be found in long paragraphs that have a topic sentence as well as in longer compositions.

OUTLINING

The organization of thought in a piece of writing, stripped of all developmental material, is revealed in an outline. The outline has certain essential parts:

1. statement of the thesis, labeled as such
2. statement of the main points
3. statement of subpoints

Below are two forms that may be used to indicate the relationship of the basic ideas in the outline. Your instructor will indicate which one you are to use when a formal outline is required.

A	B
Thesis: _____	**Thesis:** _____
I. Main point	1. Main point
A. Subpoint	**1.1** Subpoint
B. Subpoint	**1.2** Subpoint
II. Main point	2. Main point
A. Subpoint	**2.1** Subpoint
B. Subpoint	**2.2** Subpoint
1. Subpoint of B	**2.21** Subpoint of 2.2
2. Subpoint of B	**2.22** Subpoint of 2.2

If subpoints are indicated, there should be more than one. The subpoints divide the main point. If there is only one subpoint, the idea should be incorporated in the main point.

Certain aspects of writing are not essential in the outline. Ways of developing the main points are not essential in the outline of basic structure except as you want to insert them in words or phrases for your own benefit. The introduction and conclusion are not necessary either, for they relate the subject to your audience—the former to catch reader interest, the latter to make the reader remember your subject and think about it.

The outline _is_ concerned with the relation of the subpoints to the main points and the relation of the main points to the other points and to the thesis. In other words, the outline is a picture of the organization of what you say in the body of the composition. When you plan the organization of your material, follow a consistent pattern. For example, if your overall plan is topical, do not switch to a cause-effect plan, though a different organizational pattern may be used in arranging the subpoints.

When is outlining necessary, and when in the process of composition should it be done? Not everything you write will need to be outlined, and outlining does not always have to be done before you start writing. Some writers write more freely by letting the ideas pour forth in a first draft. You can then sort them out, decide on a logical sequence, and revise. For a short composition this works quite well. In somewhat longer compositions, however, before writing a first draft you may want to list the aspects of your subject that you want to discuss and arrange them in a manner that seems best. At this point you have made a topic outline. Then you may need to phrase the thesis, the main points, and the subpoints in sentences that will establish the relationships among them. Such an outline (1) provides the writer with well-worded statements of the points that he or she can use in writing the paper and (2) is useful when the writer is devising a transition from one main point to the next.

Before you read the selection "The Influence of the Frontier" later in this lesson, study and compare these outlines that preceded the writing:

Topic outline
Influence of American Frontier

I. Influences (causes)
   A. Lasted 300 years
   B. Settlement of empty land important
   C. Difficult living conditions
II. Results
   A. To individual
      1. Gave opportunity
      2. Promoted restlessness
      3. Developed self-reliance
      4. Promoted friendliness
   B. To nation
      1. Local government for local needs
      2. Federal government for national needs

Sentence outline

Thesis: The American frontier had a profound influence on the character of Americans and on the nation.

I. Certain aspects of the frontier were to prove influential.
  A. Although its geographical location kept changing, the frontier for 300 years provided escape for the discontented.
  B. The settlement of the frontier land would also affect the individual and the nation.
  C. Difficult living conditions on the frontier were another influence.
    1. Each man had to solve his own problems.
    2. Isolation and loneliness were a part of life.

II. These aspects of frontier life produced certain effects.
  A. There were numerous effects on the individual.
    1. The frontier gave people opportunity and hope.
    2. The frontier led to a certain restlessness.
    3. The frontier developed self-reliance.
    4. The frontier developed a feeling of equality among men of varied backgrounds and abilities.
    5. Frontier isolation developed a naive friendliness toward strangers.
  B. The frontier developed attitudes toward government.
    1. Local government concerns local needs.
    2. National government concerns matters that local governments cannot handle.

EXERCISE 1.

Answer these questions on the outlines of "The Influence of the American Frontier."

1. At a glance, which outline gives the better picture of the organization?
2. Which outline do you think was initially more helpful in sorting out the writer's ideas?
3. Which outline gives a better picture of the content?
4. Which outline would help the writer more in phrasing ideas as he or she writes the composition?

THE INFLUENCE OF THE AMERICAN FRONTIER

(1) In the United States of America we find a teeming nation of people derived from all

corners of the world and bound together in a federal system of government. To understand how such a diverse mass of people--originally speaking different languages and adhering to different customs and religions--could eventually develop common characteristics that distinguish them from people of other nations of the world, we must understand the influence of the frontier on the development of the country. According to American historian Frederick Jackson Turner, the frontier was the greatest single influence in shaping what the country was to become. Regardless of whether one accepts this evaluation, the influence of the frontier on American character and institutions was profound.

(2) Several aspects of the frontier made it influential. First, though its geographic location moved constantly westward, the frontier was always there. For 300 years--from the early 1600s to the later 1800s--discontented and ambitious people could escape from organized society and retreat to a relatively empty land. The first frontier existed just west of the colonies along the Atlantic coast. In the seventeenth century, pioneers followed the rivers to the Appalachian Mountains, and these mountains became the frontier. During the Revolutionary War, Americans crossed the Allegheny section of those mountains. By 1820 settlements were found along the banks of the Ohio River clear to the Mississippi and down the Mississippi to Louisiana. Settlements had advanced into Kansas and Nebraska by 1850. Then gold was discovered in California, and pioneers passed through the Great Plains and Rocky Mountains heading for the West Coast. After the plains and mountains were settled in the last quarter of the nineteenth century, the geographic frontier ceased to exist.

(3) This westward movement of settling the empty frontier land followed a consistent pattern of development that would affect the

individual and the country. First came
explorers, who forged paths through the
wilderness. Close on their heels, sometimes
accompanying them, came fur traders and
sometimes priests and missionaries, who made
contact with the indigenous Indian population.
The white man had entered a land, however, in
which he recognized no law. Only after
ranchers, then farmers, had established
permanent homes did towns spring up and people
become aware of the need for government.

(4) Throughout this period when the country
went from a primitive society to an organized
one, conditions on the frontier were difficult.
Those who explored the new land were on their
own in meeting new conditions, finding food and
shelter for themselves in all sorts of weather,
and fending off Indian attacks. Those who
settled there had to build their own homes,
break the soil, raise crops, and protect their
families from danger. The pioneer settlers had
to be their own priests, their own doctors. If
marauders came or if one's right to the land was
questioned, the pioneer had to be his own law.
Whatever corner of the earth a person came from,
no matter what one's station or wealth in
another society, the frontier made the same
demands of everyone. In the vast emptiness of
the open land, the settler was often lonesome.
Another human being was a welcome sight. Anyone
passing through the country was urged not only
to spend the night but to stay for days. When
settlers left their homes to go for
supplies--journeys that sometimes took many
days--they often left their cabin doors
unlocked, and any traveler was welcome to come
in and cook what food there was.

(5) Those who lived on the frontier could not
help being affected by the conditions of their
life. Certainly the frontier offered new land,
and the settler went with a hope that a better
life was possible. The presence of this new land
may have developed a sense of restlessness in
Americans. However, because people faced the

same dangers and had to do for themselves, the land also fostered a spirit of self-reliance, a sense of competence, and a feeling of being the equal of everyone else. Persons were judged not for social status but for what they themselves could do. The settler lived in a relatively empty country, and the passing stranger broke the loneliness. Americans developed a naive friendliness and belief in the goodness of others. Visitors from abroad are sometimes baffled by the instant heartiness with which Americans meet them, because it seems to imply more friendship than a quick meeting can bring. This immediate friendliness is a legacy of the frontier.

(6) The dual system of loyalty to the community and to the federal government that developed on the frontier affected the nation. The frontiersman, who had at first been a loner, became tied to the community in unexpected ways. It was easier for a group to hunt down a thief than for one man to do it. The yearly journeys that the settlers made back to civilization to get salt often had to be made in groups to avoid or repulse Indian attacks. Such events developed the frontier people's loyalty to the community. Yet they became aware that they were dependent on the national government for things the local government could not manage. Among these were roads, disposition of public lands, railroads, and national defense. Thus regional loyalty came to exist side by side with recognition of the need for and loyalty to a federal government. Yet historian Alice Felt Tyler reminds us that the frontiersman "was a believer in . . . limitation of government to the barest necessities for individual freedom."* Like the frontiersman, contemporary Americans resent undue government interference.

(7) Today the geographic frontier of the United States has gone, but 300 years of frontier life have left their stamp on the country--on the attitudes and personality of

the individual, on the state, and on the nation.
The frontier today is a symbol for great
challenge and great reward, for starting a new
way of life. As such, it has been used in titles
of books, in names of corporations, and in
political campaigns. One example was John F.
Kennedy's labeling of his plans for improving
the nation "The New Frontier."

   *Alice Felt Tyler, <u>Freedom's Ferment</u> (New
York: Harper & Row, 1944), p. 6.

EXERCISE 2.

Answer these questions on the organization of "The Influence of the
American Frontier."

1. Is the overall organization of the essay by time, space, topic, or
   cause and effect?
2. What is the purpose of paragraphs 2, 3, and 4?
3. What is the purpose of paragraphs 5 and 6?
4. In paragraph 2, is the pattern of organization by time, space, or
   topic?
5. Is the pattern of organization in paragraph 3 by time, space, or
   topic?
6. What is the pattern of organization in the section that lists the
   effects of frontier life?

EXERCISE 3.

Discuss in class what method of organization—topical, chronological, spatial, cause-effect—might be used in expanding each of the
following into a composition of three or four pages. Be prepared to
defend your answer.

1. The boundaries of my country have changed several times
   since ___(date)___.
2. The territory in my country has been acquired in several
   ways.
3. ___(Person)___ was one of the foremost figures in the
   development of ___(country or section of country)___.

4. ___Electronics (Oil, Tourism, Agriculture)___ is the backbone of the economy of my country.
5. ___(School, Museum)___ has developed a program unique in my country.
6. ___(Name of national hero)___ truly deserves the title of Father of His Country.
7. No (activity, group of performers, composer, artist, writer) is more widely acclaimed in ___(nation)___ than ___(name___.

TRANSITIONS, INTRODUCTIONS, AND CONCLUSIONS

Transitions, introductions, and conclusions are ways in which the writer clarifies the thesis for the reader and helps him follow the line of thought.

Transitions

Throughout a composition, in order to keep the central idea or purpose of an essay clearly in the mind of the reader and show the relevance of each main point to the central idea and to other main points, you as a writer may use various devices. Sometimes the central idea is restated or referred to several times during the composition. A convenient time to call the reader's attention to it is when you move from one main point of development of the idea to another. You may use transitional words or phrases such as "The next reason for this condition is" or "Not only . . . but also" or "Then" or "In addition" to refer to your previous point or your central idea and to introduce what is to come. The transitional device you use in a given spot depends on your method of organization. Transitional words and phrases appropriate to each type of organization will be discussed as each method of organization is treated in succeeding lessons.

Introductions

So far in this lesson, we have been studying the relationships (1) between main points and the thesis, (2) between subpoints and main points, and (3) between the supporting points themselves. Another important aspect of writing is to relate your subject to the reader. You do this by considering the following:

1. Will your readers already be interested in your subject, or will you need to capture their interest? Do you need to make an

astonishing statement of fact or opinion, tell a story, give an apt quotation, or focus in from a wide subject to a narrow one?

2. Does your reader need background information to understand your subject? Do you need to explain terms or give a history of the subject?

3. Do you need to tell the reader why he or she needs to know what you have to tell?

This type of material is included in the introduction. The introduction generally ends with a statement of the thesis.

Conclusions

In the conclusion you will try to say something that will ensure that the reader cannot possibly forget or misunderstand what you have said. Here are some common ways of ending a composition:

1. a summary
2. an illustration that reminds the reader of the central idea
3. a quotation that restates the central idea in a forceful way
4. a reference to a point made in the introduction, which again brings the central idea into focus

EXERCISE 4.

Answer these questions about the introduction, conclusion, and transitional devices in the essay "The Influence of the American Frontier."

1. Of the possible ways to introduce a subject, which is used in paragraph 1?

2. Circle words that link the thought of one paragraph to the preceding paragraph or to the main point or central idea.

3. What other devices besides transitional words and phrases does the author use? Give examples.

4. In a short article, an author cannot develop assertions in as much detail as in a chapter of a book on the subject. If this article were expanded, which points would you like to see developed in more detail? What developmental devices would you use?

5. What method is used in the final paragraph to bring the central idea into focus?

EXERCISE 5.

Following is a group of sentences, some of which belong in an outline, some of which do not. In outline form arrange the sentences that belong in an outline, labeling the thesis sentence, identifying main points and subpoints, and so on.

1. Endomorphs are fat, dominated by their digestive systems.
2. At school the extreme endomorph is called "Fatty."
3. People differ in physique.
4. Vicerotonic people turn to other people to help them out of trouble.
5. Human beings differ in many ways.
6. People differ in mental ability.
7. A genius has extraordinary intelligence.
8. Mesomorphs have hard, muscular bodies and strong bones.
9. A moron has an IQ of 50 to 60 and is incapable of developing mentally beyond the ages of 8 to 12.
10. Somatonic people are adventurous and move in an assertive way.
11. Ectomorphs are lightweight and have little muscular strength.
12. Cerebrotonic people are shy and hate to make themselves conspicuous.
13. People differ in temperament.
14. They are reluctant to deviate from a usual routine.
15. An idiot is a person who cannot develop beyond the mentality of a person from 3 to 4 years of age.

USING OUTSIDE SOURCES

In the compositions that you wrote in Lessons 1 through 4, you used information that you knew at first hand. For term papers for other courses, you will have to collect information through reading. In the Handbook, techniques for writing the term paper will be discussed in more detail. When you use secondary sources of information in a paper (information from your reading or from interviews with other people), remember these principles:

1. The facts may come from your reading but *the plan of the paper, the thesis, and the organization, must be your own.*
2. *The wording must be your own* unless you indicate that you are quoting someone else. This can be done by direct or indirect

quotations. In direct quotations of someone else's words, use quotation marks. In indirect quotations *(paraphrases)* of someone else's ideas, introduce the statement by, "____(Name)____ says that."

3. *As you read source material, jot down usable ideas in your own words.* Do not copy the wording exactly unless it is sufficiently effective to be worthy of an exact quotation or unless the content is so unbelievable that you need the exact quotation to support its authenticity.

4. *Record the author, title, place of publication, publisher, date, and page(s) of all source material.*

5. When you quote directly, check wording, spelling, and punctuation with care. What you put inside quotation marks should be *exactly the same as the original.*

6. *Give credit to your sources,* both for direct quotations and for paraphrases or summaries of someone else's ideas. See section III D in the Handbook for the footnote form.

EXERCISE 6.

Answer these questions about the use of secondary sources in "The Influence of the American Frontier."

1. Where do you think the author found the facts? Are they facts that probably appear in a number of sources on the American frontier? If so, could they be considered general information that does not need footnoting?

2. If such facts had been quoted exactly from the books they came from, what punctuation marks would probably tell you? Is there any other way in which quotations can be indicated?

3. Do you think most of the facts given in the essay were quoted directly from the source from which the author of the selection found the information?

4. The complete sentence from which the Alice Felt Tyler quotation (in paragraph 6) is taken reads as follows:

> Owing to the very nature of his life, the frontiersman was a believer in <u>laissez faire</u> doctrines and in limitation of government to the barest necessities for individual freedom.

(Note the indentation and change of spacing to indicate a quotation. This is often done when long quotations are used in a manuscript.) Why do you think only part of the sentence was quoted? How is the omission shown?

5. The statement by Frederick Jackson Turner was made in a paper read at a meeting of the American Historical Association in Chicago, July 12, 1893. Could it have been footnoted? It appears in quotation marks in a number of books on the American frontier. Why do you think it was not footnoted here?

6. The writer of the selection "The Influence of the American Frontier" may have taken notes something like this:

> *Frontier—existed 300 years*
> *First frontier—Atlantic. Then Appalachians, Ohio Valley,*
> *Great Plains, Rocky Mountains. Gold in California—1849.*

Paragraph 2 could then have been written this way:

```
Frontier living was part of American life for
300 years. At first the frontier was the
Atlantic seaboard. Then in successive stages
the following areas were settled: the
Appalachian Mountains, the Ohio Valley, Kansas
and Nebraska, the Great Plains, the Rocky
Mountains, and the West Coast.
```

What are the disadvantages of reading such a condensed list? If you were writing an essay examination, what would be the advantage of presenting a condensed list?

EXERCISE 7.

Read the following excerpt from Alice Felt Tyler's *Freedom's Ferment* and decide whether the ideas expressed here could have been incorporated into the article on the influence of the American frontier on Americans.

Three thousand miles of sea, to be traversed in colonial days with only the danger and discomfort of a long and tedious voyage, caused the European individual transplanted in America to feel himself separated from his old world. He found it easy to accept the idea of a natural, "absolute, unrelated man" who existed and had acquired property before governments were developed to make demands upon his liberty and property. Since he must combine with other colonists to meet common problems and make use of common opportunities, he accepted without question the idea that government sprang from the people and is the agent of the people. It was natural, therefore, for American political leaders to accept John Locke, the great exponent of English constitutional development, as their spokesman, the interpreter of their ideas of natural laws, individual liberties, and the right of revolution when they were oppressed by illegitimate use of authority.*

1. Write a few sentences expressing in your own words the ideas in the preceding paragraph.
2. How would you indicate in the body of a paper that you are presenting the ideas of Alice Felt Tyler?
3. Would you footnote your sentences to indicate the exact source? Note that the footnote is put at the bottom of the page on which the quoted material appears or at the end of the essay. (The use of the abbreviations *ibid.* and *op. cit.* are explained in the Handbook, section III D.)

Taking Notes

EXERCISE 8.

As your instructor reads aloud "The Influence of the American Frontier," pretend that this is a lecture being given in a history class and take notes on the lecture. In taking notes, try to be aware of the overall organization and write enough to make the notes useful in recalling what the instructor said. When you have finished, compare your notes with the topic outline on page 101.

Writing Summaries
A summary should include the following:

1. the title of the work and the author's name
2. the central idea and the main points
3. only as much of the developmental material as is necessary for understanding

A summary should not include personal opinions of the person doing the summarizing, and a summary should be in the words of the summarizer, not the phrasing of the original author.

---

*Alice Felt Tyler, *Freedom's Ferment* (New York: Harper & Row, 1944), p. 6.

EXERCISE 9.

Outside of class read the following selection written by the authors of this text. Later, in class, with your textbook closed, write a summary of it.

UNDERSEA MUSEUMS*

(1) The federal government of the United States has established many national parks at places of historic or scenic interest. At these, tourists on vacation can see spectacular caves, canyons, falls, geysers, mountains, lakes, rivers, and battlefields. Several national parks simply preserve prairie and forests as they were before Europeans came to the continent. Until recently, however, no one had thought of using the resources off the coasts as recreation areas. Now since scuba† diving has become so popular, four undersea areas have been set aside as retreats for swimmers and divers who want to get away from the crowds found in most vacation areas.

(2) The first underwater park was near Truk Island in the South Pacific. Many ships and planes were wrecked there during World War II, and the area provides adventurous scuba divers a chance to explore some 70 sunken ships in a park that is both eerie and fascinating.

(3) More recently the United States Government has established a similar park just off St. Croix in the Virgin Islands. An interesting feature of this park is the underwater markers that show pictures of the various kinds of fish found here with the name and habits of each.

(4) The first subsurface park in the continental United States was established at Key Largo, Florida. It covers about 75 square miles and gives divers their only chance to see

*Data from Thomas Giafardoni, "Underwater Parks: Keep 'Em Coming," *True*, 54 (March 1973): 30.

†*Scuba* stands for "Self-Contained Underwater Breathing Apparatus."

living coral in North American waters. To date,
more than three million people have enjoyed the
many types of coral on the reef and the
varieties of fish that go swimming by.
  (5) Another undersea museum has recently been
set aside at Big Sur, California. It adjoins a
park area along the shore.
  (6) Since the advent of scuba in 1943,
adventurers under the sea have shown that they
can venture almost anywhere. Perhaps in the
future the sea will become nearly the only place
where man can retire to find the solitude once
found in the vast, empty areas of the land.

Writing Essay Examinations

Study the techniques for writing essay examinations in section III B
of the Handbook. Then do the exercise below based on "The Influence of the American Frontier."

EXERCISE 10.

Following are some sample answers to an essay examination question. Some of them contain common errors. One is satisfactory. Be
prepared to discuss the shortcomings of each defective answer and
decide which answer is satisfactory and why.

  <u>Examination question: Discuss the effects of
the American frontier upon American life today</u>.

<u>Answer 1</u>: Made people more self-reliant. But
they were lonely. Would welcome any stranger.
Not like today when we are sometimes suspicious
of the stranger who comes to our door. But of
course times have changed. There is more crime
and so we have reason to be suspicious of
strangers. There is no place where we have those
same frontier conditions today.

<u>Answer 2</u>: To a student of American history one
of the most interesting parts of the study is
the development of the frontier--of course we
have to keep remembering that the frontier
changed and Americans moved farther and farther

west in the United States. We have to remember
too that there was a distinctive pattern of
development of the frontier. First the
explorers came and then the traders with the
Indians. Then the miners and the ranchers came
in to develop the country. Finally, when the
farmers arrived, civilization had taken over.
But Americans today are a lot like the pioneers
in many ways. They are individualistic like him
but perhaps not as resourceful. They are not
lonely either. But they still greet strangers
with the same friendliness that the pioneers
did.

<u>Answer 3</u>: The effects of the American frontier
on life today are:

1. It made Americans more individualistic.
2. It made Americans more friendly. Americans
   greet foreigners in a more friendly way than
   they are greeted by many foreigners.
3. Americans have a dual loyalty--to both state
   and nation.

<u>Answer 4</u>: The American frontier had at least
five important effects upon American life
today. On the frontier, men had to rely on
themselves to do things. This has resulted
today in making Americans more individualistic. A second effect of the frontier was to
break down social barriers, and this lack of
social barriers still exists. Still another
effect was that the loneliness of the frontier,
which fostered friendliness toward strangers,
left an impression on succeeding generations so
that Americans today tend to greet strangers
with instant friendliness and a belief in their
goodness. A fourth legacy of the frontier is
that it gave to Americans a sense of loyalty
both to their particular region and to the
central government at the same time. Finally,
the frontier has always meant a place where a
person had to work hard and risk a lot, but it

offered a great reward. Therefore, in American thinking, the frontier is a symbol for starting a new way of life.

Reviewing Grammatical Patterns

PARALLEL STRUCTURE

GRAMMAR EXERCISE 1.

Parallel structure produces clearer, more readable writing. Note the parallel structure in these sentences about the American frontier. Rewrite the idea using different wording but keeping the parallel structure.

1. On the frontier a guest was urged *not only to spend* the night *but to stay* for days.
   A guest was welcome not only *for a night* but _____ .
2. Even in Alaska the stretches of untouched land *are owned* by the federal government, the Alaskan Indians, or the Eskimos, and *are not open* for settlement.
   In Alaska *the government, the Alaskan Indians,* or *the Eskimos own the land,* and newcomers _____ .
3. In colonial days, a diverse mass of people—originally *speaking* different languages and *adhering* to different customs and religions—gradually developed common characteristics.
   In colonial days, a diverse mass of people who originally *spoke* different languages and _____ .
4. There was open land to the west *inviting* people who wanted to escape from civilization and *rewarding* them for their daring.
   There was open land to the west *that invited* people who wanted to escape from civilization and _____ .
5. Travel is a way *of meeting* new people from other countries and *of learning* about those people and those countries.
   Travel is a way *to meet* new people from other countries and _____ .
6. I have practiced a lot of sports. I like *to ski, to bicycle, to climb,* and *to hike.*
   I have practiced a lot of sports. I like *skiing,* _____ , _____ , and _____ .
7. My grandmother doesn't like cars. Cars *pollute* the air and *make* it dangerous to cross the street.

My grandmother doesn't like cars because of the *pollution* and _____ .

REPORTED SPEECH

You may report the exact words of someone by using quotation marks around the words, or you may report them indirectly. Compare these direct and indirect reports:

Direct: Frederick Jackson Turner said, "The frontier is the greatest single influence in shaping what America was to become."

Indirect: Frederick Jackson Turner said *that* the frontier *was* the greatest single influence in shaping what America was to become.

Idea in different wording: Frederick Jackson Turner considered the frontier to be the greatest single influence in shaping what America was to become.

Here is another example:

Direct: Alice Felt Tyler said, ". . . the frontiersman was a believer in . . . limitation of government to the barest necessities for individual freedom."

Indirect: Alice Felt Tyler said *that* the frontiersman *was* a believer in limitation of government to the barest necessities for individual freedom.

Idea in different wording: Alice Felt Tyler said that the frontiersman believed in limiting government in order to preserve individual freedom.

When you report in your own words, be sure you do not misinterpret what the original speaker or writer said.

GRAMMAR EXERCISE 2.

Study sections G16a, G16b, and G16c in the Handbook. Assume that a classmate has been absent and that you are going to write her a note telling her what happened in the class that she missed. Here are (1) statements the professor made, (2) questions the students asked, and (3) suggestions the professor gave the students. Report them in indirect speech in your note.

1. Statements by the professor
   a. "In the past people have used many kinds of commodities for money."

    b. "Primitive people often used stones and shells."

    c. "Shells used by American Indians were called *wampum.*"

    d. "The ancient Romans counted their wealth in terms of cattle."

    e. "The Latin word for cattle was *pecus.*"

2. Questions asked by students

    a. "Is that where we get our term *pecuniary*?"

    b. "What does *pecuniary* mean?"

    c. "When did coins begin to be used?"

    d. "Is it true that the Chinese were the first to use paper money?"

    e. "What's the advantage of paper money?"

3. Suggestions given by the professor

    a. "You had better look up *pecuniary* in the dictionary."

    b. "You can find the answers to your questions in your textbook."

    c. "Study Chapter 12 for tomorrow."

    d. "Be prepared for a test on Friday."

    e. "Get a good night's sleep beforehand."

GRAMMAR EXERCISE 3.

Here is a conversation between a French student planning to study in the United States and a friend who has just returned to France and is giving advice. Write a report of the conversation. Do not quote the direct words of the speakers. Your report will begin:

> My friend said that I ought to apply for a scholarship. I asked him whether . . .

A CONVERSATION

(1) "You ought to apply for a scholarship," Andre said.

(2) "Do you think I have a good chance of getting one?" I asked him.

(3) "The competition will be keen," he replied. "I suggest that you take a course in English."

(4) "Why do I need it?" I said.

(5) "You have to understand the language when it is spoken rapidly, and you will have to write a good many papers," he told me.

(6) Then, "Do you plan to live in a university residence hall or in off-campus housing?" he asked me.

(7) "Which do you recommend?" I asked.

(8) "I advise you to live in the residence hall. It's cheaper and you'll get to know more students," he said.

(9) "But it might be noisy," I objected.

(10) "That's true," he replied. "Ask for a single room."

(11) "I hope I get the scholarship," I told him.

(12) "I hope so too. Write and let me know what happens," he replied.

SENTENCE CONNECTORS

Review the use of sentence connectors, section A2a in the Handbook.

GRAMMAR EXERCISE 4.

Join the following pairs of sentences into one sentence, using appropriate sentence connectors (not conjunctions). Put the sentence connector at the beginning of the second clause and use suitable punctuation. When you have finished the exercise rewrite the sentences, changing the position of the sentence connector and making necessary changes in punctuation.

1. It is raining. We will go to the meeting.
2. He passed the examination. He received his certificate.
3. One can make a great deal of money in that profession. The hours are long and the work difficult.
4. The assignment was very difficult. We did not finish it as soon as we had expected.
5. This is the most beautiful design of its kind that I have ever seen. It is the only one I have ever seen.
6. The city is famous for its art gallery. It has a fine symphony.
7. It was a very cold night. We decided to stay at home.
8. The competition is keen. You must work hard if you want to be successful.
9. The car ran out of gasoline. They had to remain there for the night.
10. He does the work very slowly. He usually does it well.

SUBORDINATORS

You know the meaning expressed by the common conjunctions *and, but, or,* and *for* and by the clause connectors *therefore, however, nevertheless,* and so on. Other words that express relationship between two ideas are subordinators, which introduce dependent clauses. Knowing how to use them helps you express your ideas more exactly and with more variety of sentence structure. Review section H23 in the Handbook for the use of subordinators.

GRAMMAR EXERCISE 5.

In the example sentences, note the relationship between the two ideas as expressed by the italicized subordinator. Then complete the sentences that follow.

Examples: These sentences express approximately the same idea.

I'll wait *until* he comes.
I won't go *unless* he comes.
If he doesn't come, I won't go.
In case he does come, I'll go.

1. I won't take the plane *until* (till) _____ .
2. _____ *unless* I get an unexpected check from home.
3. In case _____ I will take the plane.
4. _____ if I win the lottery.

Examples:

I gave Paul my car keys *so that he* can go downtown this afternoon. (planned result)
I don't have my car *so* I can't take you to your lesson. (unplanned result)
I can't take you to the lesson *unless* Paul brings the car back soon. (condition, after a negative statement)
I can take you to the lesson *provided* Paul brings the car back soon. (condition, after an affirmative statement)

1. I didn't wear my coat *so that* _____ .(Give a reason.)
2. I didn't wear my coat so _____ . (Give a result.)
3. I can go Friday unless _____ . (Explain a condition.)
4. Provided _____ I will cancel my doctor's appointment. (Tell what circumstance will make you cancel your appointment.)

END NOTES

1. Note the inversion of subject and verb in the use of *did* in this sentence:

   Only after ranchers, then farmers, had established permanent homes *did* towns *spring up* and people *become* aware of the need for government.

   This structure is used for emphasis in literary rather than spoken English.

2. Note that in quotations the punctuation mark precedes the final quotation mark. When there is a quotation within a quotation, single quotation marks are used.

3. Titles of short articles, articles that are part of a longer collection, and chapters of books are put in quotation marks. Titles of books are underlined.

   "The Influence of the American Frontier"
   Alice Felt Tyler's book <u>Freedom's Ferment</u>

   In printed material, italics take the place of underlining.

4. Underlining (italics) is also used in these cases:

   a. A word used as a word.

   The word *people* is singular in form.

   b. A foreign word or phrase.

   opus citado

5. In possessives, the apostrophe goes before the *-s* when a single thing is referred to. When the noun is plural, the apostrophe goes after the *-s*

   Organization helps the reader to follow the *writer's* line of thought.
   Writers' problems cannot always be solved in this way.
   The *settlers'* ideas of government were influenced by the Iroquois Indians.
   The *people's* ideas of government were influenced by the frontier.

Lesson 6

ANALYZING A CONDITION, SOCIAL PRACTICE, OR BELIEF

Rhetorical Principles	Grammatical Patterns
Topical organization	The passive voice
Deductive and inductive order	Past tense versus present perfect
Devices for coherence in topical organization	Past perfect
	Modals
Use of reference material and footnoting	The subjunctive
	Infinitives as complements
	Infinitives to show purpose
	Avoiding dangling modifiers

Writing a Composition

Assignment: If you wish to make clear just what a condition, social practice, or belief actually is, you need to examine various aspects of it. You may want to give evidence that the condition exists or reasons why you believe a certain practice is good or bad or should be changed in some way. Therefore, for this lesson (1) choose a social practice or an economic or political condition that you are familiar with and write a paper of two or three pages explaining to your reader just what it is, or (2) choose a belief you hold that your readers may not agree with and give reasons why you believe it.

Stage I. Prewriting

STEP 1. BRAINSTORMING FOR IDEAS

EXERCISE 1.

Following are some questions that you might answer in a composition. Choose one of them (or another not listed) about which you feel competent to write, and be prepared to discuss with your classmates how you might limit and develop it.

1. What ethnic groups have influenced society in your country?
2. Is polygamy desirable in your culture?
3. Are stiff penalties for crimes justified?
4. Should a father (mother) have custody of children in case of divorce?
5. What economic problems do young couples encounter in your country?
6. What traffic problems exist in your (city, country)?
7. Are people in (city, country) happier without a car?
8. Should everyone have a chance to go to college?
9. Does any group in your country feel apart from the rest of society? (e.g., Catalonians in Spain, citizens of Quebec in Canada)
10. Should the hunting season for (an animal or bird) be extended?
11. What is the significance of Yom Kippur (or some other religious celebration)?
12. Should women study some things that are different from the things that men study?
13. What qualities other than physical strength are required in order to be a good (golfer, tennis player, and so on)?

14. What traditional customs in your country preserve the national heritage?
15. Are chopsticks better eating implements than forks?
16. What are the distinguishing characteristics of a particular genus of plants or animals?
17. Should certain books be banned from the schools?

EXERCISE 2.

Formulate topic sentences you could use for three of the topics suggested by the questions in exercise 1. If you choose another subject to write on, present the topic sentence you will use.

STEP 3. JOTTING DOWN IDEAS AND REFINING A POINT OF VIEW

EXERCISE 3.

Here are some notes for a composition. After you read them, answer the questions that follow.

The influence of the Indians on North American culture
1. Names: states, cities, rivers, geographical features
2. Government: League of the Iroquois
3. Art: jewelry, rugs, painting, dances, architecture
4. Food: potatoes, peanuts (tobacco?)
5. Sense of history

1. Suggest a possible thesis sentence for the composition. (Note that the thesis sentence is *not* the title.)
2. What method of organization will the author probably use?
3. What method of development will the author probably use for most of the points listed? Which points cannot be developed in this way? Suggest a possible method of development for these points.

EXERCISE 4.

Jot down ideas for the composition you will write. Group similar ideas together and state your thesis.

Stage II. Giving Form to the Composition and Studying Techniques

STEP 4. WRITING A FIRST DRAFT

EXERCISE 5.

Write a first draft of the composition. As you write, think of revisions you will make, both in organization and in wording. The study of rhetorical techniques that follow may give you suggestions for your writing.

STEP 5. STUDYING RHETORICAL PRINCIPLES

Topical Organization

When a writer analyzes a subject he may discuss different aspects of it according to some logical division of ideas called *topical organization*. This is probably the most common organizational pattern in expository writing. Topical order is a method of classification. Here are some ways of classifying material.

1. By fields of inquiry
   a. physical
   b. mental
   c. moral
   d. social
   e. economic
2. By kinds of causes or effects
   a. causes: primary, contributing, precipitating
   b. effects: immediate, long range
3. By physical characteristics
   a. color
   b. size
   c. atomic weight
   d. relation to other elements

These are only a few of the classifications that might be used. Usually a writer presents the most important point last so that it is the idea that stays in the reader's mind the longest and so that the lesser points do not seem trivial in comparison.

Note the sections into which the textbook *Psychology and Language**
is divided:

1. Language
2. Comprehension
3. Production
4. Acquisition
5. Meaning and Thought

EXERCISE 6.

Fill in the missing topic in each of the following groups.

1. men, women, and _____
2. elementary school, high school, and _____
3. Buddhism, Islam, and _____
4. economic, social, and _____
5. meat, dairy products, and _____

Deductive and Inductive Order

The rhetorical patterns of organization listed in Lesson 5 (time, space, topical, cause-effect, problem-solution) are determined by the relationship of the main points to the other points. Deductive and inductive order refer to the relative placement of the thesis sentence and the main points. In deductive order the writer states the thesis, then develops it; in inductive order the the ideas are developed first and the thesis stated at the end. The nature of the subject, the reader, and the situation—all are factors in determining which order is best for a given piece of writing.

Note that inductive and deductive order of the arrangement of ideas are quite different concepts from inductive and deductive reasoning. The similarity in vocabulary is unfortunate and sometimes confusing to students.

(1) *Deductive order:* Deductive order is by far the most common in expository writing. It is an aid to both the writer and the reader. By stating the thesis at the outset, a writer is more likely to keep to the subject and relate the main points to the central idea as well as to the other points. When the thesis sentence is at the beginning of a book or a chapter, a composition or a paragraph, it is in the expected place.

---

*Herbert H. and Eva Clark, *Psychology and Language, an Introduction to Psycholinguistics* (New York: Harcourt Brace Jovanovich, 1977).

For a researcher, this often saves time, and it helps any reader get oriented. One of the important uses of deductive order is writing essay examinations.

(2) *Inductive order:* A common use of exposition is to explain a point of view. While this use may result in persuasion, its primary purpose is to give reasons, and it makes use of the devices of arrangement and support of ideas that we studied in previous lessons.

The attitude you anticipate in your readers affects whether you proceed inductively or deductively. If you think your readers will have no quarrel with your conclusion, you will probably proceed deductively, stating your conclusions at the outset. If you think your readers will be hostile to your conclusion, you give your reasons first, hoping they will agree with them one by one until they have to reach the conclusion that you did.

NORTH AMERICA'S DEBT TO AMERICAN INDIAN CULTURE

(1) Stephen Vincent Benét, the American writer, said that when the British first came to America they thought they would be English even though they lived in another country. But, Benét said, they would never be English again. The country and the Indians who already lived in it would change the immigrants. Almost unnoticed, certain aspects of Indian culture seeped into their lives and contributed to making them "American."

(2) Indian influence may be seen everywhere today in the names that were given to states, cities, and physical features of the country. The states of Delaware, Iowa, Illinois, and Alabama were named after Indian tribes. Many rivers--the Seneca and Susquehanna, for example--have Indian names; so do the cities of Spokane, Omaha, and Biloxi, to name only a few. The Mojave Desert, the Ute Pass (through the Rocky Mountains), and Lakes Huron and Erie--these too have Indian names.

(3) In the form of federal government in the United States every American owes a particular debt to the Iroquois Indians. Living in what is now New York State, the Iroquois were perhaps

the most politically sophisticated of all the Indian tribes of North America. Several nations of one branch of the Iroquois (called the Five Nations) were joined in a confederacy called the League of the Iroquois. Under the League, each of the five nations remained sovereign in its own domestic affairs but acted as a unit in matters that concerned relations with the other Indian nations. The confederacy kept the tribes of the Five Nations from fighting one another, and the federation proved valuable in diplomatic relations with other tribes. When a chief said, "I speak for all the Five Nations," the opinion was not to be regarded lightly.*

(4) When the thirteen colonies in America were considering what kind of government to establish after they had won independence from England in the latter part of the eighteenth century, Benjamin Franklin suggested that they establish a confederacy similar to that of the Iroquois. The convention agreed, and the government of the United States under the Articles of Confederation was influenced by the federated government of the Five Nations of the Iroquois.

(5) Art is another field in which the United States has been influenced by Indian culture. Indian jewelry in silver and turquoise is featured in many stores. Many homes, especially in the southwestern United States, contain Indian rugs and are decorated with items of Indian origin, such as sand paintings and pottery. Indian dances, too, engage the interest of Americans of all racial and national backgrounds, and people travel for hundreds of miles to see the ceremonial dances in such cities as Gallup, New Mexico, and Flagstaff, Arizona.

(6) Indians affected the country's eating habits too. They introduced many new foods to the people of Europe; the white potato and the sweet potato, maize (corn), peanuts, and avocados are but a few. Indians also introduced

tobacco to the early European settlers. It was
the crop that brought wealth to the colonies,
and it remains one of the leading products in
the country today.

(7) Concerned as he was with America's past
and future, President John F. Kennedy advocated
making the study of Indian history required for
all young Americans. Perhaps he sensed that for
a relatively new country, many of whose
citizens have been recently transplanted from
other continents, the Indians' greatest
contribution lies in the feeling of permanence,
the sense of continuity, which their history
furnishes the nation.

*Details about the federation of the League of
the Iroquois were obtained from William
Brandon, The American Heritage Book of Indians
(New York: Dell Publishing Co., Inc., 1961).

EXERCISE 7.

Answer these questions about the selection you have just read.

1. What is the purpose of the first paragraph?
2. How is the essay organized?
3. What is the thesis?
4. Does paragraph 3 use the same method of development as
   paragraph 2? Explain.
5. What is the relationship between paragraphs 3 and 4? Why do
   you think the material in paragraph 4 was not included in
   paragraph 3?
6. What is the purpose of the last paragraph? Does it introduce a
   new idea or does it summarize what has already been said?
   Explain.
7. Is the material in paragraph 3 presented by topic, by time, by
   space, or by cause-effect?
8. Do you find any place within the essay where cause-effect
   order is used? Explain.
9. Complete the following outline of the essay, using complete
   sentences.

Thesis: Certain aspects of Indian culture seeped into American
    life.
  I. Indian influence may be seen everywhere today in the names
     that were given to states, cities, and physical features of the
     country.
  II. In the form of federated government of the United States,
      every American owes a particular debt to the Iroquois
      Indians.
III. _____ .
IV. _____ .

Devices for Coherence in Topical Organization

As discussed in the previous lesson, transitional words and phrases
review for the reader what has just been discussed and show its
relationship to a new topic that will be introduced. In material organized by topic, common transitions are:

- First of all (My first point is)
- Next (Second, In addition, Also)
- The last advantage (reason, feature, point)
- In conclusion

Sometimes the thesis sentence of an essay organized by topic indicates the order.

> There were three types of reasons for the war between the American
>   States: social, political, and economic.

The writer should then discuss the topics in the order presented in
the thesis sentence.

EXERCISE 8.

Study the transitional devices in the essay "North America's Debt to
American Indian Culture" by answering these questions:

1. What words in the first sentence of paragraph 2 link it to
   paragraph 1 and show that the writer is dealing with the first
   topic?
2. What words in the first sentence of paragraph 3 introduce the
   second topic?
3. What sentence introduces the third main topic?
4. What words in the last paragraph indicate a summary?

Use of Reference Material and Footnoting

The previous lesson explained that when you use material that you did not know or that was not generally known, you must *put the information in your own words or use quotation marks*. In either case you must *credit the source*.

EXERCISE 9.

Answer these questions about the source for the material for "North America's Debt to American Indian Culture."

1. The author is a native of the United States. Where do you think she got the information about Indian names? Indian art? Indian influences on food? Does she need to credit the sources? Why or why not?
2. Note the footnote for the information about the Five Nations of the Iroquois. Do you think the author put the information in her own words? What makes you think so?
3. Do you think the information about John F. Kennedy was obtained from reading? Why does it not need to be footnoted?

Stage III. Critiquing and Revising

STEP 6. ANALYZING AND REVISING THE FIRST DRAFT

EXERCISE 10.

Bring the first draft of your composition to class for analysis by your classmates and instructor. But first check the following points:

1. Is the thesis clearly stated?
2. Have you followed a consistent organizational pattern? Is it one that is suitable for your subject?
3. Have you used transitional devices to make the main points clear?
4. Is each main point sufficiently developed?
5. Does the introduction catch the interest of your readers?
6. Does the conclusion summarize what you have said?

If possible read your composition aloud to someone to check for sentence structure and wording.

Following are two student compositions on the subject for this assignment. Note the differences in method of organization and the topics they treat.

MANY PEOPLE'S FOOLISH HOPE FOR LIFE
Hyum Kim, Korea

(1) Everyone knows how precious life is and wants to live forever. There are many stories about people who have searched for something that would keep them alive forever. Even nowadays some people practice cryonics, which will revive them when technology has improved. However, I believe for many reasons that these efforts merely represent people's foolish hopes.

(2) First of all, living forever violates the moral code of the human race by defying God. According to the Bible and human thought from primitive times, if a person dies, his or her soul is taken back to the Creator. The human body should be buried in the earth because of the biological fact that our bodies developed from the earth. Basically all organic life gets its nutrition from the earth. If we live everlastingly, we cannot put nutrition back into the earth; and in a short period of time, the earth will no longer nourish life. This means that there would not be any animals or green plants left. Thus it also means that human beings could not live on this planet.

(3) Second, if people live forever, there will not be any living space for new generations. The population on the Earth will increase rapidly because nobody will die and babies will keep on being born. The Earth's surface area is limited. Where will there be space for the new generations? As far as we know, there is no planet like Earth in close distance to us. Even if there were planets that had conditions similar to those on Earth and even if we traveled at the speed of light, we could never get there. Therefore, finding space on another planet is an impossible dream.

(4) Like others, I want a long life. But living forever violates our moral code and breaks our ecosystem. Therefore, even though we have a foolish hope for everlasting life, we must die and give a chance to new generations. Instead of searching for a cure for death, while we are living we should make the most of all the things we encounter.

EXERCISE 11.

Answer these questions about the composition.

1. What is the central idea? Is it one with which most people will agree? Does it make you want to keep reading further?
2. What method of organization is followed in the composition? What are the main points into which it can be divided?
3. Could paragraph 2 have been made into two paragraphs? What further development would be needed if this were done?
4. Do you find any examples of cause-effect arrangement in the composition? Explain.
5. Do you find the argument convincing? Is there other information you would like to have?
6. Is the conclusion effective? Why or why not?

THE KOLLEGSTUFE OF A GERMAN GYMNASIUM
Werner Hillebrand, West Germany

(1) When I was in the eleventh grade of the gymnasium, I looked forward to the next two years to come. Indeed, I had a very good reason to do so: I would soon enter the Kollegstufe. In the Kollegstufe, the last two years of the gymnasium, the student chooses two main subjects which together contribute 50 percent to the total grade-point average.

(2) This sounded like a wonderful idea. We students liked the idea because it meant that we could finally get rid of our most uninteresting subjects and study what we really liked. For me, this meant I could get rid of chemistry and, above all, mathematics. I could, instead, concentrate on my favorite subjects, which at that time were English and, even more, history

and sociology. The Ministry of Education was
also fond of this system, which was introduced
only a few years ago. They assumed that the
students would benefit from an early specialization in that their ability to study on an
academic level would be enhanced.

(3) Unfortunately, the idea didn't turn out to
be as wonderful as I had thought. Actually, I
benefited most from the Kollegstufe in that I
could recognize from a more in-depth study of
history and sociology what I should not study at
the university--history and sociology. Once I
had graduated from the gymnasium, I chose to
study business and economics. After I had
studied for a few semesters, I knew that I had
made the right choice. There were problems,
however. The mathematical requirements in my
courses uncovered my deficiencies in mathematics. I had to study hard to be able to comprehend mathematical approaches to economic or
business problems. During the first two
semesters I even thought of leaving the
university because my difficulties seemed to be
unmanageable. My general education, which I was
supposed to get in the gymnasium, was not
general enough.

(4) Although not all my former classmates had
such grave problems as I had, I favor the former
educational system with a more general
selection of courses. Furthermore, an early
specialization to me seems to limit people in
various ways. For example, students tend to
choose subjects in the university that they
already have specialized in at the Kollegstufe
and thus do not have the broad education that
they need. Another defect of the limitation
caused by early specialization is that
specialists in a certain area, who are not
generalists, seem often to be unable to
perceive the interrelation between their
particular field and other fields.

(5) For these reasons, then, I think that the
seemingly old-fashioned demand for a general

and thorough education is of value in our world
of specialists.

EXERCISE 12.

Answer these questions about the composition.

1. What are the two main divisions of the essay?
2. What is the thesis? Where is it stated? Would it have been
   more effective if it had been stated earlier? Explain.
3. Is the arrangement deductive or inductive?
4. What is the function of the first paragraph? Why is it
   necessary?
5. Into what two parts might paragraph 2 be divided?
6. What is the central idea of paragraph 3?
7. What is the main idea of paragraph 4?
8. What is the function of the last paragraph?
9. Is the author's purpose to explain or persuade?
10. Following is an outline of the composition. How does the
    order in which the material is presented differ from the
    order in the paper? Do you think the outline was written
    before the composition to help the writer decide what to say,
    or afterward in order to check the organization?
    Explain.

Thesis: I think the seemingly old-fashioned demand for a general
and thorough education is of value in our world of
specialists.

I. Specializing in Kollegstufe seemed like a good idea.
   A. We students liked it because we could drop disagreeable
      courses and take more of the courses we liked.
   B. The Ministry of Education liked it because the students'
      ability to work on an academic level would be enhanced.
II. Such specialization turned out to be not a good idea.
    A. It was not a good idea for me because I changed my major
       field and did not have the background that I needed.
    B. Students are limited when they choose the same courses
       in the university that they specialized in in the
       Kollegstufe.
    C. Specialists do not perceive the interrelation of fields of
       study.

STEP 7. WRITING THE FINAL DRAFT

EXERCISE 13.

In preparing the final draft of your composition, check it carefully for spelling and punctuation. Check also the use of tenses—past, present perfect, and past perfect. Have you used passive forms correctly? Are there sentences that require the use of the subjunctive? Read the composition again for wording and sentence structure. Then copy it neatly and hand it in to your instructor in the form required. Remember that your instructor may ask for both the first and final drafts.

Reviewing Grammatical Patterns

THE PASSIVE VOICE

Study the uses of the passive in sections E12 and E13 in the Handbook.

GRAMMAR EXERCISE 1.

Which of these sentences from "North America's Debt to American Indian Culture" can be stated in the active? If the sentence cannot be stated in the active, why can't it? Tell why you think the passive was used in each case.

1. Indian influence *may be seen* everywhere in the names that *were given* to the states, cities, and physical features.
2. These states *were named* after Indian tribes.
3. Several nations *were joined* in a confederacy.
4. The opinion of the chief *was not to be regarded* lightly.
5. The government of the United States *was influenced* by the government of the Five Nations of the Iroquois.
6. Art is another field in which the United States *has been influenced* by Indian culture.
7. Indian jewelry *is featured* in many stores.
8. Many homes *are decorated* with items of Indian origin.
9. President Kennedy *was concerned* with America's past and future.
10. The study of Indian history should *be required* for all young Americans.

GRAMMAR EXERCISE 2.

Here are some sentences written by students in classes in English as a foreign language. Choose the correct verb form.

1. All decisions in business (influenced, are influenced) by these factors.
2. We should (be concerned, concern) about these problems.
3. (We suggested, It was suggested) the solution.
4. In this century many things (happened, was happened).
5. The buildings (are belonged, belong) to the government.
6. Everybody (surprises, is surprised) about this.
7. Three countries (involved, were involved) in occupying America in the early years.
8. The room (filled, was filled) with antiques.
9. Bills and statements that (prepare, are prepared) in the accounting office help people.
10. The palace (used, is used) to be the palace of kings.

PAST TENSE VERSUS PRESENT PERFECT

The simple past tense is used to make statements of fact or opinion about conditions in the past or about a completed event.

> My grandmother's garden contained many varieties of flowers. (statement of fact that was true once but is true no longer)
> The concert last night was not well done. (opinion about a past event)

The relationship between past time and the present moment is shown by the use of *has (have)* plus the past participle. This form is called the *present perfect.* To understand its uses, study section B8C in the Handbook.

GRAMMAR EXERCISE 3

Tell why the italicized verb forms in the following sentences are used, and fill the blanks appropriately with either the present-perfect or past-tense form of the verb.

1. Science *has* not yet *determined* all the means by which birds navigate. Some scientists believe they are guided by Polaris, the North Star; others think birds sense magnetic fields. Many scientific observations _____ (take) place in this area.

2. Antarctic seas may have a temperature of 5.4°F below freezing. What keeps the fish alive? Scientists recently _____ (find) that these fish contain a substance called glycoprotein, a pure white substance that acts like the antifreeze in the radiators of our cars.

3. Is there life on other planets? To date mankind _____ (discover; in the negative) the answer.

4. An *albino* is a human being or animal with no coloring matter in the skin, but even among certain plants, flowers _____ (appear) as albinos.

5. China, which suffers frequently from earthquakes, *has enlisted* all its farmers and other citizens as part-time observers to help make predictions about earthquakes. Last year some individuals _____ (prove) the value of such activity.

6. The cockroach *has been* on the earth 280 million years, even though exterminators _____ (discover) many ways to get rid of them.

7. The dragonfly _____ (be) on earth 320 million years, but *has* always *been* man's friend because it eats flies and mosquitoes.

8. People who live in a very high altitude, such as that of Bolivia and Tibet, _____ (adapt) themselves to the scarcity of oxygen by developing chests and lungs far larger than normal and by carrying a quart more blood than the average human of equal size.

9. Smoke detectors *have proven* so effective in alerting people to fires that many states are beginning to require them in public buildings. Last week we _____ (install) one in our home.

10. Since 1952 people _____ (dredge) over half a million carats of diamonds off the southern coast of Africa.

PAST PERFECT

Study the uses of the past perfect in section D9 in the Handbook.

GRAMMAR EXERCISE 4.

In the following sentences, based on the selections "The Influence of the American Frontier" and "North America's Debt to American Indian Culture," tell which of the italicized words is farther in the past.

1. *By 1850,* settlements *had advanced* to Kansas and Nebraska.
2. When the settlers *established* themselves on the frontier, the white man *had entered* a land in which he recognized no law.
3. After farmers *had established* homes, towns *sprang up.*
4. The frontier people, who at first *had been* loners, *became* tied to the land in various ways.
5. The thirteen American colonies *considered* what kind of government to establish after they *had won* independence.
6. Before the white man *came,* the Iroquois Indians *had lived* in North America for many years.
7. The Americans *based* their system of government on a system the Iroquois *had established.*

GRAMMAR EXERCISE 5.

Write a paragraph using the sentences that follow and choosing the verb form that you think is best.

1. Before I left Japan, I (had often eaten, often ate) a meal with a knife and fork but I (had never slept, never slept) in a Western-type bed.
2. Until I came to America, I (had always lived, always lived) in a rural community on the island of Kyushu and (had never stayed, never stayed) in a big, Western-type hotel.
3. When I got to America, I (was eager, had been eager) to find out what a Western bed would feel like.
4. I (had always thought, always thought) it would be too soft.
5. I (was afraid, had been afraid) I would fall out of bed.
6. The first night in the United States I (stayed, had stayed) in a hotel in San Francisco.
7. I (liked, had liked) the bed and didn't fall out.
8. Now I (am, have been) used to American beds.
9. Yesterday I (wrote, have written) to my parents in Japan.
10. I (told, have told) them that I (decided, have decided) to sleep on a futon when I return home.

MODALS

Study the uses of modals in section F14 in the Handbook.

GRAMMAR EXERCISE 6

Supply the correct modal *(can, could, may, might, will, would, shall, should, have (has) to, had to, ought to)* for the blanks in the following sentences.

1. In the eleventh grade of my school in Germany I was happy because I _____ soon enter the Kollegstufe, or junior college.
2. In the two years of the Kollegstufe, the student _____ choose the subjects he or she wants to study.
3. This meant that I _____ get rid of my most uninteresting subjects.
4. I _____ not have to study mathematics and science anymore.
5. The Ministry of Education assumed that students _____ benefit by early specialization.
6. I benefited in that I _____ recognize from a more in-depth study of history and sociology what I should *not* study in the university.
7. Once I had graduated from the junior college, I decided that I _____ study business and economics.
8. A student _____ pass an examination to be admitted to the university
9. I _____ study hard to comprehend mathematics.
10. I decided that I _____ studied mathematics in junior college.
11. I think that everyone _____ have a good general education.
12. This type of education _____ prepare a person best in this age of specialization.

THE SUBJUNCTIVE

Study the forms and uses of the subjunctive in the Handbook, section G16b. Note the sequence of tenses in sentences expressing conditions.

If I *were* you, I *would* go. (present condition)
If I *had* understood her, I *would have* answered. (past condition)

In the composition "Many People's Foolish Hope for Life" there is an example of the subjunctive form of the verb used to express a hypothetical (unreal) condition. Note its use and the sequence of tenses.

> Even if there *were* planets that *had* conditions similar to those on Earth and even if we *traveled* at the speed of light, we *could* never get there.

GRAMMAR EXERCISE 7.

Tell what you would do under each of the following conditions. Begin your sentences as indicated.

1. If I were a millionaire, I _____.
2. If I could speak ten languages, I _____.
3. If I lived in a cold country, I _____.
4. If I lived in a hot country, I _____.
5. If I had 17 children, I _____.
6. If I were famous, I _____.
7. If we had known that there would be a test, _____.
8. If I had not opened the door, _____.
9. If the professor had arrived earlier, _____.
10. If I had only studied the lesson, _____.

GRAMMAR EXERCISE 8.

Assume that your friend John has just been recommended for promotion in his company. Complete the following sentences telling about him.

1. The head of his department suggested that John be _____
   _____.
2. His supervisor requested that he _____.
3. The personnel director asked that John _____.
4. The board of directors agreed that John _____.
5. John said that if he _____ , he _____.
6. If John receives the promotion, he _____.

INFINITIVES AS COMPLEMENTS

Note the following uses of the infinitive in the selections you have been reading for this lesson.

> The Iroquois chief's opinion was not *to be regarded lightly.*
> I chose *to study* business and economics.

Students tend *to choose* subjects . . . that they have already specialized in.

In the Handbook, section G17, study the list of verbs that can be followed by infinitives.

GRAMMAR EXERCISE 9.

Write a short paragraph on one of the subjects below.

1. Your college career, telling the following things:
   a. what you *want to do* with your life
   b. what you *expect to get* from a college education
   c. what courses or people have *inspired you to do* this
   d. what required courses you *dread to take*
   e. what courses you *plan to take* next semester
   f. when you think it is *possible for you to reach* your goal
2. The requirements for a job in your field of study, include the following:
   a. what an employer will *expect you to do*
   b. what an employer might *tell you not to do*
   c. what kind of employee you intend *to be*
   d. what aspects of the job you will most *enjoy doing*
   e. what aspects you will *dislike doing*
   f. what kind of promotions you *expect to get*

INFINITIVES TO SHOW PURPOSE

Study section H24 of the Handbook for examples of infinitives to show purpose. Examples from the selections in this lesson follow.

People travel for miles *to see* ceremonial Indian dances.
I had to study hard *to be able to comprehend* mathematical approaches to business problems.

GRAMMAR EXERCISE 10.

Write sentences telling what you must do in order to (to) accomplish each of the following purposes:

1. to enjoy real adventure
2. to get along with a roommate
3. to get along easily in a foreign country
4. to climb to the top of a mountain

5. to learn a foreign language
6. to prepare a favorite food

AVOIDING DANGLING MODIFIERS

When a participial phrase is placed at the beginning of a sentence, the noun that the phrase modifies should immediately follow the phrase.

> Wrong: Floating down the river, rocky cliffs rise up.
> Right: Floating down the river, *you* see rocky cliffs.

GRAMMAR EXERCISE 11.

Finish the following sentences.

1. Racing toward the beach, _____.
  (You failed to see what?)
2. Looking up at the plane in the sky, _____.
  (You noticed what?)
3. Getting on the bus, _____.
  (You made what awful discovery?)
4. Sitting near the window, _____.
  (You observed what?)
5. After arriving late for class, _____.
  (You made what mistake?)

Rewrite the following sentences, correcting the humorous mistakes from student compositions—mistakes caused by the fact that the noun is not placed next to the phrase that modifies it.

1. Standing at one end, the alley of trees appears to be a tunnel.
2. Looking backward into the past, it was a great time to be in school.
3. Coming closer and closer to the enormous stairways, the castle grows bigger and bigger.
4. After having a look at how they make this product, it's time to go.
5. Skiing downhill at breakneck speed, the snow blew in our faces, almost blinding us.

END NOTES

In good writing, sentence structure and sentence length are varied to avoid monotony. In each group that follows, the italicized parts of the sentences from "North America's Debt to American Indian Culture" express similar ideas in different wording.

Paragraph 1, sentence 1: *Benét says that*
Paragraph 1, sentence 2: But, *says Benét,* they
Paragraph 2, sentence 2: The states of Delaware, Iowa, . . . *were named* after
Paragraph 2, sentence 3: Many rivers . . . *have Indian names.*
Paragraph 2, sentence 4: "The Mojave Desert . . . and Lakes Huron and Erie—these too *are Indian names.*

Paragraph 5, sentence 1: Art is *another field* in which the United States *has been influenced* by Indian culture.
Paragraph 6, sentence 1: Indians *affected* the country's eating habits *too.*

Lesson 7

EXPLAINING A PROCESS OR HISTORICAL DEVELOPMENT

Rhetorical Principles	**Grammatical Patterns**
Organization by time	*For, since,* and *ago* in expressions of time
Coherence by words or phrases indicating time progression	Other prepositions in expressions of time
Introductions—Reference to what is close in time or space	Expressions of degree and comparison
Organization by space	Expressions of measure
Coherence by words or phrases indicating spatial organization	*It* as a sentence starter
Spatial organization in introductions	Review of use and omission of articles
Use of reference material and footnoting	

Writing a Composition

Assignment: In writing on scientific subjects you will often have to explain the steps in a process. In the social sciences you will have to trace the history or development of a movement or area of knowledge. Write a composition of two to three pages (500 to 800 words) explaining a process or tracing the development of a movement, belief, or area of knowledge. As an alternative, you may trace the stages in a journey. You may need to use outside sources in writing this paper.

Stage I. Prewriting

STEP 1. BRAINSTORMING FOR IDEAS

EXERCISE 1.

Here are some topics that might be used for this assignment. Choose two or three, or others of your choice, for class discussion. What point of view might you take toward the topic? How might you develop it?

1. *A process*
   a. How to raise wheat (dates, rice, pineapple, avocados)
   b. How to build or make something (a boat, a gourmet dish)
   c. How to prepare for some competition (in sports, music)
   d. How to prepare for an extended stay in another country
   e. How to read a book (take notes, prepare for an examination)
2. *History of a movement*
   a. How ideas about evolution have changed
   b. How the practice of medicine has progressed
   c. How the automobile has evolved
   d. How the study of astronomy has developed
   e. How the Industrial Revolution came about
   f. How man's knowledge of the ocean has increased
   g. How weapons have changed since caveman days
   h. How___(country)___became a unified nation with its present boundaries
   i. How certain marriage or burial customs developed

3. *A personal experience that has been important in your life*
4. *A change in territorial boundaries of your country or city over a period of time*
5. *The stages in a journey*

EXERCISE 2.

Choose a topic on which you plan to write.

STEP 2. PHRASING THE THESIS SENTENCE

EXERCISE 3.

Write out and bring to class possible thesis sentences for three of the topics suggested in exercise 1 or other topics suggested in class. This may include the topic on which you plan to write. Discuss with your classmates your selected topics. Consider also the organizational pattern and method of development that might be used in the writing.

STEP 3. JOTTING DOWN IDEAS AND REFINING A POINT OF VIEW

EXERCISE 4.

Here are some notes for the essay "Evolving Knowledge of the Nature of the Brain," which appears later in this lesson. After you read them, answer the questions.

Collis, John Stewart, *Living with a Stranger*. New York: George Braziller, Inc., 1979.

Early civilizations—brain not source of thought	Sumerians—liver is organ of thought, soul, emotion
	Egyptians—brain not necessary for future life; remove when embalming
	Bible—organ of thought not brain
	David—"My liver shall sing praise to Thee (God) and not be silent."
	<u>Brain</u> not used in Bible.
	"His bowels yearned with compassion."
	"His veins instruct him in the night season."
	"The Lord trieth the heart

and the kidneys."
Assyrians- 300 years later- liver
source of thought. p. 78
St. Augustine- 4th century A.D.
"Men go abroad to wonder at the
height of the mountains, at
the long courses of the rivers,
at the vast compass of the ocean,
at the circular motion of the
stars, and they pass by themselves without wondering." p. 80
1848- Phineas Gage- workman- railroad engineer.
Blasting rock- rod 3½ ft. long, diameter of a penny-
went through skull beneath left eye. Senses unimpaired. Personality changed. Became violent, ill-
tempered, obscene. Could not hold job. Head and
rod on display at Harvard Medical School.
Result- research on compartments of brain. p. 80.

Lennart Nilsson, <u>Behold Man</u>. Boston: Little, Brown and
Company, 1973.

Hypocrates- first to theorize that mental life was
embodied in cavities of brain. Fluid of brain
gave life to rest of body. 4th century B.C.
Aristotle- brain fluid cooled blood from heart.
Heart- organ of thought, soul, emotion. Beats
according to emotions. p. 165

"How the Brain Works," <u>Newsweek</u> CI (Feb. 7, 1983).

Surgery for epilepsy- hippocampus removed. Short-
term memory gone.
Sensations from outside brain- send electrical
impulses to amygdala.

This and hippocampus and nucleus basalis—
send messages to cortex. Messages stored
permanently.

Neuroscientists discovered that chemicals acetylcholine and vasopressin help in retention.

Thinking, planning, imagining believed to take
place in frontal lobes of brain. Damaged
frontal lobes—no planning. p. 42-43

Dr. George Ojemann (University of Washington)—
stimulated brains electrically during surgery.
Some spots store nouns, some verbs, etc.
Bilinguals—vocab. for one language in one
place, for another in another. p. 42

Dr. Patricia Goldman-Rakie (Yale), "We have an
understanding of the neurology of vision. In
principle we can have a neurology of cognition."
p. 42

1. The writer used outside sources in the composition. What information about the sources did she need to write down? Why?
2. What will the next step in writing the composition probably be?
3. What plan of organization do you expect the composition to follow (time, space, topic)?
4. Suggest a possible thesis sentence for the composition.

EXERCISE 5.

Take notes for the composition you will write. If you need an outside source for further information, be sure you include in your notes the following information: author, title, source (see section 11 in the Handbook). If you find a quotation to use, be sure it is in the *exact words* of the source *with quotation marks*. Otherwise, the *material in your notes should be in brief form, in your own words.*

Stage II. Giving Form to the Composition and Studying Techniques

STEP 4. WRITING A FIRST DRAFT

EXERCISE 6.

Organize your material and write the first draft of your composition. Before you write, you may want to make a tentative outline and study the section on rhetorical techniques in Step 5.

STEP 5. STUDYING RHETORICAL PRINCIPLES

Organization by Time

A common type of arrangement of the major ideas in a composition is by time. This arrangement is usually used when tracing the history of a subject.

In a book called *Evenings with Music,* * the author devotes one chapter to a thumbnail history of music. The thesis sentence is as follows:

> The music that we know today, the musical instruments with which we have become familiar, the forms that we have studied all have been the subject of slow evolution.

Succeeding paragraphs begin as follows:

> Before he was able to speak, <u>prehistoric man</u> . . .
> At the beginning of <u>the seventh century</u> . . .
> Then <u>about the year 1000</u> . . .
> The story of music <u>for the next four centuries</u> . . .
> With the discovery <u>in the fifteenth century</u> of the East and its rich treasures, and with the opening up of commerce and trade . . .
> Toward <u>the middle of the 1720s</u> . . .
> <u>The deaths of Bach (1750) and Handel (1759)</u> brought the polyphonic period to a close . . .

The material about music in this chapter has obviously been arranged in a time sequence. Note how the introductory words of each section indicate time. This order is used to mark time in stories, to show the development of a science, or to mark the steps of a process,

*Syd Skolsky, *Evenings with Music* (New York: E. P. Dutton & Co., Inc., 1944).

and it is widely used in history books. It may be used to organize material in a paragraph or in a longer piece of writing.

Coherence by Words or Phrases Indicating Time Progression

A piece of writing that is organized according to a time sequence makes use of certain familiar phrases to indicate that progression. The progression may be by milleniums, by centuries, by years, months, days, hours—or by historical eras. Time may also be indicated by certain common phrases, as is seen in the following exercise.

EXERCISE 7.

Put the following groups of time phrases in a logical sequence. Phrases that seem to indicate a similar period of time can be bracketed together.

1. quite a while after that   toward the end
   then   somewhat later
   at last   finally
   in the beginning   today
   later   long ago

2. before the discovery of   during the Middle Ages
      America   at the time of the Industrial
   in the Middle Ages   Revolution
   at the dawn of history   in modern times
   during the Renaissance

Introductions—Reference to What is Close in Time or Space

People are interested in what is close to them in time or space. The current, the latest, and what is happening nearby get attention and help the writer tie the topic to the reader. The reader is also intrigued by learning something new about a common object. As you read the following composition, be aware of the techniques used to capture reader interest in the introduction as well as the organization by time.

EVOLVING KNOWLEDGE OF THE NATURE OF THE BRAIN

(1) Interest in computers has led to people's increasing interest in their own brains--that super computer--three pounds of jellylike matter the color of an overcast sky. This intense interest in the brain is astoundingly new. For most of mankind's millions of years of existence, it never occurred to individuals to

wonder how they thought. Only in relatively recent times have people scientifically probed the source of their thoughts and emotions.

(2) Six thousand years ago, the Sumerians believed that the liver was the organ of thought, soul, and emotion.[1] The ancient Egyptians, whose civilization also extends milleniums B.C., did not regard the brain as the source of thought either. When they entombed their Pharaohs and provided them with food and other things they would need for a future life, they spooned out the nonessential brain through the nose to keep it from corrupting the embalmed body.[2]

(3) A thousand years B.C. the Jewish psalmist David said, "My liver shall sing praise to Thee [God] and not be silent." Other biblical authors revealed that they too (perhaps because of the influence of other Middle Eastern civilizations) were not aware that thought processes originate in the brain. The word *brain* is never used in the Bible. Other organs are credited as the source of thought and emotions: "His bowels yearned with compassion," "His veins instruct him in the night season," and "The Lord trieth the heart and the kidneys." The Assyrians 300 years later still were championing the liver as the source of thought.[3]

(4) The Greek philosopher Hippocrates seems to have been the first to theorize, in the fourth century B.C., that mental life was embodied in the fluid-filled cavities of the brain and that the fluid sparked life in the rest of the body. Aristotle, just decades later, thought that brain fluid cooled the blood from the heart, which was the organ of thought, soul, and emotion because it beats fast or slow according to the emotions.[4]

(5) Hippocrates' theory about the source of thought was not pursued for over a thousand years. St. Augustine, in the fourth and fifth centuries A.D. commented, "Men go abroad to wonder at the height of the mountains, at the

long courses of the rivers, at the vast compass
of the ocean, at the circular motion of the
stars; and they pass by themselves without
wondering."[5]

(6) However, something happened in 1848 that
set scientists to wondering. Railroad engineer
Phineas Gage was preparing to blast a rock on a
railroad track when the tamping iron he was
using to make a hole for the dynamite backfired.
This rod--3 1/2 feet long and with the diameter
of a penny--entered his skull beneath his left
eye and came out the other side of his head.
However, his eyesight, his speech, and all his
other senses were left unimpaired. There was
only one problem. The rod had taken out a chunk
of his personality. Phineas, who had been a man
of high character and sweet disposition, became
ill-tempered, violent, and obscene. He also
became irresponsible. He could not hold a job,
and to support himself, he had to go around to
fairs exhibiting his head and the rod, which are
today at the Harvard Medical School.[6] This
accident stimulated research on the
compartments of the brain and the intimate
connections among those compartments.

(7) Today, to find out more about how the brain
functions, scientists are using microscopic
electrical probes and injecting humans with
chemicals that shine with radioactivity. By
such means they have found out how the brain
controls the body--how certain brain areas
supervise metabolism, movement, and reflexes.
Now they are looking for the parts of the brain
that govern memory, emotions, and thought.

(8) A surgical incident helped to throw light
on the nature of memory. A young man had his
hippocampus (a small structure in the middle
brain) removed to relieve his epileptic
seizures. The surgery was successful in
stopping the seizures, but it destroyed his
short-term memory. He could not remember what
happened five minutes ago, but memories formed
before his operation remained. This and
subsequent research confirms the fact that when

sensations come from outside the brain, these
sensations (sights, sounds, and so on) are
fired electronically into the brain and go to a
way station, the amygdala, which, with the
hippocampus and nucleus basalis, sends
important messages to the cortex (the top of the
brain). The message is stored there
permanently.[7] Neuroscientists have also
discovered that the chemicals acetylcholine
and vasopressin help the cortex retain the
imprint of incoming information.[8]

(9) Thinking, imagining, and planning for the
future are brain activities that are much more
difficult to analyze. Scientists believe such
activities take place in the frontal lobes and
all of the cortex that is not involved with
sensing the outside world and moving the body.
People with damaged frontal lobes might be able
to paint pictures but they could not plan to
paint a picture for a friend's birthday next
week.[9]

(10) Of interest to students of language is
the fact that scientists find there is not only
a place where the brain stores vocabulary
items, but that it stores all the nouns in one
spot, verbs in another, prepositions in
another. Dr. George Ojemann of the University
of Washington discovered this when he asked
patients to read a passage while he probed spots
on their brains with electrodes. When he
touched one spot, a patient could read
everything except the nouns. Touching another
spot would knock out the verbs. So apparently
the brain can parse a sentence. For a bilingual
person, vocabulary of one language is stored in
one place, and vocabulary for another language
in another.[10]

(11) Scientists admit that there are many
questions about the brain that are not yet
answered. What sparks the imagination? What
brain function produces emotion? What
biochemical or electrical impulse governs will
and consciousness? Researchers do not have the

answers yet, but they are hopeful. Patricia Goldmann-Rakie of Yale University is typical. She says, "We have an understanding of the neurology of vision. In principle we can have a neurology of cognition."[11]

[1]John Stewart Collis, <u>Living with a Stranger</u> (New York: George Braziller, Inc., 1979), 78.
[2]Ibid.
[3]Ibid.
[4]Lennart Nilsson, <u>Behold Man</u> (Boston: Little, Brown and Company, 1973), 165.
[5]Collis, op. cit., 80
[6]Ibid.
[7]"How the Brain Works," <u>Newsweek</u> CI (Feb. 7, 1983): 42.
[8]Ibid., <u>passim</u>.
[9]Ibid., 46.
[10]Ibid., 46-47.
[11]Ibid., 46.

EXERCISE 8.

Answer these questions about the composition you have just read.

1. List the key phrases that indicate the organization by time.
2. To which period of time is the most explanation devoted?
3. What feature of the article makes you feel that the author knows what he is talking about?
4. What methods of development are used to explain the brain research that is going on today?
5. What kinds of development are used to show lack of knowledge about the brain in ancient times?
6. By what means does the author relate the topic to the reader in the introduction of the article?
7. By what means does the author conclude the article?

Organization by Space

Sometimes material in an essay is arranged as it would appear in space—from left to right, north to south, inside to outside, far to near. Spatial arrangement may be the pattern for an entire composition when the author's purpose is (1) to give a picture of the arrangement of items in a wide area or (2) to show progression in travel or in the

conquest of territory. In his book *Why We Behave Like Americans,* *
Bradford Smith uses spatial organization to describe America by
telling his readers about a trip he took from the East Coast to the
West Coast. Spatial organization is perhaps more commonly used in
a paragraph, as Victor Hugo does in *Les Miserables* when he describes
the battlefield of Waterloo. It may be used in an introductory paragraph to narrow the subject from a wider geographical focus to a
more restricted one.

Note the use of spatial arrangement in the following composition.

ADVENTURE ON THE COLORADO†

(1) One of the major tourist attractions of
the United States is the Grand Canyon of the
Colorado River. Every year thousands of visitors come to gaze into its awesome purple depths
from vantage points along the road at the rim of
the canyon or from the safety of a hotel window.
Some of the more daring may venture down into it
on mule back for a closer view. At the bottom is
the Colorado River, considered by some to be the
roughest to navigate in the world. To test the
truth of this assertion and to see the most
awesome aspects of the canyon, you should take a
three-week trip down the river in a small boat
that carries only an oarsman-guide and one or
two other persons.

(2) At first you do not realize how exciting it
is to make the trip. You start where the river is
calm, some miles upstream from the canyon. Here
the boat floats slowly along on clear water
between limestone cliffs some 2,000 feet high.
Farther down the river the view changes as the
boat drifts between rock walls on which
abstract sculpture has been produced by the
force of the water against the rocks over a

*Bradford Smith, *Why We Behave Like Americans* (Philadelphia: J. B. Lippincott Company, 1957).

†Facts taken from Robert Wallace, "Wooden Boats Plus Colorado River Equals
Adventure," *Smithsonian* 5 (May 1974): 37–43.

period of two billion years. Above these walls
rise high promontories green with pine.

(3) As the boat glides on, you become
conscious of a distant roar. The river narrows
and suddenly you find yourself in turbulent
water, its churning dark green crests edged in
foam. Your boat drops dizzily. You are going
through the first of the rapids. Before you have
time to recover, you plunge through another
series of rapids, then another. Caught in a
whirlpool, the boat spins out of control,
stands straight up on its stern, then shoots
downward into a hole. You recall what the guide
has told you--that the current of the river is
so strong in some places that it can peel a man
like a banana, stripping off his pants, belt,
shirt, and shoes in a few minutes.
Unbelievably, the boat rights itself.

(4) The river channel becomes even narrower.
Now the boat is nearly crushed as it shoots down
almost perpendicularly into seething water
through a passageway between boulders. The
noise makes your chest vibrate like a drum. You
agree with those who say that few natural sounds
on the planet are more intimidating than the
thunder of the water. Then it happens. The boat
upsets, and you find yourself buffeted about in
a churning maelstrom. At first it may be
difficult for you to catch your breath, and you
may wonder if it is possible to keep from being
sucked under. Somehow your life jacket keeps
you afloat, and the guide pulls you back into
the boat, which is built to be unsinkable and
which in a moment heads on down the river.

(5) As you go the rest of the 285 miles down the
canyon you will have many more adventures such
as this. The river makes a 2,000-foot drop in
the course of your journey, and you will
negotiate 150 rapids. At night the guide will
find a flat, sandy spot big enough for a
campsite. He will build a fire and later, after
a warm meal, you will crawl into your sleeping
bag too exhausted to stay awake.

(6) Eventually the boat finds safer going.
There are fewer boulders in the water, the
rapids become less treacherous, and you finally
float into Lake Mead, which is formed by Boulder
Dam. The river will go on to the West Coast, but
your boat trip is over. You have survived the
dramatic run through the canyon, and the thrill
will remain. Perhaps, like others, you will be
so delighted with the trip that you will want to
experience again the adventure of the water and
the beauty of the canyon.

EXERCISE 10.

Answer these questions about the preceding composition.

1. What is the thesis sentence?
2. What details in the composition support it?
3. How is the author's awareness of space shown in the
   introduction?
4. Does this adventure build to a climax? Explain.
5. What is the purpose of paragraph 5? Why did the author not
   give more details in this paragraph?
6. Which idea expressed in the final sentence is not developed
   much in the composition?
7. Is the composition to some degree organized by time as well as
   by space? Give words or phrases that indicate this.

Coherence by Words or Phrases Indicating Spatial Organization
Devices for coherence to show the pattern in spatial organization
depend on the type of spatial pattern used. The readers of Bradford
Smith's chapter about what America looks like can sense the westerly
direction of his journey by his mentioning the states he goes through.
Here are some examples:

When the sun comes up over the . . . rocky
coast and offshore islands of <u>Maine</u> . . .
Crossing from <u>New England into New York</u>, the
traveler gets onto a parkway . . .
. . . at the rush hour one can slip through New
York City itself and westward onto the <u>New</u>
<u>Jersey Turnpike</u> without stops or delays.
Not only the shape of the land, but even the

color of the earth changes as the car speeds
west. (The author takes us through
<u>Pennsylvania, Ohio</u>, and <u>Illinois</u>.)
    Even <u>Kansas</u> (west of the Mississippi) . . . is
full of variety.
    In <u>New Mexico</u> you learn to spot a river by the
clouds of dust blowing out of it.
    <u>Arizona's</u> strewn rocks and cliffs rising like
masonry walls . . . look like a city in ruins.
    At <u>San Bernardino (California)</u> the desert
ends.

In describing a scene one might use such phrases as "on the left,"
"in the middle," "on the right." In describing the process of washing
a car a writer might say, "You begin with the top. . . ." "Then the
body. . . ." "Last, you wash the wheels."

EXERCISE 11.

Answer these questions on the devices for coherence in "Adventure
on the Colorado."

1. What words in paragraph 2 indicate the part of the river that
   is to be described first?
2. What is the transitional device to tie paragraph 3 to paragraph
   2?
3. Why is the material in paragraph 3 put in a paragraph by
   itself?
4. What words link paragraph 4 with paragraph 3?
5. What words link paragraph 4 with paragraph 5?
6. What part of the journey is described in the last paragraph?
   What words and phrases indicate this?

Spatial Organization in Introductions

When motion picture cameramen want to focus closely on something, they sometimes "zoom in" on it. That is, they narrow their
focus from a wide area to a smaller one. This is sometimes done in
writing also. For example, if you were describing a person, you might
begin by telling how he or she looked from a distance, such as a block
down the street, then add details as the person comes closer or enters
a room, and add still more details as you observe him or her sitting
across from you in a restaurant. This method of arrangement may be

used in the introduction to a composition to give readers a wide view of a familiar field before introducing them to an aspect of it they may know little about. Note the use of the narrowing technique in the following selection.

THE ANTARCTIC: HOME OF THE WIND*

(1) Now that we have followed the story of its [Antarctica's] discovery in detail, it is time that we had a look at the continent as a whole.

(2) If we began with its appearance as seen from the moon by the first human to reach it, the Antarctic would remind him strongly of what the astronomers see when they look at the planet Mars. A more or less round patch of dead white would surround the Pole itself, and it would wax and wane as winter passed into summer, though not so markedly as on Mars.

(3) If an observer contented himself with a space ship only a few thousand miles above the earth's atmosphere, he would make out more interesting details. . . . A closer view would show that calm and silence are the very last adjectives to apply to the Antarctic, for it is the Home of the Wind. If our observer from above could see the wind . . . he would see a continent covered with a moving sheet of air flowing always to the left as is the way with winds in the Southern Hemisphere.

(4) If he were hovering only a few hundred feet up . . . he would see, on three days out of every four, the loose snow being driven over the firm snow, a spindrift of tiny particles veiling the furrows caused by the wind and building long streamers of hard snow behind every obstacle, pointing outwards towards the edge of the continent. The details of this wind-sculptured surface could be seen through a thin drift in a light wind, but as the wind grew stronger the layer of whirling snow would get thicker till in

*Frank Debenham, *Antarctica* (New York: Macmillan; and London: Herbert Jenkins, Ltd., 1961), 124–126. © Frank Debenham 1959. Reprinted by permission.

a full blizzard it would be 100 feet thick and so dense that visibility would be reduced to a single meter's distance.

EXERCISE 12.

Answer these questions about spatial organization in the selection you have just read.

1. What progression in space is used in "The Antarctic: Home of the Wind"?
2. What words indicate the pattern?
3. What sentence gives you a clue to the fact that this is part of a longer piece of writing?
4. What information do you think the author will present following the paragraphs presented here?

Use of Reference Material and Footnoting

The composition "Evolving Knowledge of the Nature of the Brain" is based largely on facts gained through reading rather than on facts generally known or on the writer's first-hand knowledge of the subject. It is the type of paper you might have to write for one of your school courses. The following exercise provides an opportunity for you to analyze how reference material is used and credited.

EXERCISE 13.

Be able to justify your reasons for answers to these questions on the use of reference material in the selection "Evolving Knowledge of the Nature of the Brain."

1. Why are there no footnotes for paragraph 1?
2. Why is the material in paragraph 2 footnoted? Are the facts probably general knowledge or are they found in a specific source?
3. Is the material in paragraph 2 in the words of John Stewart Collis (see footnotes 1 and 2) or in the words of the author of "Evolving Knowledge of the Nature of the Brain"? What is the reason for your answer?
4. Is the material in paragraph 2 probably merely a paraphrase of the words of Collis? If it were a paraphrase, how should the writer of the selection indicate this fact?

5. In paragraph 5 a quotation from St. Augustine is given. Why is it footnoted to Collis?
6. Why are there no footnotes for paragraph 7?
7. Is paragraph 9 probably a paraphrase of *Newsweek*? Why or why not?
8. Why is *passim* used in footnote 8?
9. Why is *ibid.* used for footnotes 2, 3, 8, 9, and 10?
10. Why is *op cit.* used in footnote 5?

EXERCISE 14.

The essay "Adventure on the Colorado" is based partly on visiting the Grand Canyon and talking to people who have taken the trip and partly on reading. How do you account for the difference in the footnoting from that used in the essay on the brain?

Stage III. Critiquing and Revising

STEP 6. ANALYZING AND REVISING THE FIRST DRAFT

EXERCISE 15.

For this composition you may have added to what you know about your subject by looking up additional information in the library. If you use such material, be sure to (1) credit your sources, (2) put the material into your own words unless you are quoting directly, and (3) put direct quotations in quotation marks. Check your composition for organizational pattern, for clear transitions between the major points, for clear statement of the central idea. Does your introduction catch the interest of the reader? Are the points sufficiently developed? Read your composition, preferably aloud, for sentence structure and wording and bring it to class for critiquing.

CHANGES IN ATTITUDES TOWARD TEACHERS IN JAPAN
Fumiko Kasai, Japan

(1) Many changes have taken place in Japan since World War II. Since then American customs, systems, and modes of behavior have been introduced. In some cases attitudes have changed 180 degrees. One of these attitudes is the respect with which teachers are regarded. The change is going on even today.

(2) The tradition of respect for teachers goes back to feudal times. Teachers then had absolute authority over the students and were regarded with utmost courtesy. An anecdote shows the relation between teacher and student that existed at that time. Hundreds of years ago, there was a famous <u>katana-shi</u>, a sword maker. The sword was the "soul" of the samurai, and this <u>katana-shi</u> had high dignity. Many samurai asked him to make their "souls." A young boy who was apprenticed to him grew to be a pretty good <u>katana-shi</u>, but still could not make a <u>katana</u>, a sword, that was as good as those his master made. He wanted to know the delicate water temperature for hardening the sword, no matter what the cost. Finally, eluding the <u>katana-shi</u>, he put his right hand into the water which the master had prepared. The teacher saw him, however, and taking a sword, cut off the hand at the wrist so that it might not remember the touch of the water temperature. The apprentice had offended against courtesy.

(3) When temple schools developed, the teacher taught youths what he knew, what he thought, and even what he felt. Students could not be against him. They followed him with the idea that "A teacher does nothing wrong." A Japanese saying, which might have been born in one of these schools is, "Be 3 feet away from a teacher in order not to step on his shadow." The teacher was not the same as other people.

(4) This background of ideas from feudal times continued for a long time. Until the end of World War II it was still the basis of the feeling between teacher and students. The occupation of teaching was respected almost as though it were one of holy orders. Students were in awe of their teachers. They stood when he entered the room. They did not dispute anything he said. The teacher sat on a platform in front of the class. He was above the students both physically and in the way they regarded him.

(5) After World War II this feeling completely vanished. Nobody could get along then without

having more or less to do with the black market. This included teachers, who had to support their families. Because of economic conditions they had to go on strike or demonstrate in order to get a raise in pay or a bonus. Students and their parents began saying "A teacher is a man as we are!" They wanted to respect the teachers, but when they saw them dealing in the black market or opposing the government they could not. The teacher was no longer a saint as before.

(6) The platform in the classroom was broken down. The teacher's desk was taken away. The teacher was told he must stand at the side of the room when speaking, or take a seat among the students and discuss with them. It was diffi-cult for both the teacher and the students to know how to relate to each other. Outside of school what should their relationship be?

(7) Not only the students and parents but the teachers as well were concerned about this new state of affairs. Having self-respect, the teachers worried when they must patronize the black market or go on strike. They lost confi-dence in their occupation. As a consequence, people of talent did not want to be teachers. Because the great respect in which they had been held disappeared, they felt worse than if there had been little respect from the beginning.

(8) Twenty years after the war, social and economic conditions had gradually improved. During this time the teacher's desk was brought back to the classroom, and from it the teacher could impart knowledge to the students rather than merely being part of a discussion on the same level as those he taught. Students had to know so many things in order to pass the entrance examination to high school or college that they could not depend just on discussion. But students and teachers thought only of getting the best results on an examination, and nothing else. Students studied and memorized

desperately. The parents helped them in this. There was neither cooperation nor a spiritual bond between teachers and students, except the common aim to pass the examination.

(9) Now there is a movement for new reform in education in Japan. Many feel that too much emphasis is given to merely passing examinations. "Build up good youngsters," the government said recently. The teacher should be a guide and example to the students, not merely a drill master. We need to get back to the spiritual bond that once existed between student and teacher without the excessive idolizing that existed in the past.

EXERCISE 16.

Answer these questions on the composition you have just read.

1. Which of the following statements do you think is the best expression of the central idea of this composition?
   a. Respect for teachers in Japan changed 180 degrees after World War II.
   b. The radical change in respect for teachers in Japan that took place after World War II needs to be balanced today by mutual cooperation.
   c. Changes in respect for teachers in Japan that began after World War II are going on today.
2. Is the statement of the central idea clear? If not, how would you change it?
3. What is the method of organization of the composition? What are some transitional phrases that show this organization?
4. Are there other methods of development that might have improved the composition?

STEP 7. WRITING THE FINAL DRAFT

EXERCISE 17.

Make revisions as suggested in Exercise 15. Check your paper for spelling, punctuation, and grammatical accuracy, and hand it in in the form required by your instructor.

Reviewing Grammatical Patterns

FOR, SINCE, AND *AGO* IN EXPRESSIONS OF TIME

Since is used with the present-perfect form of the verb. *Ago* is used with the past tense. *For* may be used with either present perfect or past, but the sentence has a different meaning with a different verb form.

> I *have studied* English *since* 1978. (specific date or period of time)
> I *have studied* English *for* five years. (a period of time up to the present moment)
> I *studied* English *for* five years. (at some past time)
> I *studied* English five years *ago*. (a point in time measured from the moment of speaking)

GRAMMAR EXERCISE 1.

Rewrite the following sentences in three ways to include expressions of time with *since, for,* and *ago.* The first sentence serves as an example of what you are to do.

> I studied history. (1980)
>   a. I have studied history *since 1980.*
>   b. I have studied history *for four years.*
>   c. I began studying history *four years ago.*

1. I wrote letters to my grandmother. (1978)
2. I study in the United States. (1979)
3. People have telephones. (1877)
4. Paul has an apartment. (January 1983)
5. I ski. (1976) ●
6. My friend works at the university. (1970)
7. Men know about fire. (primitive times; thousands of years)

OTHER PREPOSITIONS IN EXPRESSIONS OF TIME

GRAMMAR EXERCISE 2.

In the following selection underline the prepositions *on, in,* and *at* in the phrases indicating time.

CELEBRATION OF PRESIDENTS' DAY

In 1865 Abraham Lincoln died, and because he was a great president, for many years Americans had a national holiday on his birthday, February 12, to honor him. But George Washington, America's first president, was also born in February. So recently, celebration of both birthdays has been observed on a Monday between the two dates, February 12 and February 22. This holiday is known as Presidents' Day, but few public ceremonies occur at this time. In contrast with the Fourth of July celebration of Independence Day, on Presidents' Day there are no parades in the morning, no picnic lunches at noon, no speeches in the afternoon. However, Republican party members often have Lincoln Day dinners at night to honor the famous Republican. Such dinners are formal, expensive, and start late in the evening, often at 8:00 P.M.

Using the preceding paragraph as a guide, supply an appropriate preposition *(in, on, at)* in the following blanks.

_____ 1983 (year)	_____ noon
the summer (season)	night
the evening	midnight
the morning	eight o'clock
the afternoon	1:30 P.M.
_____ Monday (day of the week)	
January 25 (calendar day)	
Christmas	
weekends	

GRAMMAR EXERCISE 3.

Write six sentences about some activity that you do or do not do, using time expressions including *in, on,* or *at.* Underline the prepositions.

> I ski *in* the winter, often *on* holidays, but I do not ski *at* midnight.
> I do not regularly drink coffee *in* the morning, but I like a cup *at* noon or night, especially *on* weekends.

EXPRESSIONS OF DEGREE AND COMPARISON

In the selections you have read in this lesson, the following expressions of degree or comparison occur:

1. "Adventure on the Colorado"
   a. current *so strong that*   c. how *exciting* it is *to*
   b. *such a delightful* trip *that*   d. *too* exhausted *to*
2. "Antarctica: Home of the Wind":
   a. big *enough for*
   b. *not so markedly as*

These and other structures of comparison are illustrated in the Handbook, section K32.

GRAMMAR EXERCISE 4.

Use structures of comparison to write two advertising slogans for each of the following, using a different structure in each. Read your slogans to the class.

> soap (gentle)
> This soap is *gentle enough to use* on a baby.
> This soap is *so gentle that it* will soothe your skin.

1. automobile (fast)
2. house paint (durable)
3. suit (well tailored)
4. wine (old)

Describe each of the following, varying the structures you use.

1. someone you like
2. someone you don't like
3. a pet you have
4. a pen you own
5. a class assignment you object to

EXPRESSIONS OF MEASURE

In the selections you have read for this lesson the following expressions of measure occur. Alternative means are indicated in parentheses.

- cliffs 2,000 feet high (2,000-foot cliffs)
- a three-week trip (a trip three weeks long)
- a 285-mile-long canyon (a canyon 285 miles long)
- a 200-foot drop

GRAMMAR EXERCISE 5.

Write sentences describing the age, height, length, or width of each of the following. Use two ways of expressing the measure for each.

> a friend (age)
>
> I have a 14-year-old friend.
> I have a friend 14 years old.

1. a pole (length)
2. a boat (width)
3. a mountain (height)
4. a student (age)
5. a wall (thickness)

IT AS A SENTENCE STARTER

Review the use of "It is" plus an adjective as a sentence starter, section A1h in your Handbook. Here are examples from this lesson.

> *It* may *be difficult for you to catch* your breath.
> *It is* exciting *to make* the trip.
> At first you may not realize *how exciting it is to make* the trip.
> *It was difficult for* both teachers and students *to know how* to relate to each other.

GRAMMAR EXERCISE 6.

Restate these sentences orally or in writing, as your instructor requests. Begin each sentence with *it*.

> *For us to go today* is important.
> *It is important* for us to go today.

1. That student tickets to football games are the same price as regular tickets is unfair.
2. For students to have to pay fees for football games if they don't like to watch football is unfair.
3. That the team doesn't win is the coach's fault.
4. That the greatest football player in the nation will participate in the game here Saturday is exciting.
5. For us to get tickets was a piece of good luck.
6. To get them so easily at the last minute is practically unheard of.

7. That you can't go with us is too bad.
8. For it to rain on Saturday would be a disaster. (Note impersonal *it* in expressions of weather.)
9. To find a place near the stadium to park a car is difficult.
10. For us to start early is necessary.

GRAMMAR EXERCISE 7.

Complete each of the following sentences using a clause beginning with *that* or an infinitive structure.

It is true that _____.
It is true that living in a foreign country can be difficult.

It is difficult to _____.
It is difficult to learn a new language.

1. It is true that _____.
2. It is necessary to _____.
3. It is sometimes frightening to _____.
4. It is regrettable that _____.
5. It is exciting to _____.
6. It is delightful to _____.
7. It is certainly fortunate that _____.
8. It is extraordinary that _____.
9. It is amazing that _____.
10. It was thoughtful of you to _____.

REVIEW OF USE AND OMISSION OF ARTICLES

Review uses and omission of articles in the Handbook, section 53, if necessary before doing these exercises.

GRAMMAR EXERCISE 8.

Explain why *a* or *the* or no article is used in these expressions from "Adventure on the Colorado."

Paragraph 1
1. one of the major tourist attractions
2. thousands of visitors
3. the river at the bottom
4. a closer view

5. a small boat

Paragraph 2
   6. the beginning of the trip
   7. the boat moves slowly
   8. pure abstract sculpture

Paragraph 3
   9. a distant roar

Paragraph 4
10. the noise vanishes

Paragraph 5
11. a place along the bank where you can build a campfire

Paragraph 6
12. the number of boulders in the water

GRAMMAR EXERCISE 9.

Write in complete sentences the answers to the following questions based on "Adventure on the Colorado." When you have finished, check your answers with the original. Did you use articles correctly?

1. For tourists with a sense of adventure, what is becoming popular?
2. To feel the overpowering force of the water in the canyon, how should you see it?
3. At the beginning of the trip what does the boat move between?
4. How old are the rock formations?
5. What happens after you pass the rock formations and when the river narrows?
6. What will happen before you get to the end of the trip?
7. As you near the end of the trip, what happens to the rapids?
8. Why do some visitors want to take the trip a second time?

END NOTES

Place the word *only* near the word or phrase it modifies. Generally it is placed before the word or phrase.

Compare the meanings:

Only John came to the party. (No one else came.)
John only came to the party. (He did not do anything else.)
John came to the only party. (There was only one party.)

EXPLAINING CAUSES AND EFFECTS

Rhetorical Principles

Organization by cause and effect (or effect-cause)

Devices for coherence in cause-effect and effect-cause organization

Grammatical Patterns

Infinitives as subjects, objects, and modifiers

Reduction of clauses to infinitives

Conjunctions and sentence connectors

Sentence recognition and use of commas

Punctuation and capitalization in sentences

Writing a Composition

Assignment: Much scientific reporting is a matter of describing causes and effects, and many liberal arts studies are concerned with the cause-effect relationship. Write a three-page composition. (1) Describe some condition that you consider good or bad and analyze the causes, or (2) describe some event, movement, or invention and tell what has happened to people as a result. As in the previous lesson, you may need to use material from outside sources in addition to your own ideas for this paper.

Stage I. Prewriting

STEP 1. BRAINSTORMING FOR IDEAS

EXERCISE 1.

Here are some suggested topics for this assignment. Out of class, choose two or three that you think you might use, or choose some not listed that you might like to write about. Consider what point of view you would take about the topic and how you might develop it. Be prepared to discuss these in class.

1. Explain the effects of some historical event on your country, city, or family.
2. Describe some recent improvement in cars, planes, computers, and so on, and tell what the effect has been.
3. Describe some scientific discovery and the effects it has had on people, the environment, and so on.
4. Tell about some recent law or election in your country or hometown (or in another country or city) and tell how it has affected people, crime, driving habits, production of some product, and so on.
5. How has some person affected your family, your school, your government, your society?
6. Does some newspaper, magazine, radio, or TV have great influence on your country? If so, what is it? Is this influence good or bad?
7. How have improved methods of communication affected the relationship between countries?
8. What has caused the growth of some recent industry (manufacture of mobile homes, computers, and so on)?
9. How does the climate in a certain area affect how people make a living, how they run their daily lives, what they hope for or dread?
10. What people, what events, what books, what circumstances have made you what you are?

11. Speculate about how some recent event will affect your country. Will the results be a chain reaction (one result causing another and that one causing something else), or will there be several results that are independent of each other, or both?
12. In what ways is your family or your town a different one from what it was ten years ago or five years ago? What has made the difference?
13. Prolonged lack of change produces effects on a country too. Are there traditional customs or beliefs that people have in your area that affect their lives in distinct ways?

STEP 2. PHRASING THE THESIS SENTENCE

EXERCISE 2.

Write a possible thesis sentence for each of the three topics you selected in exercise 1, and discuss with classmates and your instructor the suitability of the sentences and the phrasing of each. Let classmates suggest which topic they would most like to read about. Consider if that is the one you are best prepared to write about. Discuss, if there is time, what is the best form of organization for the topic.

STEP 3. JOTTING DOWN IDEAS AND REFINING A POINT OF VIEW

EXERCISE 3.

The subject you select will probably be one you already know something about. You have seen certain results that you think are good or bad (or both good and bad). Or you have observed that certain actions or conditions produce certain results. (1) Jot down in phrases your own ideas on the subject, or write a preliminary draft to express them. (2) Looking at these ideas, decide whether the thesis sentence you have written does indeed reflect the exact point of view you want to explain. (3) Consider how you can best develop these ideas. Review the methods of development discussed in Lessons 1 and 2. (Are there examples you can use, comparisons you can make, figures available, quotations from people who are in a position to know a great deal about the subject?)

EXERCISE 4.

Decide whether you need to get additional information from the library or by interviewing someone, and, if so, take notes, phrasing the ideas in your own words unless you plan to use a particular sentence or phrase as a direct quotation.

In taking notes, be sure to record the name of the author, title of the book or magazine article, publisher, page numbers of the material to be quoted, and so on.

Stage II. Giving Form to the Composition and Studying Techniques

STEP 4. WRITING A FIRST DRAFT

EXERCISE 5.

Write a first draft of your composition. Many writers prefer to write the body of the composition first, leaving the writing of the introduction and the conclusion until the last. The theory is that the body of the composition tells what you really want to say. The introduction only relates the subject to your reader, gaining his interest, showing why the topic is important, or explaining that you are writing about only one aspect of a larger subject. The conclusion tries to reinforce the central idea in a remarkable way.

STEP 5. STUDYING RHETORICAL PRINCIPLES

Organization by Cause and Effect (or Effect-Cause)

One way to arrange ideas in sequence is to discuss causes and then the effects or results of the causes. Often the order is reversed, with an analysis of a condition and an exploration of what caused it. This arrangement is effective to explain mechanical or historical processes —electric refrigeration, jet propulsion, a civil war, the development of mass production in industry.

Sometimes the result is well known to the reader and need not be developed in as much detail as the causes. Sometimes there are several causes or there may be a cause that itself is the result of something else, which was caused by yet a third factor. In using cause-result order, the writer takes into account what his reader probably knows—and what he needs to know. Note the order in the following selection.

TV: MONSTER OR MIRACLE*

(1) According to the A. C. Nielson Company, a
company that measures television audiences, 80
million households own television sets in the
United States today. In 1981, this company
claims, a record level of 6 hours and 44 minutes
per day was the average listening time in these
households--a sharp rise from the 1970s. Almost
all Americans watch their sets for a number of
hours every day. Those who spend the greatest
amount of time in television viewing are the
very young and the very old. Women, minorities,
shut-ins, and those in hospitals are the most
frequent watchers of TV. Heavy users are
usually less educated than those who spend less
time before the "tube." A panel of educators has
determined that by the age of 16 most children
have spent 10,000 hours watching television--
more time than they have spent in school. Some
of the programs are educational and
informative, some merely entertaining. Some
contain many scenes of sex and violence.
Watching such programs for hours on end cannot
help having an effect on American thinking, on
society's moral values and cultural standards,
and on the knowledge of the world that the
average person has. Is television in America a
monster or a miracle? Opinion on its effects is
divided.
(2) It is easy to point to unwanted effects
that may have come from watching television. An
increase in violence has been linked to
television watching. After a recent program in
which the hero played "Russian roulette," 29
people are said to have shot themselves as they
tried to imitate the hero. The National
Institute of Mental Health, as a result of a
five-year study of 732 children, concluded that
"violence in television does lead to aggressive behavior by children and teenagers."
This included several kinds of aggression--

*Data from *U.S. News & World Report*, 93 (August 2, 1982): 27-30.

conflicts with parents, fighting, and delinquency.

(3) Television is also blamed for a decay in moral values. According to author and actor Steve Allen, the effect of TV in this respect is "horrendous." He believes "Television is creating people who think it is perfectly O.K. to grab what they want and the only bad thing is getting caught."

(4) Yet another undesirable aspect of television is the effect it has on the minds of children. Hour after hour of watching pictures lowers a child's attention span and conditions children to enjoy only what is fast paced and entertaining. By comparison, study in school seems slow and boring. Scores on Scholastic Aptitude Tests given to high school seniors have dropped some 50 points on the average since the 1960s, and although the cause-effect relation has not been proved, this drop is blamed in part on television.

(5) Yet television is not all bad in its effects on American society. News is now brought into the home, and television has increased people's knowledge of the world. Many educators think that television has given Americans a wealth of experience that is not being measured by today's school tests. Millions of preschool American children have learned reading and arithmetic through such programs as "Sesame Street" and "The Electric Company." One study has suggested that children who watch television are more curious and read more widely than children who do not. Veteran broadcaster Eric Sevareid argues that "Television has had an enormously positive influence on America, partly because in presenting the news, it is free of government control." And there are those who credit television for making Americans more tolerant of racial and religious differences in the country.

(6) The direct effects of television are

difficult to measure. The hope is that the new
video age will benefit from past mistakes and
successes in the television industry and that
television will ultimately do the country more
good than harm.

EXERCISE 6.

Complete the following outline of the article about the amount of
television viewing in the United States and its effects. Then compare
your outline with those of your classmates.

Thesis sentence: Television is a widely used form of entertain-
ment in the United States, but opinion on its effects is divided.
 I. Television is widely used.
II. Effects of television are both good and bad.
   A. There are several bad effects.
      1. _____ .
      2. _____ .
      3. _____ .
   B. Yet there are good effects too.
      1. _____ .
      2. _____ .
      3. _____ .

EXERCISE 7.

Answer the following questions about the television article and
about the outline that you have just completed.

1. Is the plan of organization cause-effect or effect-cause?
2. Is the material in the first paragraph of the composition
   developmental (examples, figures, and so on) or organizational?
   Is the outline concerned with developmental material or with
   organizational material? What developmental details are used
   under points IIA and IIB that are not included in the outline?

3. According to the outline, would you expect the author to think that the good effects of TV outweigh the bad or vice versa? Do you think this is the case? Why or why not?
4. Which of the following kinds of support are used for point I: facts, figures, examples, quotation from authority, illustration, comparison, explanation? Be able to give examples.
5. Which of these groups of phrases is more effective in introducing evidence to support a point?

    One study has suggested. . . .
    There are those who credit television with. . . .

    or

    The National Institute of Mental Health, as a result of a five-year study of 732 school children, concluded. . . .
    According to author and actor Steve Allen. . . .
    Scores on Scholastic Aptitude Tests given to high school seniors. . . .

6. What assertions in this article are not developed by giving facts, figures, examples, and so forth? Which assertions will you agree with even though they are not developed? Which ones need development?
7. Steve Allen and Eric Sevareid both earn their livings by appearing on TV. Sevareid believes that TV has a positive influence on children; Steve Allen believes it is bad. What is the reader to conclude from this conflicting testimony?
8. Would it be desirable to have testimony about the effects of TV from someone outside the television industry? Why or why not? What kinds of people are best fitted to give reliable testimony?

EXERCISE 8.

Many people might look at the title of the TV article and say, "I don't need to have a writer tell me whether TV is good or bad. I know what I like and don't like." Write an introduction to this article that will lure a person to read it. Choose one of the following magazines to publish the article, and gear your introduction to that readership.

1. *Parents Magazine*
2. *Time (Newsweek, U.S. News & World Report)*
3. *Modern Maturity* (for retired people)
4. *Spring* (for high school girls)

Would you or would you not alter the content of the article to fit the readers? Explain.

Devices for Coherence in Cause-Effect and Effect-Cause Organization

Signposts that keep the reader reminded of cause-effect relationship are the italicized words in the following phrases and sentences.

- What *causes* this?
- What *brought this* about?
- What *contributed to this state of affairs?*

and

- The *result* is. . . .
- The *effect* of all this is. . . .
- Then this *happened.* . . .
- Certain people (institutions) were *affected* (changed).
- The expected *happened.*

EXERCISE 9.

List devices for coherence that keep the reader of the article on TV aware of the organizational pattern.

Stage III. Critiquing and Revising

STEP 6. ANALYZING AND REVISING THE FIRST DRAFT

EXERCISE 10.

Before you write your final draft of the composition, check the first draft for the following points:

1. Is the subject limited sufficiently for you to cover it adequately in three or four pages?
2. Is the thesis clearly stated?

3. Are the main points clearly stated and have you shown the relationship of each to another main point and to the thesis?
4. Is each main point developed sufficiently? Have you used a variety of developmental material?
5. Is any material irrelevant?
6. Are the introduction and conclusion adapted to the reader?
7. Is your organizational pattern consistent?

Bring the first draft to class for possible critiquing by your classmates or for a conference with your instructor.

While you are critiquing and revising your first draft, study the composition that follows.

THE CAR AND MY NATIVE PLACE
Werner Foster, West Germany

(1) Before World War II nobody owned a car in my home place. A lot of people say that was the golden age of man. After the war, more and more inhabitants were able to afford an automobile. After almost 40 years of living with the car, the people and the town are different from what they were without the car. How did the car change the social life of the inhabitants of my town, and how did it change the town itself?

(2) The automobile brought some advantages such as more comfortable and cheaper traveling, but it also brought great disadvantages like the change of social life. Today, people are very busy. Nobody has time for other persons. Time is money. The car is one reason for this stress. After work everybody hurries to his automobile and drives home. Of course there are traffic jams during rush hours. Drivers get more and more excited and angry, and when they finally arrive home, the family suffers because the driver is in a bad mood.

(3) Especially since the 1960s and 1970s the car has become a status symbol in my native place. A lot of people are jealous of their neighbors because the neighbors can afford a bigger Mercedes or BMW than they can. I know of families who live only for their cars. They save every penny only to be able to afford a bigger

car. These people have created the Saturday afternoon cleaning fever. They vacuum, wash, and polish the automobiles the whole afternoon. They are authorities on what wax is best, what gets white sidewalls on the tires the cleanest, what dressing to put on vinyl tops. They have the attitude: First my car and second my family. They have no time to play with their children. They have no time to read a book. They have time only for their car.

(4) The automobile has not only made men crazy; it has also changed my native place. In the 1950s we got our first tar street. In the 1960s and 1970s all our streets were covered with tar or concrete. More cars, more streets, more concrete--that was the devilish circle. The streets became broader and broader, and the sidewalks became smaller and smaller. Sometimes it seems the cars are more important than men. In former days there was a nice big park next to my home. I remember those happy days when I played soccer with my friends on the soft green grass under the big oak trees. Today we have a concrete desert next to our house. The municipality decided to build more parking spaces downtown.

(5) The energy crises of 1974, 1979, and 1983 stopped the automobile boom in Germany. The high gasoline prices are responsible for a new car mentality in Germany. Now a lot of people use their cars only if it is necessary. But in my opinion this change has come almost too late because the car has already destroyed too much.

EXERCISE 11.

Answer the following questions about the composition.

1. Why did the author spend little time on explaining the cause?
2. What two advantages of automobiles does the author mention? Why is it effective to admit certain advantages?
3. According to Foster, in what ways has the automobile affected people? Do you think the author has thought considerably about his subject?

4. In paragraph 2, study sentences 2, 3, 4, and 5. Is the relationship between the ideas in these sentences made completely clear? Combine the ideas into one sentence and delete any idea that seems irrelevant.
5. In stating his thesis, how does the author try to arouse reader interest? Does the author know the answer to the questions? How would the thesis be stated differently in an outline?
6. What is the primary way in which the author develops his points?
7. What unexpected idea is introduced in the conclusion? Does it invalidate the thesis?

STEP 7. WRITING THE FINAL DRAFT

EXERCISE 12.

Prepare a final draft of your composition making use of suggestions for revision in exercise 10. Check carefully matters of grammar, spelling, and punctuation. Be sure sentences are complete. Copy the composition neatly and hand it in in the form required by your instructor.

Reviewing Grammatical Patterns

INFINITIVES AS SUBJECTS, OBJECTS, AND MODIFIERS

In the material that you have been reading in this lesson, you have encountered infinitives used in the ways indicated in parentheses under each of the following excerpts.

1. One way *to arrange ideas in sequence* is *to discuss*. . . .
   (modifier of a noun)   (complement)
2. Cause-effect organization is often used *to explain a process*.
   (adverb)
3. . . . what his reader knows and what he needs *to know*.
   (object)
4. It is easy *to point to unwanted effects*. (*To point to unwanted effects*
   (subject)
   is easy.)
5. . . . it is perfectly OK *to grab* what they want. (*To grab what*
   (subject)
   they want is perfectly OK.)

GRAMMAR EXERCISE 1.

Following are several facts about Napoleon's life. The sentences contain infinitives used as subjects, objects, or modifiers. Copy these sentences and label the use of the infinitive as is done in the preceding example sentences.

1. To get away from French punishment, Napoleon fled to England after his defeat at Waterloo.
2. But the British thought it would be difficult to keep him in England.
3. Therefore, the British wanted to send him to St. Helena.
4. To confine him on a remote island would solve their problem.
5. That was a way to get rid of him, to please the French government, and to be humane to Napoleon.

GRAMMAR EXERCISE 2.

Dr. Mortimer Adler believed that the best way to make the ideas in a book your own is to mark up the book. Only in that way can you make the content of the book a part of your life. Following are his suggestions for the marking. Use a correct form of the verb in parentheses to complete each sentence.

1. Adler says that he underlines _____ (indicate) major points or forceful statements.
2. He uses vertical lines at the margin _____ (emphasize) a statement already underlined.
3. He puts a star or an asterisk _____ (mark) the 10 or 20 most important things in the book.
4. He puts numbers in the margins _____ (indicate) the sequence of points the author uses to develop his central idea.
5. Adler puts numbers of other pages in the margin _____ (remind) himself where else in the book the author makes a point relevant to the point marked.
6. He uses circles _____ (indicate) key words and phrases.
7. He uses the margins _____ (record) his comments on what he reads.

REDUCTION OF CLAUSES TO INFINITIVES

Clauses are often reduced to infinitives or infinitive phrases with subjects and/or objects.

1. To get away (so that he could get away) from French punishment, Napoleon fled to England. (infinitive as adverb expressing purpose)
2. That is a suggestion for them to act upon (that they should act upon). (infinitive as a modifier of a noun)

GRAMMAR EXERCISE 3.

Change the following italicized clauses to infinitive phrases. Indicate the function of the infinitive in the sentence.

1. That is something *scientists should investigate.*
2. The coach gave his football players a new play *that they must practice.*
3. We were assigned a composition *that we must finish in an hour.*
4. The ambassador carried papers *that he would deliver to the king.*
5. I brought you books now *so that I can avoid doing it at the last minute.*
6. Please tell me something *that I can do.*
7. Here is a micrometer *that you can measure the inside dimensions with.*
8. Please find someone *that I can go* with.
9. *So that you can be wide awake for the examination,* get a good night's sleep.

CONJUNCTIONS AND SENTENCE CONNECTORS

GRAMMAR EXERCISE 4.

Note how paragraph 2 in the following selection is made more vivid and more unified by the use of conjunctions and sentence connectors to show the relationship of the ideas.

(1) The small town of Concord, Massachusetts, has played an important part in American political history. It has played an important part in American literary history. It was through the towns of Concord and Lexington that the British soldiers marched in 1775 to keep the rebellious colonists under control. It was at the old stone bridge in Concord that the first battle of the American Revolution took place. In the early part of the nineteenth century, Concord was the home of a group of American writers and philosophers. It became a center of literary activity. Ralph Waldo Emerson, the poet, essayist, and transcendentalist

philosopher, made Concord his home. For a time
the novelist Nathaniel Hawthorne lived there.
Henry David Thoreau was a resident of Concord.
Thoreau is known for his book *Walden,* an account
of his life in the woods. He is known for his
essay "Civil Disobedience." This essay
reflects Thoreau's opposition to slavery. In
brief, this quiet, charming New England town
has figured importantly in the development of
the American nation. Many tourists visit it
each year.

(2) The small town of Concord, Massachusetts,
has played an important role *not only* in
American political history but in American
literary history *as well.* It was through the
towns of Lexington and Concord that the British
soldiers marched in 1775 to keep the rebellious
colonists under control, *and consequently* it
was at the old stone bridge in Concord that the
first battle of the American Revolution took
place. *Moreover,* in the early part of the
nineteenth century, Concord was the home of a
group of writers and philosophers, and
therefore became a center of literary activity.
Ralph Waldo Emerson, the poet, essayist, and
transcendentalist philosopher, made Concord
his home, and for a time *so did* the novelist
Nathaniel Hawthorne. Henry David Thoreau was
also a resident of Concord. Thoreau is known *not
only* for his book *Walden,* an account of his life
in the woods, *but also* for his essay "Civil
Disobedience," which reflects Thoreau's
opposition to slavery. In brief, this quiet,
charming New England town has *thus* figured
importantly in the development of the American
nation. *Therefore,* many tourists visit it each
year.

GRAMMAR EXERCISE 5.

Rewrite the following passage, adding conjunctions to show addition, contrast, comparison, or result, as has been done in paragraph
2 of the preceding exercise.

CALIFORNIA GOLD

In 1849 gold was discovered in California. Many people went there to seek their fortunes. A great migration to the West was begun. People moved into California in large numbers. Some towns doubled in population almost overnight. Buildings were hastily constructed. They were not built to last. As the gold mines were exhausted, the settlements became "ghost towns." The Wild West in those days was a place of excitement, glamour, danger, and lawlessness. Later permanent settlements were made. A few of the "forty-niners," as these early settlers were called, made the fortunes in gold they had come to seek. Others made more modest fortunes in merchandising or farming or ranching. Still others returned home, as poor as when they had left.

SENTENCE RECOGNITION AND USE OF COMMAS

Study section A3 in "Conventions in the Mechanics of Writing" in the Handbook for the uses of commas.

EXERCISE 6.

Listen as your instructor reads aloud each of the following word groups. Then read the word group aloud with your instructor. After that, punctuate with periods and commas the sentence(s) you have just read. Finally, discuss the necessary punctuation.

Be able to tell whether a given comma is used (1) to indicate an appositive, (2) to separate an interrupting (nonrestrictive) element, (3) to separate a long adverbial element at the beginning of a sentence, (4) to separate words in a series, (5) to separate figures, or (6) to separate a city from a state or after a state when the city and state are mentioned together.

1. In one of the United States's least-known mountain ranges the Black Hills of South Dakota is America's great treasure chest.
2. The beautiful Black Hills are a treasure in themselves and present-day Americans are not the only ones who have thought so the Indians considered the Black Hills the home of their gods.

3. Under the trees and rocks that give the Black Hills their spectacular beauty lies yet another treasure: gold.

4. The Homestake mine near Lead South Dakota is the richest gold mine in the United States it has been producing gold for over 100 years.

5. Miners now have to go down into the earth $1\frac{1}{2}$ miles but treasure is still there.

6. When the Homestake began to yield vast quantities of gold the Oglala Sioux Indians sued the company for 6 billion dollars for "tresspass of its property."

7. The gold is recovered now only at tremendous costs because $3\frac{1}{2}$ tons of ore need to be broken hauled hoisted over a mile crushed separated and refined in order to get 1 ounce of gold.

8. In 1907 when a fire broke out in the mine 80 million cubic feet of water had to be poured into it to put out the fire and then all the water had to be pumped out all this was very expensive yet the mining operation was so valuable that the mine continued to operate.

9. There are also the costs of forcing cool fresh air one mile down into the mine shafts so that the workers can work since the temperature where they work is 134°F they could not work if the fresh air were not forced down there.

10. The Homestake has yielded 31410612 ounces of gold and 7285784 ounces of silver.

11. The shafts and tunnels of the Homestake are so numerous under the town of Lead South Dakota that residents became concerned that the town would sink into the honeycombed mountain beneath the town.

12. Now to prevent the town from sinking the miners pump gold-depleted sand back into the caverns the miners created.

13. Although extraction of gold from the Homestake gets more expensive every year it is not likely that mining here will slow down soon unless the veins of gold run out.

PUNCTUATION AND CAPITALIZATION IN SENTENCES

GRAMMAR EXERCISE 7.

Study IIIA1 to IIIA4 and IIIA12, in the Handbook. Then in the following sentences insert the needed punctuation and capitalization.

1. contact sports like football and wrestling involve a certain amount of physical risk to the player nevertheless many

young men and even some girls are attracted to such activities

2. college athletic teams originally played intramurally that is against other teams in their own college however such activity did not affect a students belief that his academic work was the major goal of his college life

3. many college athletic stars go on to become players on professional teams consequently some outstanding college athletes focus their attention on athletics rather than on their academic work

4. some outstanding athletes have shown almost a mania for sports for example paavo nurmi of finland one of the greatest distance runners of all times tried to stretch his infant son's feet so that he too could be a great runner

5. some people protest the emphasis on college sports today arguing that the athletic department costs too much nevertheless many athletic programs are financed with money earned by the football team

6. with the widespread interest in professional football baseball and hockey it is not likely that college sports will be deemphasized at least it is not likely in the near future

7. critics of big-time sport such as football baseball and tennis say that it is no longer a sport in contrast big time sport is a business played for headline popularity of the players and for spectator gambling

8. professional athletes get fantastically large salaries on the other hand they are subjected to harrowing pressure to perform

9. the little boys playing baseball on a vacant lot play for the fun of it in contrast to the professional player baseball is part of the days and nights work

10. players on professional athletic teams have to be away from home a lot are under great pressure to perform and have a comparatively short working life as a result they often have emotional and financial as well as physical problems

GRAMMAR EXERCISE 8.

Punctuate the following passage correctly, indicating the beginning and end of sentences.

MARK TWAIN AND THE MISSISSIPPI

Mark Twain's success as a writer has been attributed by some to his skill in the use of language his gift for apt understatement and his ability to recount a tale in the words and rhythms of actual men and women these are qualities of his style and may have been developed through his encounters with people in Nevada and California mining camps undoubtedly the West influenced the style of the writing of the impressionable observant Mark Twain a more pervasive influence in his themes and subject matter however was the Mississippi River the young Sam Clemens spent his boyhood in Hannibal Missouri where the arrival of the river steamer always brought life to the sleepy little town and afforded an escape from the petty problems of everyday living the boats and the river had a special fascination for the boy thus in his early adult life he became a pilot on the Mississippi and his pen name Mark Twain is taken from river-pilot terminology his writing reflects more than a mastery of style however the river developed within him certain perceptions certain attitudes that form the theses of his novels.

GRAMMAR EXERCISE 9.

In class with books closed, summarize the selection "Mark Twain and the Mississippi."

END NOTES

Avoid overuse of "There is (are)" as a sentence starter. The construction often makes the sentence unnecessarily wordy.

> *There is* a new president *who* has come to our school.
> A new president has come to our school.

Use the passive voice sparingly. Generally if the actor is not known or if the action is more important than the actor, passive is correct. Otherwise the active voice is preferable.

Lesson 9

DEFINING AND DISCUSSING CAUSES OF A PROBLEM

<table>
<tr><td>Rhetorical Principles</td><td>Grammatical Patterns</td></tr>
<tr><td>Problem-solution order—defining a problem and its causes

Coherence by words and phrases indicating a problem and its causes

Using an outline in the planning stage</td><td>Review of verb forms
Subordinators and sentence connectors
Verbs followed by participles
Verb-preposition combinations
Agreement of subject and verb</td></tr>
</table>

Writing a Composition

Assignment: Write a composition of three or four pages (700 to 1000 words) in which you define a problem and explain some of the causes of it. Try to pick a subject (1) that you know something about from personal experience and (2) that you can suggest solutions for (in the next lesson).

Stage I Prewriting

STEP 1. BRAINSTORMING FOR IDEAS

EXERCISE 1.

Here are some topics that might be used for this assignment. Choose two or three, or others if you like, for class discussion. Be sure to pick ones in which you have a real interest.

1. Educational problems
   A. Problems caused by lack of personal contact between students and professors in large classes
   B. Problems in having a grade reflect what a student has gained from a course
   C. Problems of living in a different culture while going to school
   D. Problems that arise when students of unequal ability and unequal background in subject matter are in the same class
2. Social problems
   A. Problems presented by elderly people who can no longer take care of themselves but who are kept alive by advanced medical technology
   B. Problems presented by hijackers, arsonists, terrorists, or drug traffickers
   C. Problems of the generation gap (children feeling that their parents do not understand them)
   D. Problems that arise when women work outside the home
   E. Problems that occur from a rising divorce rate
3. Economic problems
   A. Problems presented by organized labor
   B. The problem that arises when a nation supported by one big industry (such as oil production) finds that that industry can no longer be carried on

   C. The problem of a rising population that outruns a nation's ability to feed that population
   D. Problems presented by underdeveloped nations
4. Political problems
   A. Problems presented by activist minorities
   B. Problems of discovering appropriate representation in voting (e.g., should only property owners be allowed to vote on matters of property taxes?)
   C. Problems in discovering the right form of government for a given society

STEP 2. PHRASING THE THESIS SENTENCE

EXERCISE 2.

Write a possible thesis sentence for each of the three topics selected in exercise 1, and discuss with classmates and instructor the suitability of the topic and the phrasing of each. Division of the class into small groups may allow longer discussion about which of your topics is most desirable to write on. Try to choose a problem of general interest.

STEP 3. JOTTING DOWN IDEAS AND REFINING A POINT OF VIEW

EXERCISE 3.

As you have done in previous lessons, either jot down ideas about your subject or start writing a preliminary sketch to express your own ideas on your subject. Then look over what you have written to see whether your original thesis sentence does indeed express your exact point of view. Also, after your first jotting or writing, consider what developmental material you can use to make your point clear. Decide whether you need facts and figures beyond your present knowledge to show the problems. Or do you need other forms of support—explanation, examples, contrast, or quotation of authority?

Getting additional facts and the opinions of others often helps convince your reader of the seriousness of the problem. As in former lessons, take notes in your own words and record accurate information about the source of your outside material.

Stage II Giving Form to the Composition and Studying Techniques

STEP 4. WRITING A FIRST DRAFT

EXERCISE 4.

Before you write the first draft, read the rhetorical principles of cause-effect organization in step 5. Your composition for this lesson will contain two parts. First you will *give evidence* that the problem exists. How much detail you use will depend on your subject and on whether your classmates probably know little or much about the problem. If they know quite a little about it already, you can proceed quickly to the second part—a discussion of the causes. (In this composition do not try to give a solution.)

STEP 5. STUDYING RHETORICAL PRINCIPLES

Problem-Solution Order—Defining a Problem and Its Causes

The problem-solving sequence of John Dewey (adapted from methods of scientific experimentation) presents a basic patterning of thought commonly encountered in writing and reading. As a writer using this pattern of thought, you should follow these steps:

1. Define the problem or give evidence that the problem exists. Tell how you know that a situation exists that calls for action. Who are affected? How are they affected? Is the problem becoming more acute? In the definition of the problem, you often describe conditions or use explanations to make your point clear. For some subjects you need facts and figures. You may want to use examples and illustrations so that your reader can picture the conditions. Again, you may want to contrast present conditions with past conditions.

2. Report causes of the problem. Here you tell why the conditions exist. Are several causes operating at the same time? Or is one cause produced by another that comes about because of yet another condition, in a kind of chain reaction? For example, suppose a certain college does not have adequate library facilities. Its facilities are not adequate because of increased enrollment. Its enrollment is increased because more people have money to go to college because wages are high.

Wages are high because—and so forth. Operating simultaneously is another cause of the problem—the income of the college has not increased in proportion to increased enrollment.

3. Suggest possible solutions to the problem. Many problems one might discuss have no simple or easy solution. The best one can hope to do is point out areas in which improvement has been made and in which further improvement might be brought about if certain things were done.

4. Defend the solution that seems most practical. To be worthy of consideration, a proposed solution must hold reasonable hope for solving the problem. It must also be something that can be financed and for which adequate personnel can be provided. Defense of a given solution must include these considerations.

Coherence by Words and Phrases Indicating a Problem and Its Causes

Following are words and phrases that are often used in compositions dealing with problems and their causes.

the evidence is all around us	since
the trouble started	and so
consequently	for this reason
therefore	at last
as a consequence	finally
that is why	because
for this reason	so
as a result	

EXERCISE 5.

Complete the following sentences by stating the cause or effect and inserting devices for coherence as needed.

1. Students spend sleepless nights before final examinations _____ .

2. _____ students often postpone daily study, they often _____ .

3. _____ ; for this reason they often have to spend sleepless nights before an examination.

4. Students have not studied for this examination. The evidence is all around us; _(Supply items of evidence.)_
5. Students often neglect library assignments _____ we see them cramming just before the final examination.
6. One student was caught in the examination with atomic weights written on his hand _____ .

PHYSICIANS' EXORBITANT FEES: THE EVIDENCES AND THE CAUSES

(1) My neighbor, a retired person in good health, recently had a routine physical examination that cost $350. Another friend with a small infection in a thumb complained of spending an hour and a half in the doctor's office taking preliminary tests seemingly unrelated to the ailment that took her to the doctor. The bill for the office call itemized procedures that seemed to her unnecessary. Such reports force the suspicion that there is something wrong with medical fees and medical practice.

(2) Are these instances merely local, or do physicians across the nation charge outrageous prices for their services and often recommend unnecessary procedures? A survey of current magazines shows that the problem is widespread. U.S. News & World Report reveals that since 1965 physicians' fees have jumped 205 percent.[1] Time sees the same picture, reporting that in 1981 medical charges showed the highest gain for any consumer item.[2] Dr. William R. Rassman in Business Week admits, "In many cases an $80 illness with a loss of 3 to 5 days' work has been turned into a $1,000-plus illness with 3 to 10 times that loss of work." He goes on to say that fictitious illnesses have increased the cost of every service and "drained the customer's pocketbook."[3]

(3) Writers in Scientific American also report questionable practices.[4] They tell of a city in Maine, where if the present trend continues, 70 percent of the women will have had

a hysterectomy by the age of 75. The report also found that the rate of tonsillectomies in some areas was six times that in other areas. The overall differences in the rate of surgery in different areas seemed to be, not the result of chance variation, but influenced by the ratio of surgeons to population. Where there was an oversupply of surgeons, operations were recommended much oftener.

(4) Do physicians need to perform unnecessary tests and recommend unnecessary operations in order to survive? We must conclude not, because the average net income of private, office-based physicians is twice that of lawyers and dentists, and four times that of skilled industrial workers.[5] How, then, do physicians justify their fees, and what, if anything, can the customer-patient do about the exorbitant costs?

(5) The physician and the economist answer the questions differently.[6] Physicians claim their fees are high because they had to finance eight years of costly higher education. After graduation, the three to five years of required hospital residency bring in only a pittance, so they begin their practice deeply in debt (estimated at $20,000 to $50,000) and longing for status and wealth. They sincerely desire compensation for 12 years of working 80 hours a week. They believe they deserve that.

(6) Economists are not so sure that physicians do deserve it. They contend that physicians are not the only ones who have had expensive training, are not the only professionals who face a period of building a practice. Economists also point out that the American Medical Association prevents the law of supply and demand from keeping prices down. The AMA from the 1930s to the 1960s fought to limit the number of medical schools and the number of students who went to those schools. The association also fought federal aid to medical education. It tried to restrict the competition

of osteopaths, chiropractors, midwives, and health-maintenance organizations. The resulting lack of competition contributed to rising costs for the physicians' services.

(7) Another cause of the high prices for physicians' services is the fact that two-thirds of all physicians are paid by a third party--an insurance company or the United States government. The patient's share of the payment is smaller than the fee really is, and thus the patient often forgets that he really pays the entire bill through insurance payments and taxes.

(8) The physician, as a businessman, enjoys a peculiar advantage. There is little chance for comparison shopping. When you are ill, you are in no position to go from doctor to doctor to ask about prices. You would never rush to an automobile dealer the night before you started on a vacation by car. You would never let the salesman pick out the car and decide the price. However, that is exactly what you do when you go to the doctor. Doctors do not have a fixed price for an appendectomy or other procedures.

(9) Still another factor contributing to the high cost of physicians' services is the peculiar doctor-patient relationship. A person feels very close to his doctor, has a certain child-like dependence on him, feels that the doctor is a friend. The emotional bond between patient and physician is often stronger than the patient's feeling of outrage over the high prices the physician charges; hence the patient is reluctant to protest overcharging.

(10) Yet the patient fusses about his bills, grumbles about the unnecessary tests, often questions procedures that kept him hospital-ized so long. Is there a way out? Can physicians' fees be kept at a reasonable level, and can we eliminate unnecessary services?

[1]"Exploding Cost of Health Care," U.S. News & World Report 89 (September 1, 1980): 44.

[2]J. Greenwald, "Those Sky-High Health Costs," Time 120 (July 12, 1982): 54-55.

[3]William R. Rassman, M.D. "Why Health Care is a Costly Disgrace," Business Week 2672 (January 26, 1981): 16.

[4]John Wennenberg and Alan Gittelsohn, "Variations in Medical Care among Small Areas," Scientific American 246 (April 1982): 120-126.

[5]As reported by David Osborne, "Rich Doctors, Poor Nurses," Harper's 265 (September 1982): 14.

[6]Ibid., 10-14.

EXERCISE 7.

Answer these questions about the selection that you have just read.

1. Is the thesis stated in the expected place? Explain.
2. What is the topic sentence in paragraph 2? How does the topic sentence influence the order of presentation of the reports from the three magazines quoted in that paragraph?
3. Might the material in paragraph 3 have been put in paragraph 2? What word in the first sentence of paragraph 3 lets you know that the ideas in paragraph 3 are closely related to the ideas in the last part of paragraph 2? If the ideas are closely related, is there justification for making a separate paragraph of the material in paragraph 3?
4. Which sentence in paragraph 4 refers to what has been said in paragraphs 2 and 3?
5. In what paragraph does the author change from discussing evidence of the problem to discussing the causes? What sentence tells you of this change?
6. In what way are the first sentences of paragraphs 2 and 4 similar? Why are the sentences structured in this way?
7. The first sentence of paragraph 5 could be considered a topic sentence covering both paragraphs 5 and 6. Why are two paragraphs made of the explanation?
8. In this article why is it important to give the physicians' justification for their high charges? What advantage do debaters have if they present the opponents' point of view before the opponents can present it?

9. What paragraphs present the economists' reasons for high doctor bills?
10. In paragraph 8, the author is still discussing a principle presented by the economists. Yet the comparison of purchasing a doctor's services and getting a car is the author's. What change in the tone of the writing alerts you to this?
11. In paragraph 9, the author contributes what she thinks is another factor in producing the high cost of medical care. Do authors have a responsibility to add what they know or believe in order to justify their writing on the subject? How does the author's type of contribution in paragraph 8 differ from the contribution in paragraph 9?
12. Would the conclusion be different if there were no prospect of finishing the composition in the next lesson?

Using an Outline in the Planning Stage

EXERCISE 8.

Often an outline is written after the first draft of a composition has been prepared. In this way the author tests the organizational pattern and then rewrites. However, in a longer composition more preplanning may be necessary. Making an outline before the first draft guides a writer's thinking and helps him or her see the relationship among the ideas to be expressed. For long writing projects, an outline is a time-saver.

Here is the working outline from which the preceding composition developed. Notice that (1) the thesis covers both subjects discussed (the problems and the causes), (2) the main points are indicated in the thesis, (3) subpoints support main points, (4) developmental material (figures, examples, and so on) is not mentioned here, but the author might well jot it down briefly.

Outline of "Physicians' Exhorbitant Fees: The Evidence and the Causes"
Thesis: There is something wrong with physicians' fees, but there is disagreement about the causes.
I. Physicians often charge exhorbitantly for their services.
   A. Doctors often charge too much for routine care.
   B. Doctors sometimes order unnecessary procedures in order to charge a patient more.

II. People have different theories about what causes the exorbitant rates.

    A. Physicians say that the high cost of a doctor's training justifies their high charges.

    B. Economists differ with physicians about the causes.

        1. Other professional people with costly education charge less, so cost of training cannot be justified as a cause.

        2. The American Medical Association has prevented competition.

        3. Doctors' bills are mostly paid by a third party.

    C. Doctors know that the peculiar doctor-patient relationship is likely to prevent a patient from protesting the exorbitant price.

Stage III. Critiquing and Revising

STEP 6. ANALYZING AND REVISING THE FIRST DRAFT

EXERCISE 9.

Before you revise the first draft of your composition, critique it and make corrections. Then make a clean revised copy to bring to class. Here are points to consider.

1. In the introduction, do you need to show the readers why the subject is an important one and how it relates to them? (Is there a similar problem in many countries, or could the effects of the problem affect life beyond the boundaries of one city or country?)

2. Is the central idea (thesis sentence) clearly stated somewhere near the beginning?

3. If you do not have space to explain all the causes in detail, explain a few well and indicate that these are only some of the things that contribute to the problem.

4. Have you given sufficient facts and figures, examples and testimony to convince your reader that you know what you are talking about? (You may need to obtain some of the supporting material from library research or interviews with experts in the field.)

5. Have you made clear to your readers just when you change from a discussion of the evidences of the problem to a discussion of the causes?

6. Have you paragraphed in a logical way, putting ideas together in logical groups?
7. Have you phrased the ideas in each succeeding paragraph in such a way that they show a relationship with the ideas in the preceding paragraph?
8. Look over past compositions that have been returned to you. Consider the mistakes in grammar, punctuation, and spelling that you have made, and check this composition for these matters.

Read the following composition. Outside of class, prepare answers to the questions about it that follow the selection. In class, discuss its strengths and weaknesses.

LITTERING IN CURAÇAO
Stephen de Haseth, Curaçao

(1) If you are driving in Curaçao, do not be surprised if you see the person in the car ahead of you open the window and throw an empty beer bottle or some other junk out of the window. This is part of everyday life in Curaçao and part of one of the island's biggest problems-- pollution. Littering starts a string of troubles that plague our once-beautiful country.

(2) I suppose the trouble starts with the attitude of the people. They are easygoing and live with the least exertion possible. It is much easier to throw something on the ground than to walk over to a garbage can and throw it in there. Such an attitude is hard for the Western world to believe but quite common for the Latin American one. So trash piles up, with serious consequences to the island.

(3) One of the consequences is that a whole neighborhood can be destroyed as a result of littering. Heavy littering in an area discourages normal people from living there, while others, like transients, get attracted by it. This is particularly what happens in neighborhoods where older people live. These people often do not have the power to do

anything against the deterioration of the neighborhood. A good example is Scharloo. Scharloo is the neighborhood where most of the rich, old Curaçao families used to live. The houses were built 100 to 175 years ago, and each house was a work of art on its own. Tour groups used to go to Scharloo because it was a truly beautiful place.

(4) Nowadays, most of the people who used to live there have moved to a place farther away from the city. Only the older people who have lived there all their lives insist on staying. In no time at all, the yards of empty houses have become junkyards for the slums close by. The houses have become a paradise for rats and transients. After a couple of years of being empty, a deserted house is in ruins, is a drug-dealing center and/or a whorehouse. People who were born in Curaçao and have come back after 20 or 30 years are shocked by what they see. This is the last thing they expected to happen to the neighborhood. Of course, you cannot say that littering was the only cause of all this, but it is definitely one of the main causes.

(5) Another consequence of a highly polluted island is that it prevents tourists from coming to Curaçao. Even for our own people it is not a pleasant sight to see trash around everywhere. So why should the cruise ships stop here and passengers see the filth when they can go to places that are more beautiful? Fewer and fewer cruises have Curaçao on their itinerary in recent times, and this has hurt the economy immensely.

(6) Unsightliness is not the worst problem caused by littering, however. The piles of refuse along the roads and in the yards of abandoned houses are a paradise for bacteria, rats, and mosquitoes. The *aedes egypti* mosquito, which was almost exterminated in Curaçao by the end of the sixties, has managed to multiply in a short time into the huge

quantities that appear in Curaçao today. Then
an epidemic of screwworm broke out. The
screwworm gets food by eating its way through
animals. Those animals die a horrible death in
less than two weeks, if they are not released
earlier from their suffering by an injection.
The screwworms can multiply very fast if the
eggs are laid in a wound. The *aedes egypti*
spreads the screwworm plague by sucking blood
from an infected animal and then from a healthy
animal. If blood containing eggs of the
screwworm is dropped on the wound of a healthy
animal, the eggs are very likely to hatch. This
is how the plague spreads, and the farmers and
stockmen suffer terrific losses.

(7) You might wonder why nothing is done to
stop this polluting and to clean up the litter
that is already all over the place. The reasons
why nothing is done are part of the problem too.
The government does not have the money for oil
and chemicals to stop the breeding of
mosquitoes, and people often do not see the need
to stop littering. Most of them think as long as
people don't die, who cares?

(8) Yet another cause of people's indiffer-
ence to the problem is that it is hard to notice
something if you have never seen anything else
to compare it with. I myself did not think that
other places in the world, especially big
cities, could be much cleaner. I was surprised
to see how clean big cities such as Chicago and
Boston are. It made a big impression on me. It
was only when I went back to Curaçao after a
visit to the States that I came to realize that
we have a serious problem there. I can
understand that people who have not seen
anything better do not notice the litter all
over the island. Another thing is that people in
Curaçao do not like to take responsibility upon
themselves. This accounts for the people who
are aware of the current situation but do not
try to do anything about it.

(9) Something quite drastic has to be done in

the near future to change the situation. It is
going to be a difficult task. Assistance from
the whole community is needed to change it, but
if we do not want the situation to get worse, we
should start acting now.

EXERCISE 10.

Answer these questions on the composition you have just read.

1. What indicates that this is a subject the writer is truly
   concerned about?
2. Why do you think the writer has not incorporated material
   from books and magazines as did the author of the selection
   about doctors' exorbitant fees?
3. Cite a chain reaction of causes and results found in this
   composition.
4. What word links the last sentence of paragraph 1 with the first
   sentence of paragraph 2? Is there a word that links paragraph 2
   with paragraph 3? Paragraph 3 with paragraph 4?
5. What alerts the reader to the fact that the author is going to
   change from evidences of the problem to a discussion of the
   causes of the problem?
6. What methods of development are used in this composition?
   Be able to cite examples.
7. What kind of testimony do you find? Do you accept it as
   being correct? Explain.

EXERCISE 11.

In class, exchange with a classmate the composition you wrote for
exercise 9. Each of you will critique the other paper. Consider all the
questions in exercise 9. Then make *three* suggestions in writing for the
improvement of the composition. Each critic will sign his name to the
critique and each of you will hand in the first revision and the critique
along with the final draft.

STEP 7. WRITING THE FINAL DRAFT

EXERCISE 12.

Prepare the final draft of your composition, making use of your
own analysis of your first draft, your outline, and the suggestions

in your classmate's critique. With your final draft, hand in the following:

1. the outline you used to check your basic thinking (This could have been made before writing your first draft or after the first draft was written.)
2. your classmate's critique
3. your first revision

Reviewing Grammatical Patterns

REVIEW OF VERB FORMS

Review the following in the Handbook: verb forms, tense and time, sections D8 to D10; the passive, section E12; modals, section F14; and verbals as modifiers, section A2d.

GRAMMAR EXERCISE 1.

Fill the following blanks with appropriate forms of the indicated verbs.

1. South American place names such as Llao Llao or Iguassu _____ (be) strange, but rhythms in names such as Cartagena, Machu Picchu, or Bariloche _____ (please) to the ear. These places _____ (be) as famous south of Mexico as New York City or Fujiyama.
2. If you _____ (be) in South America only once, you _____ probably _____ (return) some day. If you _____ not _____ (study) much about South American countries before you _____ (go), you probably _____ not fully _____ (appreciate) much of what you _____ (see).
3. Traditionally, travellers _____ (go) to South America only after they _____ (be) everywhere else—so _____ (say) South American guides. Yet vacationing in this part of the world _____ (have) certain advantages.
4. Because vacationers _____ (be) not there in swarms, they _____ (avoid) the queues and the jostling that often _____ (precede) the sight of some choice treasure in Europe or the Orient. Your South American guide

_____ (have) time to tailor a tour to the interests of your group.

5. Always, everywhere are new adventures for the eye: the blaze of flowers _____ (climb) up walls; long peaceful valleys; mountains _____ (wreath) in clouds; angry rivers _____ (dash) themselves into foam against the rocks; and a procession of volcanic cones, each as perfect as Fujiyama, _____ (march) down the continent.

6. Everywhere you _____ (note) differences in the way of life. Aggressive and witty boys _____ (entertain) you in a dozen cities as they _____ (keep) your shoes glossy and try _____ (prepare) you for an exorbitant charge.

7. On country roads Indians _____ (trot) along _____ (bend) over as though they _____ (carry) heavy burdens even though there _____ (be) nothing on their backs. In contrast, as 9:00 P.M. _____ (approach), the elevators in the big hotels _____ (crowd) with ladies in exquisite gowns and jewels _____ (be) _____ (escorted) down to dinner by prosperous-looking men.

8. Plane and train travel in South America _____ (take) a little getting used to. Schedules _____ not _____ (respect) in this area as they _____ (be) in Germany or the United States, for example. Mail _____ (be) uncertain, so _____ (plan) _____ (carry) souvenirs and gifts back home rather than _____ (mail) them.

9. Hunting addresses _____ (be) a challenge, for each city _____ (seem) to have its own system of identifying a certain residence. In Caracas, a city of three million, no home _____ (have) a number.

10. In Bogota, _carreras_ (avenues) _____ (run) parallel to the mountains. _Calles_ (streets) _____ (be) perpendicular to the mountains and _____ (be) _____ (number) beginning downtown. If you _____ (hunt) for Avenue 5, number 11–50, you _____ (find) the door on Avenue 5, 50 meters from the corner of street 11 as you _____ (walk) toward street 12. It _____ (make) sense to the

Colombians, but the visitor _____ (find) it easier
_____ (take) a cab.

11. In spite of petty annoyances, traveling to South America
_____ (hold) one supreme advantage. Before you
_____ (depart) for better-known tourist spots abroad,
friends _____ (tell) you that you must _____
(see) a certain thing, and _____ (predict) that you
_____ (love) something else.

12. For the person who _____ (dislike) being informed
ahead of time about what he or she _____ (admire),
South America _____ (be) a place that _____
(lend) itself less to such instructions and prophecies. Here
each traveler _____ (be) an explorer, and _____
(carry) home in mind and luggage his or her own peculiar
treasure.

SUBORDINATORS AND SENTENCE CONNECTORS

In the Handbook, review sentence connectors, section A2a, and
subordinators, sections A2b and H23.

GRAMMAR EXERCISE 2.

Complete the following sentences and punctuate them.

1. I like classical music but (What music don't you like?) .
2. I like classical music *even* though (In spite of what?) .
3. I can go tomorrow evening *provided that* (Give the
circumstances under which you can go.) .
4. I would like to go to your dinner *only* (What prevents you
from going?) .
5. I would agree with your argument that a college education
makes one more employable *except that* (What makes you not
agree entirely?) .
6. I cannot go *unless* (Explain the circumstances that would
make you able to go.) .
7. Please get me a book from the library *in case you* (Name
circumstances that may be convenient for the listener.) .
8. I like rice *but* _____.
9. I like rice *so* _____.

10. I like rice *because* _____ .
11. *Once* you like rice _____ .
12. I bought 50 pounds of rice *so that* _____ .

VERBS FOLLOWED BY PARTICIPLES

Review section G18 in the Handbook.

GRAMMAR EXERCISE 3.

Read the following selection aloud with your instructor. Then write it from dictation.

> I intend to <u>avoid making</u> mistakes that other travellers often make. I <u>dislike having</u> things go wrong when I am away from home. Thus, I <u>start planning</u> early, and I don't <u>postpone doing</u> certain things I need to do. I don't <u>enjoy applying</u> for a passport, but I do it, and even though I <u>dread taking</u> shots, I go and get them anyway.
>
> I <u>begin packing</u> a week in advance and <u>finish packing</u> at least a day before I depart. I don't <u>put off getting</u> travellers' checks, but get them instead of just <u>talking about getting</u> them. I leave the dairyman a note that tells him to <u>stop delivering</u> milk several days before I depart. Sometimes I <u>consider stopping</u> the daily paper a week in advance too, but somehow I can't <u>resist wanting</u> to know what is going on even though I am aware that I <u>risk having</u> the papers dropped daily on my doorstep while I am gone.
>
> By doing these things promptly, I <u>miss rushing</u> around frantically at the last minute trying to do what needs to be done. I suppose I will <u>keep on planning</u> ahead in the future, for I <u>prefer going away</u> relaxed rather than frantic.

VERB-PREPOSITION COMBINATIONS

Certain prepositions regularly follow certain verbs. (See section I26 in the Handbook.)

GRAMMAR EXERCISE 4.

Listen as your instructor reads aloud the following selection, noting the italicized verb-preposition pairs.

THE WESTWARD MOVEMENT

The Westward Movement of Americans across the continent has been an intriguing epoch in American history, but it has probably <u>accounted for</u> many family quarrels. When a man <u>objected to</u> life in a settled community, he could <u>look for</u> a better place farther west. If he was married, he might not even ask his wife if she <u>approved of</u> his idea. If she <u>objected to</u> his going, she might <u>argue with</u> him, but he might not even <u>listen to</u> her, or he might <u>laugh at</u> her arguments. He might say that he had <u>heard about</u> a gold strike in South Dakota, and she might scornfully comment that he seemed to <u>believe in</u> any rumor he heard, and that if he <u>cared for</u> his wife and children, he would stay home and <u>provide for</u> them. She would <u>remind him of</u> other gold strikes he had <u>heard of</u> that proved fruitless. He would say that he <u>looked forward to</u> having a fine home for her and the children some day, but staying home gave him no chance to <u>provide for</u> his family in the way he hoped to. But she would not <u>agree with</u> him. If he went west, what would the neighbors <u>think about</u> it, and she would hardly ever <u>hear from</u> him. Whom could she <u>depend on</u> to provide the family with a home and food and fuel? "Let's not <u>talk about</u> this any more," she would say. "I will never <u>consent to</u> your going." He would <u>look at</u> her in a peculiar way. He had already <u>decided on</u> going, and he would not <u>wait for</u> her to change her mind. Even though she would <u>blame him for</u> deserting her, she would eventually be <u>convinced of</u> the wisdom of his decision, he thought.

Now, without looking at the story you have just heard, fill in the blanks with the proper preposition in the version of it that follows.

THE WESTWARD MOVEMENT

The Westward Movement in American history has probably accounted _____ many a family dispute. When a man grew dissatisfied _____ life in a settled community and told his wife that he had decided _____ a move to a new location farther west where he counted _____ finding new opportunities, she might object _____ the idea of a move. Perhaps she would say, "You never asked me what I thought _____ it, and I don't approve _____ the idea at all."

"But I've heard _____ a wonderful opportunity," he might say. "You should listen _____ what some of our neighbors say. They tell _____ good land there, and I can provide _____ my family better on a larger farm. Maybe we won't even have to depend _____ farming. I've heard _____ people who found gold in the West. If we get rich, I'll provide you and the children _____ the best home you ever had."

"But I'm satisfied _____ things right here. Let's not talk _____ a move," she might reply. "I will never consent _____ going. I've heard _____ people who died on the way west or who were killed in Indian raids. I'm looking forward _____ bringing up my children in a peaceful community."

He might laugh _____ her fears. "I'll protect you _____ Indians," he might say. "Don't you believe _____ taking advantage of a good opportunity?"

She might then remind him _____ the problems they had had when they settled the home in which they were living and blame him _____ wanting her to undergo all those difficulties again. But he probably didn't listen _____ her. He was convinced _____ the wisdom of his decision and concerned only _____ the wealth he might have if he struck gold. Women usually didn't know what they were talking _____ anyway, he may have thought. They should rely _____ the wisdom of the men.

AGREEMENT OF SUBJECT AND VERB

Four types of problems arise that cause mistakes in subject-verb agreement. The following examples show the structures that give rise to the problems.

1. When the subject is singular and not compound, the verb is singular also.

   The amygdala, with the hippocampus and nucleus basalis, *sends* important messages. . . . (There is no compound subject.)
   The instructor, as well as my classmates, *is* coming to the party. (In reality they are all coming, but grammatically only the instructor is the subject.)
   Compare this sentence with:
   The instructor and my classmates are coming.
   The couch in addition to the chairs *shows* signs of wear.

2. With fractions and words such as *part* or *all* the verb agrees with the noun in the prepositional phrase that follows.

   Half (all, part) of the eggs were broken when we got them.
   Three-fourths (all, part) of the *land is* under cultivation.

3. Compound subjects connected by *and* require plural verbs. Compound subjects connected by *or* require verbs that agree with the subject nearest the verb.

   Either the mayor or the *councilmen are* to be invited.
   Either the councilmen or the *mayor is* to be invited.

4. Careless mistakes in subject-verb agreement occur in the inflection of third-person-singular present tense and present perfect form of most verbs.

   They arrive today. *He arrives* today.
   They have already *come. He has* already *come.*

GRAMMAR EXERCISE 5.

Keeping in mind the rules for agreement of subject and verb, complete the following sentences by supplying the correct verb form.

1. King David, as well as the Sumerians, _____ (be) wrong in thinking the liver was the organ of thought.

2. Hippocrates, but not the other Greeks, _____ (have) been credited with discovering that the brain is the seat of thought.

3. Almost all of the ancients _____ (have) been pictured as not understanding the role of the brain.

4. Almost all of the information we have gained about the brain _____ (have) been discovered in the last century.

5. Scientists today _____ (be) optimistic that they can learn more about the brain.

6. Patricia Goldmann-Rakie _____ (be) perhaps the most optimistic of all.

7. One is confident that doctors or computer engineers _____ (be) going to discover exactly what produces creativity.

8. One is confident also that some scientist or physician _____ (be) going to discover what makes man moral or immoral.

9. Thinking, imagining, and planning for the future _____ (be) brain activities that are difficult to analyze.

10. Such activity _____ (take) place in the temporal lobe.

11. Not all of the cortex _____ (be) involved in sensing the outside world and in moving the body.

PRESENTING A SOLUTION TO A PROBLEM

Rhetorical Principles	Grammatical Patterns
Problem-solution order— solving the problem Coherence Outlining	Sentence building Use and omission of articles Review of verb forms General review of grammatical patterns Spelling and punctuation

Writing a Composition

Assignment: Write a composition of three or four pages giving solutions for the problem you discussed in Lesson 9. Present first several solutions that have been proposed or tried or that you can suggest. Then explain which solution seems most workable in terms of cost, manpower, people's attitudes, and so on.

Stage I. Prewriting

STEP 1. BRAINSTORMING FOR IDEAS

EXERCISE 1.

Jot down a list of possible solutions to the problem you discussed in Lesson 9. Some may be modifications of past attempts to solve the problem; some may be new suggestions of your own. Make clear to your reader whether your solution will wipe out the whole problem or whether it is designed to help in some small way. Some problems are so complex that there is no easy or complete solution. Since problems are solved by eliminating their causes, it is desirable to review the causes that you presented in your last composition. Check printed matter to see whether others have proposed or tried certain solutions and with what success.

EXERCISE 2.

Prepare and give a three-minute speech to your classmates (1) refreshing their memories about the problem you are concerned with and (2) reviewing the causes of the problem. Then discuss the solution(s) you propose, and invite comments about the workability of your proposed solutions.

STEP 2. PHRASING THE THESIS SENTENCE

EXERCISE 3.

In light of your brainstorming for ideas with classmates and your own search for solutions to your problem, phrase a thesis sentence that reveals what the problem is and indicates to what extent you believe the solution you propose will solve the problem.

STEP 3. JOTTING DOWN IDEAS AND REFINING A POINT OF VIEW

EXERCISE 4.

Outline the proposal, indicating major points. Jot down developmental material you can use to make your points clear. In developing points, you may make more of a line of reasoning than you have done in previous writing because you will be defending a point of view by giving a clear explanation.

Stage II. Giving Form to the Composition and Studying Techniques

STEP 4. WRITING A FIRST DRAFT

EXERCISE 5.

Before you write the first draft, read the rhetorical principles presented in step 5. Revise your outline after studying the one prepared for the article "Physicians' Exorbitant Fees: Solutions." Then write your composition about solutions to the problem.

STEP 5. STUDYING RHETORICAL PRINCIPLES

Problem-Solution Order—Solving the Problem

In offering a solution to a problem, two stages are often involved: (1) suggesting possible solutions—the solutions must be practical and reasonable (one way to discover solutions is to find ways to eliminate the causes of the problem); and (2) defending the solution that seems best able to solve the problem. It must be something that can be financed and for which adequate personnel can be provided. Its superiority over other solutions should be made apparent.

No big problem has a simple solution. The best that one can hope to do is point out areas in which improvement has been made and in which further improvement might be brought about if certain steps were taken. When considering solutions to a problem, one faces the same questions that physicians have to answer when they prescribe for a patient: What will I advocate to cure the patient? Will the medicine make the patient worse? Will another medicine be more effective? In your solution composition, you are not expected to devise a perfect solution. You are expected, however, to make reasonable suggestions for what might help.

The composition that follows offers a solution to the problem presented in the example composition in Lesson 9. As you read it, be aware of the order in which ideas are presented.

PHYSICIANS' EXORBITANT FEES: SOLUTIONS

(1) Scientists advocate that the best way to solve a problem is to eliminate the causes. Thus we turn first to what doctors say cause their high fees: the difficulty of being admitted to

medical school, the eight years of costly study, the three to five years of residency in a hospital at low pay, the years of building up a practice, and the heavy responsibilities. Are these justifiable reasons? Some of them could justify greater fees for lawyers, who also have difficulty in being admitted to law school, who have heavy responsibilities, and who spend years in building up a practice. Yet lawyers earn only half as much as doctors. We must, then, discount these reasons, and accept only their complaints about the high cost of education.

(2) How can we meet this problem of cost? One solution is to reduce the number of years of training required. However, patients want their doctors to have the best possible training and thus do not want the quantity or the quality reduced. Another solution is to help prospective doctors finance their education. Since the health of all citizens is of public concern, the government--national and state--might subsidize aspiring physicians and then charge them a certain percentage of their income after they have established a practice. However, to avoid doctors' charging even higher fees to repay their loans, there would have to be some government regulation of doctors' fees, and many would object to this. We are left, then, with the patients' paying for the doctors' education when they pay high fees, and we are back with the problem. Many sick people who need a doctor's services find these fees exorbitant or are unable to pay them.

(3) Since it is difficult to eliminate the causes physicians claim for their high charges, might it be easier to eliminate the causes seen by the economists? They claim that lack of competition causes high prices. A solution would be for doctors to advertise, listing prices. It is doubtful, however, that they could be encouraged to do so. The public, long accustomed to think advertising by physicians

is unprofessional, would conclude that only
incompetents advertise reduced prices.

(4) Another solution the economists would
favor is for the government to order a cutback
in fees, as General Charles de Gaulle did in
France in 1960 under emergency powers. The
United States government, however, has shown
little inclination to do this. One administration proposed a 2 percent cutback in govern-
ment-supported hospital costs for the aged, but
no mention was made of cutting payments to
physicians.

(5) A third solution of the economists is for
the government to join insurance companies in
allowing only a certain reasonable amount for a
given medical service. However, there would be
nothing to prevent physicians from charging the
patient additional personal costs. Furthermore,
there would have to be more frantic appeals from
people unable to afford high fees before any
such action would be taken, and it is difficult
to get sufficient numbers of people to protest.

(6) Although the foregoing proposed solutions
have some merit, all present difficulties.
Until one of them becomes a reality, what can we
do? Perhaps the best idea is to avoid unnecessary trips to the doctor. One way to do this is
to make more use of nonmedical services.
Advertising could acquaint the public with the
usefulness of chiropractors, acupuncture and
acupressure practitioners, and midwives.
Magazine articles and television programs
explaining the benefits and limitations of
these services could be encouraged.

(7) Another solution is to encourage health-
maintenance groups of physicians who try to
keep one well for a flat minimal monthly fee. We
could also encourage registered nurses to
establish clinics where, at reduced prices, one
could get blood pressure and diabetes tests,
immunization shots and other injections--

in fact, all types of medical help that registered nurses are allowed to give.

(8) Even more important, perhaps, would be for
each person to become aware of the importance of
health and become interested in maintaining it.
This would involve public education to make
people note messages from their own bodies.
Such education could be carried on in TV
programs, in schoolrooms, and in newspapers and
magazines. It would involve learning what to
eat, what not to eat, how to exercise. One would
also learn more about sanitation, the drugs
that can be purchased over the counter, and
first aid techniques. County agents have free
brochures and information about how to get
other free materials from government agencies.
One needs to realize, too, the importance of
knowing the family medical history and
hereditary weaknesses in order to take
precautions against disease.

(9) Avoiding health problems seems to be the
simplest way to escape the discomfort of being
ill as well as the payment of costly physicians'
fees.

EXERCISE 6.

Answer these questions on the selection you have just read.

1. If this selection were not part of a longer discussion (started in
   Lesson 9), what would need to be said in the opening
   sentences to acquaint the reader with the subject?
2. Does the writer follow the two-part organization—presentation
   of various alternatives and defenses of the most practical—that
   was suggested at the beginning of this lesson?
3. Is the reader given a reason why each of the impractical
   proposals is unsatisfactory?
4. Because of lack of space, every main point is discussed more
   superficially than desirable. Choose one of the main points that
   you think needs more development, and tell how you would
   develop it (by examples, figures, a line of reasoning, and so
   on).
5. There are some aspects of the final solutions that are less than

perfect for solving the problem. What are some? Should they have been discussed? Give a reason for your answer.

Coherence

EXERCISE 7.

Answer these questions about devices for coherence and organizational pattern in the selection "Physicians' Exorbitant Fees: Solutions."

1. Do you think the writer planned the essay by making an outline beforehand? Why or why not?
2. Would a topic or sentence outline be more useful at the planning stage? Explain.
3. Is there any word or phrase in paragraph 1 that indicates that the author is discussing first the possible solutions rather than the one that he or she thinks is the best? How do you know the writer is doing this?
4. Into what two parts is the first paragraph divided? How is this indicated?
5. What is the relation of paragraph 2 to paragraph 1? How is it shown?
6. Does paragraph 3 continue the discussion introduced in paragraph 2 or does it introduce another topic? What word or words tell you?
7. How many paragraphs deal with solutions suggested by economists? What words tell you?
8. Do all the solutions presented by the economists directly address the cause they give—lack of competition? How might this have been indicated in the composition? Do they address the basic problem—exorbitant fees?
9. What new section of the discussion is begun in paragraph 7?
10. Into how many parts is this section divided?
11. Where do you find the ideal solution summarized?

Outlining

EXERCISE 8.

Complete the following topic outline of "Physicians' Exorbitant Fees: Solutions."

Thesis: Solutions to physicians' exorbitant fees
 I. Possible solutions
   A. Eliminating causes given by doctors
     1. Causes they give
        a. _____
        b. _____
        c. _____
        d. _____
        e. _____
     2. Justification of causes
        a. Lawyers— _____
        b. Cost of education— _____
     3. Meeting problem of cost
        a. Reduction of years of training—impractical because patients want well-trained doctors
        b. _____—impractical because _____
        c. _____
           _____
   B. Solutions given by economists
        a. Competition by advertising prices—impractical because _____
        b. _____
        c. _____
 II. Best solution—avoid unnecessary trips to the doctor in these ways:
   A. _____
   B. _____
   C. _____

Stage III. Critiquing and Revising

STEP 6. ANALYZING AND REVISING THE FIRST DRAFT

EXERCISE 9.

Make an outline either before or after writing the first draft. Revise the composition as necessary, then bring the outline and the revision to class.

A SOLUTION TO THE PROBLEM
OF LITTERING IN CURAÇAO

(1) I realize that there is no easy solution to the problem of littering in Curaçao, and I realize too that people might scorn the suggestions of a student who is writing about the problem from a thousand miles away. I have done some thinking about the matter, however, and talked with people who told me how Singapore was cleaned up. I do think that I have some suggestions that might be of value. I do not claim that they are perfect answers, nor do I think that the problem can be corrected overnight. Correction has to start somewhere, however, and these are starting points.

(2) As I mentioned earlier, part of Curaçao's pollution problem stems from the attitude of the people. You may think that the obvious thing to do is to make people use trash cans, but when people are easygoing and do not like to take responsibility this is not an easy thing to do. They are accustomed to throwing their trash down on the street, and the habit is hard to break. The government could punish litterers by imposing heavy fines, and this might deter some. But it would mean continuously patrolling the streets to catch violators, and the size of the police force is not adequate for this. Also, many of the people who are the worst offenders cannot afford to pay the fines. Jailing those who cannot pay would only develop resentment against the police and against the government-- and might even lead to violence. A better plan of punishment might be to make litterers work for a certain number of hours cleaning up the refuse--the dirtier and smellier the better--and carrying it to a central disposal place where it could be buried, burned, or destroyed chemically. Again, an overseeing force of some sort would be necessary, and this would involve expense.

(3) Instead of punishment, a system of rewards could be tried. Prizes could be offered for the neatest neighborhood or city block; this would give people an incentive to deposit litter in covered bins provided for the purpose. The plan would make for cooperation on the part of neighbors but would require education.

(4) Cities can be clean. I have been impressed with the cleanliness of the cities I have been in since leaving Curaçao. An important key to the problem is education. This education might well begin with schoolchildren, who are impressionable, whose habits are not so strongly formed as those of their elders, and who look up to their teachers. Teachers could start by stressing keeping the classroom clean, the halls, the school yards; there could be contests with prizes for the best-kept desk, row of desks, and so on. Visiting lecturers from various health agencies could show slides on the dangers of littering and the diseases it breeds, as well as before-and-after pictures of places where litter has been cleaned up. The children could take pictures home to their parents. Public information lectures could also be arranged for adults, perhaps in connection with a social hour which would be an incentive for attendance.

(5) Along with this education program would go a cleanup campaign, with awards made publicly to encourage neighborhood and personal pride. Violators might be made to pick up the trash while others watched and thus be shamed in the eyes of their neighbors.

(6) The best solution, I believe, calls not just for one measure but for a combination of measures--education, the offering of incentives to mount a "clean neighborhood" campaign, and perhaps some kind of punishment for those who do not comply. I would put the emphasis first, however, on positive approaches. To aid in the combined program,

concerned citizens should be encouraged to write letters to the newspaper emphasizing the importance to business and to tourism that Cura çao be cleaned up so that it can once again be a beautiful island that would be the pride of its citizens and a delight for people to visit.

EXERCISE 10.

Answer these questions about the example composition.

1. What evidence does the author give that he is qualified to offer a solution to the problem?
2. What does he suggest as the best solution to the problem of littering in Curaçao? Where is it stated? Is this an effective place for his solution? Explain.
3. Does the author first present possible solutions and then the best solution? In what paragraph does he begin discussing the best solution?
4. Does he give adequate reasons why the solutions he rejects are impractical? Explain.
5. Does he give adequate reasons for accepting the solution he proposes as the best? Is there other information you would like to have? Are there arguments you could offer against his solution?

EXERCISE 11.

Exchange with a classmate the outline of your revised draft. Critique the outline and discuss your critique with your classmate. Here are questions to be considered in critiquing an outline.

1. Is the thesis a complete sentence? Does it cover all the ideas mentioned in the main points?
2. Does each main point clearly support the thesis?
3. Are the main points coordinate with each other? (Should some be subpoints under a main point?)
4. Does each subpoint clearly support the main point under which it occurs?
5. Are all points clearly stated in sentences?

STEP 7. WRITING THE FINAL DRAFT

EXERCISE 12.

Write the final draft taking into consideration previous revisions in the composition and in the outline.

Reviewing Grammatical Patterns

SENTENCE BUILDING

Professional writers express their ideas concisely by condensing into one sentence ideas that less skilled writers state in several sentences. They do this by reducing some sentences to modifiers of nouns or verbs or of the entire sentence.

GRAMMAR EXERCISE 1.

Try your hand at combining into one sentence the sentences in each group below. Do not change the idea. Avoid simply using *and.*

1. Certain reasons justify greater fees for lawyers. They have difficulty being admitted to study. They have heavy responsibilities. They spend years building up a practice. Yet they earn only half as much as doctors.
2. The doctor might charge even higher fees. There would have to be some regulation of doctors' fees. This would avoid it.
3. The doctor might advertise and list prices. This would be a solution to the high fees they charge.
4. Make people use trash cans for their litter. This is the obvious thing to do. It is difficult to do. People are easygoing.
5. The litterers might be made to work. They could clean up the refuse. They could take it to a central disposal place. It could be buried there. This might be a better plan of punishment.

GRAMMAR EXERCISE 2.

Here are some groups of ideas that students of English as a foreign language had difficulty in combining into one sentence. See if you can do a better job.

1. My city has a mountain. The mountain stands behind it. (Use a present participle.)

2. In my city is a palace. The palace is surrounded by walls. The walls are 1900 meters long. (Use a past participle.)

3. Beech trees are very popular and beautiful all over our district. Our district is located on the northern end of the main island. There is a short summer and a severe, long winter there. (Use relative clauses.)

4. The characteristic markets or bazaars of Baghdad are found in the center of Baghdad. All the banks and almost all of the businesses are located in the heart of Baghdad. (Use relative claus-es.)

5. Many people speak at Hyde Park Corner in London. Many people listen. The number of listeners depends on the speech. (Begin with *The number of* people. . . . Use relative clauses.)

GRAMMAR EXERCISE 3.

Rewrite the following selection, expressing in one sentence the ideas between the slashes. You will use clauses and verbal modifiers to do so.

AT THE AIRPORT

/At the airport I always like to conjecture about the people while I am waiting for a plane. I see many people at the airport./ That man is a grandfather. He is standing beside a toy counter. He is meeting a plane. His daughter and two small grandchildren are arriving on the plane./ That couple are newly married. I can tell this because they are paying a great deal of attention to each other and look very happy. They are weighing in their luggage./ That man seems very nervous. He is behind them. He constantly checks his watch. He keeps listening intently to the loudspeaker. The loudspeaker announces the flights./ Perhaps he has missed an important appointment. He is trying to get to his destination. He will leave on the next plane./ That man is a business executive. He is wearing a dark suit./ Perhaps he is making a trip to Washington, D.C. He wants to talk to senators. The senators can initiate legislation. The legislation will help his business.

USE AND OMISSION OF ARTICLES

Review use and omission of articles in the Handbook, section B3.

GRAMMAR EXERCISE 4.

As your instructor reads the following selection, read it silently along with him or her, noting particularly the use of articles with the numbered words. You will then answer some questions about the use of articles.

HOW DIFFERENT CULTURES VIEW TIME

All people perceive the distinction between present, past, and future time, although they may have different ways of indicating it in their languages. Yet not all *cultures* view *time*
(1)   (2)
in the same way or mark the same time distinctions in their speech.
(3)
In societies based on European *culture,* people look back on an event in the past. We say, "I enjoyed the concert last night." "Last week I went to Chicago." "I passed my examinations a year ago." In English the verb form and *the*
(4)
adverb indicate that these events are past. We say that they are behind us. Similarly we look forward to the future. We say, "I am going to

(5)
take *a trip* to Europe next year. I will leave in
(6)
March." *The future,* which is indicated in

English by an auxiliary verb with the main verb

and by an adverb, is before us. For the Quechua

Indians of Peru and Bolivia, however, the

situation is different. They speak of the
(7)
future as "behind oneself" and *the past* as

ahead. They argue, "If you think of the past or

the future, which can you see with your mind's

eye?" The obvious answer is that we can see the

past and not the future, to which the Quechua

replies, "Then, if you can see the past, it must

be ahead of you, and the future, which you

cannot see, is behind you."*
(8)   (9)
Not only is this view of *past* and *future*

different from that of many cultures with which

we may be familiar, but also different

languages mark different time distinctions

within the present, past, or future, or

different relations between periods of time.

The speaker of English may say, "I work in *the*

(10)   (11)
library," and call this *present tense* even
                          (12)
though at the *moment of speaking,* the true
                                      (13)
"present time," he is eating *lunch* with a
                (14)
friend. *Confusion* exists because what we call

present tense does not necessarily refer to the
                          (15)
present moment. *Action* occurring or a situation

existing at the actual present is marked with a

special form, the "present continuous." This

distinction between permanent condition and

present occurrence is worth making for the

speaker of English, although this distinction

is less closely observed in many languages

closely related to English.

These differences may suggest that there is

more than one valid way of viewing "the same

thing" or that there may be differences of

opinion as to what "the same thing" really is.

*Material on Quechua Indians from Eugene Nida
in *Customs and Culture* (New York: Harper & Row,
1954), p. 206.

1. Why is no article used with (1) *cultures*? Why is no article used
   with (3) *culture*? Does the same reason apply in both cases?
2. Why is no article used with (2) *time*? Can you think of a case
   where one might say *the time* or *a time*?
3. Why is *the* rather than *an* used in (4) *the adverb*?

4. Why is *a* rather than *the* used in (5) *a trip,* but *the* in (10) *the library*?
5. Explain why articles are used in (6) *the future* and (7) *the past,* but not with (8) *past* and (9) *future.*
6. Why is there no article in (13) *lunch,* (14) *confusion,* and (15) *action*? Do all three refer to abstractions?

GRAMMAR EXERCISE 5.

In class with books closed write a brief summary of the selection "How Different Cultures View Time."

REVIEW OF VERB FORMS

GRAMMAR EXERCISE 6.

Answer these questions about verbs based on the selection "How Different Cultures View Time."

1. Why is the present tense rather than the present continuous used in the discussion of the culture and beliefs of the Quechuas?
2. What are some ways of expressing future time in English?
3. Why might one say, "I *work* in the library," when at the moment he or she *is eating* lunch? Might one also say, "I *am working* in the library?" Explain.
4. What tense is used when one is referring to the present moment?
5. Would the speaker who *works* in the library say to his or her friend, "I worked in the library for three years," or, "I have worked in the library for three years."? Why?

GENERAL REVIEW OF GRAMMATICAL PATTERNS

GRAMMAR EXERCISE 7.

Rewrite the following sentences to make them grammatically acceptable.

1. Coming closer and closer the statue appeared more and more alive.
2. Throwing off our coats the day seemed colder than we thought.

3. The sun came out and shining on the snow.
4. Having been trained in sight reading of music, learning to play the piano was easy for me.
5. The rules of soccer are easier to understand than football for the spectators.
6. Getting on the bus it suddenly occurred to me that I had left my billfold at home.
7. The artist could do interesting things with clay like molding a vase or glaze it or paint it.
8. Driving along about 60 miles an hour a barricade suddenly appeared before me.
9. I have learned many skills such as typing, skiing, drive a car and sing.
10. I don't know yet many of my instructors well.
11. In comparison with soccer, you need much more equipment in football.
12. Tactics are all the means whereby a team takes into account its own strengths and its opponent's weaknesses in order to win.
13. Part of success in any sport is to keep cool always.

GRAMMAR EXERCISE 8.

Finish the following sentences with ideas that make sense.

1. This examination began at 7:30 even though _____.
2. I will do some traveling during this vacation provided that

   _____.
3. I would go to California with my roommate except that

   _____.
4. The California trip is impossible unless _____.
5. However, I have my clothes ready to pack in case

   _____.
6. My roommate just got a big check from home, so

   _____.
7. I have bought a couple of good books to read during the vacation so that _____.
8. I will do some skiing during the vacation if _____.
9. I have some skis, but _____.
10. I might go up to some ski resort by myself, only

    _____.

Spelling and Punctuation

GRAMMAR EXERCISE 9.

Write the following passage quickly as your instructor dictates it. (The instructor will put the proper names on the chalkboard. Study them for a minute or two before the exercise starts.) After you have finished writing, correct mistakes by comparing what you have written with the selection in the book.

THE JOY OF WRITING

People in all ages have enjoyed phrasing ideas. It is said that the Roman philosopher Seneca found comfort in a sentence and got joy out of making a thought captive. The Roman general Lucullus thought that nothing--not even opium or oratory--gave one a finer thrill than successfully driving a flock of clauses, rounding up an idea, and roping it in careless grace with words.

John Kennedy said of Winston Churchill, when he conferred honorary United States citizenship on him, "In the dark days and darker nights when Britain stood alone--and most men save Englishmen despaired of England's life--he mobilized the English language and sent it into battle."

END NOTES

Note the use of apostrophes in paragraph 2 of "Physicians' Exorbitant Fees: Solutions."

- . . . government regulation of doctors' fees . . . (*doctor* is plural)

- . . . the doctor's services . . . (*doctor* is singular)

- to avoid doctors' charging . . . ; . . . the patients' paying for . . . [possessive before a verb form used as a noun (gerund)]

Handbook

GRAMMATICAL PATTERNS

A. Sentence Patterns

A1. BASIC SENTENCE PATTERNS

A1a. A Complete Sentence

A sentence may be defined as "a complete thought." A complete thought indicates that a person or object *does* something (action) or *is* something (condition).

The baby cried.	John is a mechanic.
John ate the apple.	The weather is sunny.
The boy is running.	Is Mary here?
Did the guests arrive on time?	This isn't right.
I didn't see them.	This feels good.

The person or thing performing the act or being in some state or condition is the *subject* of the sentence. *The baby* is the subject of the first sentence in the left column above. *John* is the subject of the first sentence in the right-hand column.

The word indicating the action or condition is the *verb. Cried* and *is* are verbs.

A speaker may use sentence fragments like "Wait" or "Look out" and be perfectly understood because the situation gives complete meaning to the one or two words. A writer does not have that advantage. That is the reason for writing in complete sentences, that is, sentences containing a subject and a verb.

The simplest sentences have as their necessary components a *subject* and a *verb.* (Modifiers of nouns and verbs are not classed as necessary components.) All sentences are marked by a capital letter at the beginning and a period, question mark, or exclamation point at the end.

The kinds of components in a sentence are dictated by the type of verb the sentence contains.

1. An *intransitive verb* plus a subject forms a complete sentence.

   I understand.
   John ran.
   Ann is sleeping.

2. A *transitive verb* requires an *object* and sometimes is followed by both a *direct object* and an *indirect object.*

Direct Object	**Indirect Object**
Tom bought a *pen.*	Tom bought *Mary* a pen.
I wrote a *letter.*	I wrote my *brother* a letter.

   A transitive verb may also be followed by both a direct object and an *objective complement.*

   Objective Complement

   We consider him *intelligent.*
   They proved John *innocent.*
   We voted John the *leader.*

3. A *linking verb* requires a *subjective complement,* which describes or relates to the subject.

   Subjective Complement

   This tastes *good.*
   John became *president.*
   The horses appeared *ill.*

   Common linking verbs are

appear, look	feel	prove	smell	taste
seem	grow	remain	sound	turn

4. *The verb be* (*am, is, was,* and so on) is followed by a *subjective complement,* which may be a noun, adjective, or adverb of place.

   Nancy is a *student.* (noun)
   Nancy is *happy.* (adjective)
   Nancy and John are *here.* (adverb)

A1b. Auxiliary Verbs in Negative and Question Patterns

Negative patterns: Sentences with verbs (except *be*) form the negative by using *does not* or *do not* (past tense: *did not*) as follows:

Singular: This book *does not interest* me.
Plural: These books *do not interest* me.
Past: This book (these books) *did not interest* me.

Compare the affirmative patterns:

This book *interests* me.
These books *interest* me.
This book *interested* me.

Sentences with the verb *be* form the negative merely by putting *not* after the verb.

This book *is not* mine.

Question patterns: Sentences with verbs (except *be*) are turned into questions by the use of *does (do, did)* as follows:

Statement: This book *interests* me.

Singular: *Does* this book *interest* you?
Plural: *Do* these books *interest* you?
Past: *Did* this (these) book (books) *interest* you?

Sentences with *be* are turned into questions as follows:

Is the book on the table?
Are you *going?*

A1c. Participles Versus Full Verbs

Some verb forms in English consist of a verb and a participle. (See sections D and E.) These verbs are called *auxiliary verbs*. Do, be, and *have* are common auxiliaries. (See A1b above and section E.)

The boy *is running.* (auxiliary-present participle; present continuous)
The job *is finished.* (auxiliary-past participle; passive)
The package *has arrived.* (auxiliary-past participle; present perfect)
Susan *has gone.* (auxiliary-past participle; present perfect)

A noun with a participle is not a complete sentence. These are *not* sentences* even though here the word group begins with a capital letter and ends with a period.

    *The boy running.
    *The job finished.
    *Susan gone.

Note: For many verbs the past participle and the past tense have the same form.

    The package *arrived.* (past tense)
    The package *has arrived.* (present perfect)

A1d. Subject-Verb Agreement: Forms of *be,* Present-tense Forms of Other Verbs

The subject must "agree" with the verb. Singular subjects must be followed by singular verbs. Plural subjects take plural verbs. In English, only the verb *be* changes to indicate both person and number. Other verbs distinguish between singular and plural only in the third-person present tense. (See also section F, modals.)

Singular	Plural	Participle
PRESENT-TENSE FORMS OF *BE*		
I am	We are	
You are	You are	being
He (she, it) is	They are	
PAST-TENSE FORMS OF *BE*		
I was	We were	
You were	You were	been
He (she, it) was	They were	
PRESENT-TENSE FORMS OF OTHER VERBS		
I go	We go	
You go	You go	
He (she, it) *goes*	They go	
He has	They *have* (irregular)	

Note the third-person singular forms. Final *-s* on a noun indicates plural. The final *-s* on the verb indicates that the verb is singular.

*Sentences that are incorrect are indicated by an asterisk (*).

The boy*s* come every day. (plural)
The boy come*s* every day. (singular)
My parent*s* live in New York. (plural)
Helen live*s* in New York. (singular)

A1e. Patterns with *there is*

To indicate the existence of something, a sentence may begin with *There is.*

There	V	N	ADV
There	is	a building	on the corner.
There	are	many people	in the city.

The true subject of the sentence in this pattern is the noun following the verb. Note that it governs the form of the verb. One could also say, "A building is on the corner." While *be* is the verb commonly used in this pattern, other verbs sometimes used are *appear, come, exist, happen, live, occur, seem,* and *sit.*

There *appeared* a face at the window.
There *comes* a time when we must go.

A1f. Impersonal *it* as Subject

It	V	N (ADJ)
It	is raining.	
It	is	cold.
It	is	ten o'clock.

A1g. Inverted Sentences with *it*

When a clause or verbal construction is the subject of *is,* the sentence may be inverted with *it* as the subject.

It	V	ADJ	CLAUSE (PHRASE)
It	is	important	that you come. (That you come is important.)
It	is	useless	to protest. (To protest is useless.)

Sentences like this represent a transposition or "transformation" of the sentence elements for emphasis.

It would be interesting *to visit New York.* (inversion)
To visit New York would be interesting. (normal order)

It is difficult for the visitor *to imagine what it is like.* (inversion)
To imagine what it is like is difficult for the visitor. (normal order)

A2. COMBINING SENTENCE PATTERNS

Some sentences have more than one s–v or s–v–complement pattern. These patterns are summarized below.

A2a. Compound Sentences: Uses of Conjunctions, Sentence Connectors, and Semicolons

When the ideas expressed in two sentences are closely connected, the sentences are frequently put together into one sentence and linked by a conjunction—*and, but, or, nor, so,* and others. The resulting sentences are called *compound sentences.* The clauses could be written separately.

It was late, *but* the guests had not arrived.
He told me that he did it, *and* I believed him.

Note the punctuation in the patterns just given.

Sentences may also be joined by sentence connectors (*therefore, consequently, however,* and so on), which indicate the relationship of ideas.

Note the placement of sentence connectors and the punctuation in the following sentences:

I went to the meeting; *however,* I did not stay very long.
I went to the meeting. I did not stay very long, *however.*
I went to the meeting. I did not, *however,* find out what I wanted to
know.

But:

We went to California last summer. We visited the Grand Canyon, too.

When sentences are linked by sentence connectors, a semicolon (;) is used between the sentence patterns, or each pattern may be punctuated as a sentence by itself. If the sentence connector is more than one syllable long, it is generally separated by a comma from the sentence pattern in which it occurs.

Sentence connectors indicate the addition or restatement of an idea, contrast of ideas, result, and sequence of time. Following is a summary of the uses of sentence connectors.

1. markers to indicate contrast of ideas

however	I enjoy shopping in the city; *however*
nevertheless	*(nevertheless, yet)*, I would not like to
yet	live there.

2. markers to indicate addition of an idea

also	Colorado is a fine place for a vacation; *also*
furthermore	*(furthermore, likewise, too)*, it is a good
likewise	place to live.*
too	

3. markers to indicate a more forceful restatement of an idea

indeed	This is a fine place for a vacation; *indeed,* it is the best we have found yet.

4. markers to introduce clauses of result

consequently	He asked me to go; *therefore (consequently,*
hence	*hence, thus, so)*, I went.†
therefore	
thus	

5. markers to indicate time sequence

afterward(s)	First we went shopping; *afterward,* we went to a play.
later on	Early in the evening we listened to music; *later on,* we danced.
hereafter	Up to this time your assignments have been easy; *hereafter,* they will be more difficult.‡
thereafter	The accident occurred last year; *thereafter,* he was more careful.‡
thereupon	The teacher left the room; *thereupon,* the students began to talk.

Some conjunctions are used in pairs, as in the examples below.

either . . . or	You can *either* go *or* stay. *Either* you go *or* I go.
neither . . . nor	*Neither* what he says *nor* what he does is becoming to a gentleman.

*Also and *too* are usually used at the end of a clause.

†*Consequently* and *therefore* are more used in writing than in speaking, and they are in more common use than *hence* and *thus.*

‡Note the time relations expressed by *hereafter* and *thereafter,* as indicated by the forms of the verbs.

both . . . and	I like *both* what he has done *and* what he plans to do.
whether . . . or	*Whether* happy *or* sad, John is pleasant and courteous.
	Whether I go *or* I stay depends upon the news we get about Mother's health.
now . . . now (then, again)	He is *now* excited, *now* depressed.
rather . . . than	I would *rather* go to the tropics *than* trek to the North Pole.

Note also reductions of clauses after *rather than.* (For other reductions see section 28.)

I prefer going to the tropics *rather than* going to the North Pole.

Note the word order in the sentence patterns marked by the following paired conjunctions:

as . . . so	*As* the twig is bent, *so* is the tree inclined.
not only . . . but (but also, but . . . too)	*Not only* did my parents give him encouragement, *but* they gave him money too.
neither . . . nor	*Neither* can I go *nor* can I stay.

A2b. Combining with Subordinators: Adverbial Clauses

Sentences may be combined by making one idea subordinate—that is, dependent on or modifying the other. Clauses introduced by *subordinators* modify the verb in the main clause or the entire clause (sentence).

They left early. It rained. → They left early *because* it rained.
You go. I will go. → *If* you go, I will go.
We finished lunch. We took a nap. → *After* we finished lunch, we took a nap.

Adverbial subordinate clauses may show time, place, manner, or purpose, or comparison, contrast, or cause. For uses of subordinating words see section H23.

Note that clauses introduced by subordinators are *not* complete sentences. These are *not* sentences:

*Because you came
*While you were here

Do *not* join two clauses introduced by subordinators:

*Because it rained *so* we stayed home.

A2c. Combining with Relative Clauses: Adjective Clauses

Sentences can be combined by using one to modify a noun in the other. The modifier is called a *relative clause.* Relative clauses may be thought of as resulting from the combination of two sentences containing an identical word. A relative pronoun *(who, whom, whose, which, that)* is (1) substituted for the identical element and (2) moved to a position next to the word that the clause modifies.

We discussed the incident. The incident was reported in the paper. → We discussed the incident *that* was reported in the paper.

The award went to the professor. The professor taught the English class. → The award went to the professor *who* taught the English class.

The student returned the book to the library. I gave the book to the student. → The student *to whom* I gave the book returned it to the library.
or
The student I gave the book to returned it to the library.

The person was wearing a green shirt. I saw the person. → The person *whom* I saw was wearing a green shirt.
or
The person I saw was wearing a green shirt.

Note that except in the subject position the relative pronoun is often omitted in informal speech or writing.
See also section J31 for use of relative pronouns.

A2d. Combining with Reductions of Relative Clauses: Participles and Infinitives as Modifiers of Nouns

Clauses modifying nouns may be reduced to participles.

The museum contains a warship. The warship dates from 1750.
The museum contains a warship *that* dates from 1750.
The museum contains a warship *dating* from 1750. (present participle)
It contains a collection. The collection is valued at more than a billion dollars.
It contains a collection *that* is valued at more than a billion dollars.

It contains a collection valued at more than a billion dollars. (past participle)

Do *not* write a participial modifier as a complete sentence (see A1d). See section J29 for further uses of verbals as modifiers. Clauses modifying nouns may be reduced to infinitives.

This was the first spaceship that went to the moon.
This was the first spaceship *to go* to the moon. (infinitive)

A2e. Combining with Appositives and Nonrestrictive Clauses

Sentences may be combined so that one merely gives further information rather than identifying a noun in the first sentence. The resulting clause is called nonrestrictive.

The celebration honored the founder. He was an Englishman.
The celebration honored the founder, *who was an Englishman.*
(nonrestrictive)

Note the comma before the nonrestrictive clause. This clause may be further reduced to an appositive.

The celebration honored the founder, *an Englishman.* (appositive)

A2f. Combining with Noun Clauses

Clauses introduced by *that* and *what* may be used as substitutes for the complement or for the subject of a sentence.

He said *that he would come.* (direct object)
That he will come on time is doubtful. (subject)

In these sentences the word *that* is merely a connector. Noun clauses may also be introduced by *what.*

She told me. She wanted something. → She told me *what she wanted.* (direct object)
What she wants is impossible to get. (subject)

In these sentences *what* is the direct object of the verb *wants* in the noun clause.

B. Noun Indicators

B3. ARTICLES

Count nouns indicate things that can be counted *(a man, two men).* Non-count nouns represent abstract or uncountable things *(danger, excitement, honesty, oil, dust).* Non-count nouns cannot be pluralized without changing their meaning (*iron,* a metal; *irons,* devices used to press clothes). Some abstractions cannot be pluralized.

Countability and definiteness determine the use of articles before nouns in English.

B3a. Indefinite Articles (a, an) versus Omission

The indefinite articles are used with singular count nouns. Their use might be best understood by remembering that they are reductions of the word *one.* The choice of *a* or *an* depends on the sound that follows. *A* occurs before a noun or adjective beginning with a consonant or with a vowel pronounced with an initial consonant sound *(a pencil, a red apple, a unit). An* occurs before vowel sounds *(an apple, an elephant).*

Uses of the forms of the indefinite article are as follows:

1. Before a singular count noun to indicate an indefinite or unspecified item.

   a book   a cup   a chair   (any one; not a particular one)

2. Before an indefinite singular count noun that is mentioned for the first time.

   On my way here I saw *a dog.*
   I have just thought of *a solution* to our problem.

3. With units of measure.

a dozen	six times *a* day	*a* yard wide
half *a* dozen	six dollars *a* pound	*a* mile high

4. Indefinite articles are *not* used with plurals of count nouns.

   Apples are good for you.
   Children can be noisy sometimes.

5. Indefinite articles are *not* used with non-count nouns. (See C7 for types of non-count nouns.)

   I'll buy *bacon, celery, sugar, rice, coffee,* and *salt.*

   but

   I'll buy *a* pound of bacon, *a* stalk of celery, *a* package of rice, and *a* jar of coffee.
   I'll buy *a* pineapple, *a* tomato, and *a* pie.

B3b. The Definite Article *the* versus Omission

The refers to a specified thing or to specified things. It may be used with singular or plural count nouns or with non-count nouns that have been made specific by some modifying phrase or clause.

> *the apple* on *the table* (a specific apple and table)
> *the apples* on *the tables* (specific apples and tables)
> *the oil* in *the can* (specific oil)
> *the oil* you just spilled (specific oil)
> On my way here I saw *a dog. The dog* was barking excitedly. (In the second sentence, *dog* refers to the specific dog mentioned in the first sentence.)

The is *not* used before non-count nouns when they are not made specific.

> I want to buy *luggage* and *jewelry.*

but

> *The luggage I bought* was a bargain.
> None of *the jewelry in that store* appealed to me.

Uses of *a* and *the* with Count and Non-Count Nouns

	COUNT NOUNS		NON-COUNT NOUNS
	Singular	Plural	Singular (no plural form)
Nondefinitized	*a* book	books	beauty
Definitized	*the* book	*the* books	*the* beauty of nature

B4. *SOME* AND *ANY* AS NOUN INDICATORS

Compare:

> *Sóme* people like adventure. (Not all do.)
> *Some* péople came to visit us. (We do not indicate definitely who they were.)

In negative statements and in questions an indefinite amount or number is expressed by *any*—not *some.* Compare:

> I have *some* money. (an indefinite amount)
> I do not have *any* money. (none)
> Do you have *any* money? (an unspecified amount)

B5. OTHER NOUN INDICATORS

WITH COUNT NOUNS				WITH NON-COUNT NOUNS	
Indefinite Item	Definite Item	Indefinite Number	Definite Number	Indefinite Amount	Definite Amount
a	the	few[a,b]	no	little[b]	no
any	this,	a few[a,b]	all[a]	a little[b]	all
either	that	several[a]	every	some	
neither	these,	some[a]	one,	much	
	those[a]	many[a]	two, etc.	more,	
	his,	any	both[a]	most	
	her, etc.	more,			
	each	most[a]			
	another				

[a]These markers are used with plural count nouns.
[b]*Few* stresses a small number; *little* stresses small quantity. *A few* and *a little* do not stress small number or quantity.

C. Nouns

C6. IRREGULAR PLURALS OF NOUNS

Plurals of nouns are regularly formed by adding -s or -es. For most nouns, add -s (*hat–hats, boy–boys*). For nouns ending in -s, -x, -z, and -sh, add -es (*dish–dishes, dress–dresses, porch–porches, fox–foxes*). For some nouns ending in -o preceded by a consonant, add -es.

echo–echoes	veto–vetoes	tornado–tornadoes
potato–potatoes	tomato–tomatoes	hero–heroes

Exceptions:

piano–pianos	soprano–sopranos
solo–solos	Filipino–Filipinos

For nouns ending in -y preceded by a consonant, change the -y to -i and add -es.

city–cities	baby–babies
lady–ladies	body–bodies

For some nouns ending in *-f,* change the *-f* to *-v* and add *-es.*

leaf–leaves	half–halves	knife–knives
life–lives	shelf–shelves	loaf–loaves

Exceptions:

proof–proofs	grief–griefs	gulf–gulfs
roof–roofs	belief–beliefs	safe–safes

Some nouns ending in *-f* have two plurals.

elf–elfs, elves	wharf–wharfs, wharves
hoof–hoofs, hooves	scarf–scarfs, scarves

Some irregular plurals that are survivals of Old English forms are:

child–children	man–men	foot–feet	goose–geese
ox–oxen	woman–women	tooth–teeth	mouse–mice

Some foreign words (particularly Latin and Greek words) taken into English retain their foreign plurals. A few examples are:

analysis– analyses	criterion– criteria	phenomenon– phenomena
basis–bases	datum–data	radius–radii
crisis–crises	hypothesis–hypotheses	stratum–strata

Some nouns have the same form for both singular and plural.

Nationalities: Chinese, Japanese, Swiss
Animals: deer, sheep, fish, trout, salmon, fowl

C7. CLASSES OF NON-COUNT NOUNS

The nouns marked with an asterisk (*) below are also frequently used as count nouns. When used as count nouns, these nouns sometimes have slightly different meanings. Compare the following sentences:

Joy is better than sorrow.
Do you know *the joys* of raising a large family?

Group I. Abstractions

beauty,* ugliness	intelligence, stupidity	permission,* refusal*	abuse* assistance
blame, praise*	joy,* sorrow*	poverty, wealth	command* contempt

bravery,	laughter,	strength,*	deference
cowardice	weeping	weakness*	enjoyment
confidence,*	love,*	tragedy,*	faith*
timidity	hate*	comedy*	gaiety*
death,*	luck,	trouble,*	isolation
life*	misfortune*	fortune*	justice*
health,	nonsense,	victory,*	kindness*
sickness*	sense*	defeat*	neglect
ignorance,	patience,	virtue,*	opportunity*
knowledge	impatience	vice*	power*
infancy,	peace,	youth,*	right*
old age	war*	maturity	work*

Group II. Substances

Food

Solids

		Liquids
bacon	ham*	coffee
beef	ice cream	cream
bread*	jelly*	milk
butter	lamb	oil*
cabbage*	pepper	soup*
celery	pineapple*	tea
cheese*	pork	vinegar*
chicken*	rice	water*
corn*	salt	
fish*	sausage*	
flour*	sugar	
grapefruit*	yogurt	

Nonfood

Solids		Liquids	Gases
cement	lead	gasoline	air
coal	linen*	oil	oxygen
cotton*	sand*		
dirt	silk*		
dust	silver		
fur*	soot		
gold	steel		
hair*	tin*		
iron*	wool*		

Group III. Collections

	Inanimate (nonliving)		Animate (living)
architecture	information	news	humanity
clothing	jewelry	postage	man
entertainment	luggage	recreation	mankind
equipment	lumber	scenery	people
fruit*	machinery	traffic	personnel
furniture	merchandise	transportation	woman
hardware	money	weather	youth

Group IV. Phenomena and forces of nature

cold	fog*	mist*	sound*
darkness	gravity	moonlight	sunlight
daylight	hail	rain*	thunder*
electricity	heat	smoke*	water*
fire*	lightning	snow*	wind*

Group V. Areas of study and activity

agriculture	fun	art*	hiking	football
business*	leisure	chemistry	reading	hockey
commerce	play*	economics	shopping	soccer
farming	work*	linguistics	swimming	tennis
science*		literature*	writing*	
		music	(most nouns	
		philosophy*	with -ing)	
		physics		
		Spanish		
		statistics		

D. Verb Forms: Tense and Time

D8. PRESENT TIME

D8a. Present Tense

The present tense in English is used for assertions. It is used when one wishes to state what is permanently true or what is true over a period of time, not merely true for the moment of speaking. It is also used to state opinions or beliefs.

All people *perceive* the distinction between present and past.
Not all cultures *view* time in the same way.

These are statements of fact, or permanent conditions. Other examples of uses of the present tense are

The state of Hawaii *consists* of seven principal islands. (present fact)
The hiking club *goes* on a picnic every weekend. (repeated action)
This milk *tastes* sour. (opinion)

Note that the present tense adds *-s* in the third-person singular. Compare:

All people *perceive*. . . .
The hiking club *goes*. . . .

D8b. Present Continuous

To indicate action that is continuing at the moment of speaking or to describe a situation that exists at the present moment but that is not a permanent condition, the English language uses *is* or *are* plus the present participle (v + *-ing*). This verb phrase is called the *present continuous*. The following examples show the forms of the present continuous and the purposes for which it is used.

1. to express action in progress at the moment of speaking

   I speak five languages (permanent condition), but I *am speaking* English now.

2. to describe a situation existing at present

   As I write this, I *am sitting* in front of my fireplace in which a cheerful *fire is roaring*. My wife *is sitting* opposite me. She *is reading* a magazine. The cat *is sleeping* peacefully on the hearth rug. A cold wind *is blowing* outside, but we feel warm and comfortable here by our cozy fire.

   Note that present sensations are expressed in the present tense, not the present continuous:

   We feel warm.
   The food tastes good.

3. to indicate an activity or situation that is continuing over a period of time

   This year I *am studying* biology, English, mathematics, and history at the university. I *am living* in an apartment on Twelfth Street. Here I have fewer interruptions than I had in the dormitory, and I *am making* good progress in my studies. I *am working* harder than I did last year, but I *am enjoying* my work more.

D8c. Present Perfect

The relationship between past time and the present moment is shown by the use of *has (have)* plus the past participle *(-ed, -en)*. This form is called the present perfect. The uses of the present perfect may be summarized as follows, with examples contrasting its use with that of the past tense.

1. to express a condition that has existed in the past up to the present moment and is still true at present

I was in England for one year. (The speaker is no longer there.)
I *have been* in England for one year. (The speaker is still in England.)

2. to express action that has (or has not) occurred in the past and may (or may not) occur again in the future

An old man says, "I was in Paris once." (He does not expect to go again.)
A young man says. "I *have been* to Paris once." (He may go again.)

3. to express recency of action or condition

I finished my assignment. (The finishing took place at some time in the past. It is now past history.)
I *have just finished* my assignment. (The speaker expresses the recency of the completion of the action. *Just, just recently*, and other adverbs with similar meanings are often used when this meaning is expressed.)

4. to indicate that an act was complete before the m ent of speaking

Are you going to get the car repaired today? I *have already done* it.
Can you get the report done by tomorrow? I *have already finished* it.
(The speaker speaks of an act in reference to the moment of speaking. The adverb *already* is used.)

D8d. Present Perfect Continuous

Just as English uses a continuous form of the present and past tenses, there are also continuous forms of the perfect tenses. Continuous perfect verb phrases indicate both duration and recency. Compare:

Grace *has read* a great many novels. (She has read them sometime
before the moment of speaking.)
Grace *has been reading* a great many novels. (She has been reading
them over a period of time just before and up to the moment of
speaking.)
I *have lived* here for a year. (I still live here.)
I *have been living* here for a year. (I still live here, but the duration of
the condition is emphasized.)

D9. PAST TIME

D9a. Past Tense
The simple past tense is used to make statements of fact or opinion
about conditions in the past.

My grandmother's garden contained many varieties of flowers.
(statement of a fact that was true once but is true no longer)
The concert last night was not well done. (opinion about a past event)

D9b. Past Continuous
To indicate action that was continuing at a point of time in the past
or to describe a situation or condition in the past, English uses *was* or
were plus the present participle (v + *-ing*). This is the past continuous
form. Note the examples that follow.

1. to report an action that was in process or was continuing at a
specific moment in the past or at a time when another event
occurred

By 1860 the Mississippi Valley *was becoming* settled.
We *were trying* to get pictures of the parade when the wind blew our
camera over.

2. to describe a situation existing in the past

The scene, as I gazed on it in the late afternoon sunlight, was
peaceful and quiet. A few palm trees *were swaying* gently in the
breezes. The surf *was lapping* against the shore with a soothing
sound. A lone fisherman *was walking* along the beach looking
for a place to cast his nets, and a few seagulls *were flying*
overhead. There was nothing to indicate that in a very few

minutes the hurricane would transform this quiet beach into
a place of violence and destruction.

D9c. Past Perfect

The past perfect (*had* + v-*ed, -en*) is used when the writer or
speaker wants to refer to an event that happened before another
event in the past or to a condition that continued up to a time in the
past.

Mr. Howard *sank* down exhausted. He *had shaken* hands with at least
a thousand people during the political rally.
The bus finally *started*. The luggage *had delayed* the departure.

D9d. Past Perfect Continuous

The continuous form of the past perfect (I *had been studying,* he *had
been sleeping,* they *had been talking*) places emphasis on the continuing
of an act or a condition up to a specific time in the past. This form
of the verb is not common, but it is used occasionally. Compare:

They *had lived* there a year when they decided to move to the
suburbs.
They *had been living* there a year when they decided to move to the
suburbs. (The emphasis is on the continuing of the condition.)

D10. EXPRESSIONS OF FUTURE TIME

There is no one special verb form to indicate future time in English. The future is indicated by verb phrases, or sometimes by the
present tense and an adverb, as follows:

1. *going to* + VERB

I am *going to take* a trip next week. (planned or intended action)

2. *will* + VERB

I *will be* in Washington for a week. (promise or statement of simple
futurity)
My wife Sarah *will go* with me.

3. present tense + adverbial element indicating time

Our plane *leaves at eight o'clock.* (usually used for schedules)

Shall is sometimes used with *I* or *we* in expressions of future time.

I *shall be* in Washington for a week. *Will* you *be* there then?

In questions, *will* expresses futurity.

Will I *see* you when I get there?

Shall expresses advisability.

Shall I *pack* my raincoat for the Washington trip?

D11. IRREGULAR VERBS

Present	*Past*	*Past participle*
am (is)	was	been
arise	arose	arisen
awake	awoke	awakened
bear	bore	borne
beat	beat	beat(en)
become	became	become
begin	began	begun
bend	bent	bent
bet	bet	bet
bid	bade	bidden
bid	bid	bid
bite	bit	bitten
bleed	bled	bled
blow	blew	blown
bring	brought	brought
build	built	built
burst	burst	burst
buy	bought	bought
catch	caught	caught
choose	chose	chosen
come	came	come
cost	cost	cost
creep	crept	crept
cut	cut	cut
deal	dealt	dealt
dig	dug	dug
dive	dived	dived
do	did	done

draw	drew	drawn
drink	drank	drunk
drive	drove	driven
eat	ate	eaten
fall	fell	fallen
feel	felt	felt
fight	fought	fought
find	found	found
fly	flew	flown
forget	forgot	forgot, forgotten
freeze	froze	frozen
get	got	got, gotten
give	gave	given
go	went	gone
grow	grew	grown
hang	hanged	hanged (execute)
hang	hung	hung
have	had	had
hear	heard	heard
hide	hid	hidden
hit	hit	hit
hold	held	held
hurt	hurt	hurt
keep	kept	kept
know	knew	known
lay	laid	laid
lead	led	led
leave	left	left
lend	lent	lent
let	let	let
lie	lay	lain
lie	lied	lied (tell an untruth)
light	lighted, lit	lighted, lit
lose	lost	lost
make	made	made
mean	meant	meant
meet	met	met

pay	paid	paid
put	put	put
quit	quit	quit
read	read	read
rid	rid	rid
ride	rode	ridden
ring	rang	rung
rise	rose	risen
run	ran	run
say	said	said
see	saw	seen
sell	sold	sold
send	sent	sent
set	set	set
shake	shook	shaken
shine	shone	shone
shoot	shot	shot
shrink	shrank	shrunk
shut	shut	shut
sing	sang	sung
sink	sank	sunk
sit	sat	sat
sleep	slept	slept
slide	slid	slid
speak	spoke	spoken
spend	spent	spent
spread	spread	spread
spring	sprang	sprung
stand	stood	stood
steal	stole	stolen
stick	stuck	stuck
sting	stung	stung
strike	struck	struck
swear	swore	sworn
sweep	swept	swept
swim	swam	swum
swing	swung	swung
take	took	taken
teach	taught	taught
tear	tore	torn

tell	told	told
think	thought	thought
throw	threw	thrown
understand	understood	understood
upset	upset	upset
wake	waked, woke	waked, wakened
wear	wore	worn
weave	wove	woven
wed	wed	wed
weep	wept	wept
wet	wet, wetted	wet, wetted
win	won	won
wind	wound	wound
wring	wrung	wrung
write	wrote	written

E. Passive Forms

E12. USES OF THE PASSIVE

The passive (*be* + the past participle) is used in the following ways:

1. to indicate a condition or result of an action
   Generally, when we use the passive voice, we do not know or do not care who performed the act. The focus is on the condition that results from an action, not on its performance.

   The house was built by a famous architect. (The focus is on the building of the house.)
   The house was built in 1905. (The builder is not important or is not known.)

   The passive is often used in reporting a historical action when the result is better known than the performer.

   Washington, D.C., was named for George Washington.
   The American Indians are believed to have come from Asia across the Bering Straits.

   While theoretically every subject-verb-direct object–pattern sentence may be stated in the passive, many statements are not effective this way. The active form of the sentence is often more forceful and direct. Compare:

The secretaries are typing the letters. (active)
The letters are being typed by the secretaries. (passive)

2. to describe ("false" passive)

With the verb *be*, the past participle may function like an adjective, though no agent is implied. This form is similar to the passive.

John is tired.
The walls are covered with mosaics.

Note the difference in meaning in the following statements:

Jane was surprised. (Someone surprised Jane.)
Jane was surprising. (Jane surprised others.)

3. with long subjects*

Sometimes a sentence is put into the passive because it would be awkward to put a great deal of material into the subject position.

The guests were greeted at the door by the hostess, who
    shook hands with each person and called each one by name.

4. for suspense*

Delaying the statement of who performed an act until the end of the sentence is a means of creating suspense.

When we returned everything was different: the room had been
    dusted, the books neatly stacked on the table, the papers picked
    up from the floor—all done by our normally untidy youngest
    daughter.

5. for emphasis*

The final position in a sentence is the most emphatic. It also receives the most stress. Thus material to be emphasized may be put in a *by* phrase at the end of the sentence.

Not only does my sister have to endure the interruptions of her
    children when she is trying to write; she is constantly harrassed
    by telephone calls from people who want her to speak at
    meetings.

*Suggested by Virginia French Allen.

E13. SOME DIFFICULT VERBS

Verbs that, in another language, may be followed by a direct object may be intransitive in English and thus may not be put into the passive. These sentences may not be expressed in the passive:

This event happened last week.
The building belongs to the government.
This used to be the palace of the king. (was formerly the palace)

Sometimes the use of *be* + the past participle changes the meaning or there is no active form of the sentence.

The government is involved in this matter.
We are concerned in constructing a new plan.

F. Modals

F14. USES OF MODALS

F14a. *Will* + v

1. Future time
    The English language has no inflectional form for the future tense as it does for the simple past. The use of *will* or *shall* is a common way of expressing the future. *Will* also suggests willingness, or a promise or an agreement with another person's wishes, in addition to implying futurity.

We will meet you on the corner in twenty minutes.
The workmen will come tomorrow to repair the roof.
My secretary will call you tomorrow.
I will let you know as soon as the work is finished.

    The future is also expressed by other auxiliaries like *am about to* or *am going to,* by the present tense with an adverbial element denoting future time *(I go to New York tomorrow),* or by other modals with an adverbial element denoting future time *(I can go next week). I am going to* + verb stresses intention to do something.

2. Requests
    Will is used in making polite requests.

Will you please take this package to the post office for me?
Will you please be seated?

3. Questions about future matters
    These questions do not concern advisability or make requests.
(See *shall,* p. 257.)

Will we have many examinations in this course?
Will the meeting of the council take place tomorrow?

F14b. *Would* + v

1. Willingness
    The use of *would* here is similar to *will.*

I would (will) be glad to help you.

2. Desires
    Would is used with *like* to express desire.

I would like a cup of coffee.
I would like to speak to you today about my country.

3. Conditional or hypothetical situations
    Would is most commonly used to express desires or
willingness in hypothetical situations.

I would do it if I knew how.
If you would do it for me, I would be very grateful.

4. Habitual action in the past

When I was a child I would often walk in the country.

5. Past tense of *will*
    Would is used as the past tense of *will* in reported speech.

Steve says he will go. (present)
Steve said he would go. (past)

6. Polite requests
    This use of *would* is similar to that of *will.*

Would you mind opening the door for me?

F14c. *Can* + v

1. Ability
    Can expresses the ability to do something in the immediate
present or in the future. In this sense it is the equivalent of *to
be able to.*

I can speak five languages. (present)
I can help you next week. (future)

2. Permission

Can is used in statements implying permission as well as ability. *Can* in questions asking permission is colloquial. (See *may,* below.)

My secretary can help you this afternoon.
Can (may) I go with you?

F14d. *Could* + v

1. Ability

Could indicates ability to do something in the past. In this sense it is the past of *can.*

When I was six years old I could speak only one language; now
    I can speak five.

2. Conditional

Could expresses the ability to do something if other conditions are met. The past tense is expressed by *could have.*

I could buy a new car if I had the money.
I could have asked him if I had seen him.

3. Possibility

The use of *could* to express a possibility is much like its use to express a conditional situation.

I hear someone coming down the hall. It could be John.

4. Past tense of *can*

Could is the past tense of *can* in reported speech.

Susan says she can repair your typewriter. (present)
Susan said she could repair your typewriter. (past)

F14e. *May* + v

1. Permission

May is used to express permission or to indicate that something is allowed. Present or future time is indicated.

You may go now. (You have permission to go immediately.)
You may leave when you have finished the examination. (You
　　have permission to leave at a future time.)
Your name may be placed in the right-hand corner of your paper.

2. Questions asking permission
　　May is commonly used in questions asking permission. (See
can, p. 264.)

May I come in? (immediate action)
May I come tomorrow? (future action)

3. Conjectures
　　May sometimes indicates conjecture about the future. When
used in this sense, the past tense is indicated by *may have.*

It may rain tomorrow. (There is a strong possibility.)
It may have rained while we were gone. (The speaker is not sure
　　whether it did or not.)

F14f. *Might* + v

1. Conjecture
　　Might expressing conjecture is sometimes used
interchangeably with *may,* or it may have a stronger
implication that the condition is hypothetical or contrary to
fact. The past tense is expressed by *might have.* (Compare with
the use of *may.*)

It might rain tomorrow.
It might have rained while we were gone.
I might build a new house if I had the money. (The situation is
　　hypothetical or contrary to fact.)

2. Past tense of *may*
　　Might is used as the past tense of *may* in reported speech.

Steve says that I may go with him. (present)
Steve said that I might go with him. (past)

F14g. *Shall* + v

1. Questions of advisability in the first person
　　This is the main use of *shall. Shall* refers to the future.

Shall I close the window?
Shall we go to the play on Thursday night?

2. Future tense

Shall is sometimes used in the first person to express the future tense. The use of *will* is more common.

We shall know the answer to this problem tomorrow.

F14h. *Should* + v

1. Obligation

Should indicates obligation in regard to a general truth or to a specific act. It generally indicates an obligation that is recognized but that is not necessarily being fulfilled. In this sense it has a meaning close to that of *ought to*. Unfulfilled obligation in the past is expressed by *should have*.

We should be courteous to our parents. (obligation; a general truth)
I should mail this letter. (obligation regarding a specific act)
I should study tonight, but I am going to the movies. (obligation recognized but unfulfilled)
You should have answered the letters today.

2. Advisability

Should represents advisability as well as obligation.

You should have answered the letters today.
You should leave at three-thirty if you want to take the four-o'clock train.

3. Possibility

Should may also indicate a strong possibility that probably will be fulfilled.

I should get a letter from my insurance company today.

4. Questions of advisability in the first person

The use of *should* here is similar to that of *shall*. *Should* implies more of a sense of advisability than *shall*.

Should we close the windows before we leave?

F14i. *Must* + v

1. Necessity is the most common use of *must*.

People must eat in order to live.
Doctors must be concerned for their patients.
I must take the books back to the library; they are overdue.

Must expressing necessity has no past tense. Necessity in past time is expressed by *had to.*

2. Inference

Must indicates inference only with certain verbs: the verb *have;* linking verbs like *seem, appear,* and *be;* verbs expressing desire like *want, need,* and *believe;* and certain verbs expressing physical activity such as *walk, run, drive,* and so forth.

There must be a lot of stamps in that drawer; I remember putting them there.
Ms. Briggs must have an early class at the university; I see her leaving the house every day at seven-thirty.
He must take the bus to work; I see him pass this corner every morning.

Inference in the past may be expressed by *must have.*

It must have rained here yesterday; there is a lot of water on the ground.
Dorothy must have won the prize. She looks very pleased.

F14j. *Ought to* + v

Ought to + v has much the same meaning as *should,* but note the contrast in form.

I should go downtown this afternoon.
I ought to go downtown this afternoon.

We should finish this today.
We ought to finish this today. (We expect to finish it or we have an obligation to finish it.)

F15. OTHER AUXILIARIES EXPRESSING MODES

F15a. *Have to* + v

Have to + v expresses necessity in much the same way that *must* + v does. *Have to* and *must* can be used interchangeably. However, note the contrast in form.

I must leave now.
You must pay your fees today.

I have to leave now.
You have to pay your fees today.

Necessity in the past time is expressed by *had to.*

I had to leave then.
We had to pay our fees yesterday.

However, different meanings are expressed by *must not* and *do not have to.* Compare these two sentences:

You must not drive 80 miles an hour; it is against the law. (It is necessary that you not do it.)
You do not have to drive so fast. We have plenty of time to get there. (It is not necessary that you do it.)

F15b. *Am to* + v, *Am Going to* + v, *Am About to* + v

Am to, am going to, and *am about to* are all ways of expressing the future. Note the differences in meaning signaled by these expressions.

I am going to visit my sister next week. (intention to act at some indefinite future time, perhaps next week)
I am about to leave. (within the next few minutes)
I am to give a talk for her club while I am there. (The members of the club expect me to do it. They have asked me to do it. I plan to do it.)
Albert was to have gone with me, but he cannot leave his business. (He expected to go. He planned to go.)
He was going to take me in his car, but now I am going to take the train. (He planned in the past to do it in the future.)

G. Verbs Followed by Clauses and Verbals

G16. VERBS FOLLOWED BY CLAUSES

G16a. Simple Clauses

Some verbs may be followed by clauses as complements. These are generally verbs having to do with speaking or with mental states.

My friend *confessed* that she had been wrong. (speaking)
She *decided* that she should apologize. (mental state)

Other verbs used in this pattern include:

Speaking

acknowledge	mention
admit	*persuade
advise	promise
argue	propose
ask	recommend
*assure	request
command	say
complain	state
confess	suggest
deny	*tell
explain	urge
imply	warn
infer	

Mental States

anticipate	feel	recognize
assume	find	request
believe	grant	resolve
bet	guess	see
conceive	hear	seem
conclude	hint	speculate
consider	hope	think
decide	imagine	trust
deduce	judge	wish
desire	know	wonder
doubt	notice	
dream	perceive	
expect	prefer	

Many of these verbs may also be used with an infinitive complement.
(See G17a.)
* Verbs marked with an asterisk must have an indirect object before the clause.

Frances assured *us* that everything was all right.
We persuaded *the boy* that he should try again.
The professor told *the students* that he had graded the papers.

Want can be followed only by an infinitive.

They wanted *to go* home.

Suggest may be followed only by a clause. An indirect object cannot be used.

My teacher suggested *that I study English.*

G16b. Clauses of Command or Request or Expressing Hypothetical Conditions (Subjunctive)

Verbs of command or request (*command, propose, request, require, recommend, suggest,* and so on) are followed by the subjunctive form of the verb. In English, except for the verb *be,* the subjunctive is expressed only in the third-person singular—by the omission of the final *-s.* The present subjunctive of *be* is *be.*

They commanded that he *come* at once.
I suggest that we *be* there at five o'clock.

The past subjunctive of *be* is *were.* For other verbs, the conditional forms of the modals *could, might,* and so on are used with the verb. Subjunctive forms are used after the verb *wish* to express hypothetical conditions.

I wish I *were* there now.
My friend wishes she *could be* there too.

G16c. Reported Speech

Compare the following sentences and note the verb form in the reported statement.

The secretary said, "John *will* do it."
He said that John *will (would)* do it.

The secretary told me, "The meeting *begins* at noon."
He told me that the meeting *(begins) began* at noon.

Compare these sentences:

Lois asked, *"Where does* Jane work?"
Lois asked me *where Jane works (worked).*

Note the verb form and the word order in the reported question.

G17. VERBS FOLLOWED BY INFINITIVES

G17a. Verbs Followed Directly by Infinitives (*to* + verb) as Complement

I plan *to leave* tomorrow.
We want *to finish* this this evening.

Other verbs that follow this pattern:

ask	endeavor	neglect
be	expect	plan
beg	forget	prefer
begin	get (be allowed, become)	promise
care	go*	remember
cease	hate	start
continue	hope	stop
decide	intend	try
desire	learn	want
dislike	like	wish
dread	mean	

G17b. Verbs Followed by Noun or Pronoun + Infinitive as Complement

We advised *Ivan to try* again.
They asked John *to make a speech*.

Other verbs that follow this pattern:

advise	force	promise
allow	get (persuade)	remind
ask	instruct	teach
beg	invite	tell
cause	oblige	urge
command	order	want
desire	persuade	warn
encourage	prefer	wish
expect		

G18. VERBS FOLLOWED BY -*ING*

My brother dislikes *traveling*.
He denied *being there yesterday*.

*Going + an infinitive expresses future intent: *I am going to.*

admit	escape	practice
allow	finish	prefer
appreciate	hate	put off
avoid	imagine	quit
be worth	intend	remember
begin	keep	resent
cease	keep on	resist
consider	like	risk
continue	miss	start
deny	neglect	stop
dislike	plan	talk over
dread	postpone	try
enjoy		

G19. VERBS FOLLOWED BY NOUN OR PRONOUN + SIMPLE VERB

I heard *him leave* this morning.
I will have *my sister go* with me.

feel	hear	let	see
have	help	make	watch

G20. VERBS FOLLOWED BY NOUN OR PRONOUN AND PAST PARTICIPLE (-ed,-en)

He will get it *done* tomorrow.
I consider the *subject closed*.

consider	have	imagine	order
feel	hear	keep	want

H. Modification of Verbs

H21. ADVERBS AND POSITIONS OF ADVERBS

Adverbs and phrases used as adverbs may be used with a verb to show time, place, manner, or purpose.

The plane leaves *at six o'clock.* (time)
Let's meet *on the corner.* (place)
My secretary does her job *well.* (manner)
The children came *quickly.* (manner)
They came *in a hurry.* (manner)

Phrases with *to* and a verb or with *in order to* show purpose.

> I went to the store *to buy a loaf of bread.*
> We left early *in order to be there when the play started.*

The adverb is the most movable element in the sentence. The usual position is at the end of the sentence, but the adverb may also be found at the beginning of the sentence or before the verb. If the sentence is long, one adverbial element usually stands at the beginning, particularly if one is a phrase or clause of time or place.

> *In the summertime when the days are long,* I *often* get up *early* and take a long walk *before breakfast. When I go on these walks,* I can *usually* see the mountains *clearly.*

Note that except in the case of two-word verbs, the one place where the adverb is almost never placed in an English sentence is between the verb and object or complement—a common position for the adverb in many other languages. For example, it is incorrect in English to say, "You will see on your right tall buildings."

Following is a summary of the placement of adverbs.*

1. at the end of the sentence
   This is the most common position of adverbs.

> These camping places have become more and more crowded *during the last few years.*
> The fish go swimming *by.*
> Another undersea museum has recently been set aside *at Big Sur, California.*

2. at the beginning of the sentence
   Any adverbial of time, place, manner, or purpose may stand at the beginning of the sentence. In this position it modifies the sentence.

> *In 1972* the U.S. government declared this area a national monument. (time)
> *Throughout the United States* there are many campgrounds that the Department of the Interior has established. (place)
> *By swimming* you can reach these underwater museums. (manner)
> *To get to these museums,* you must use scuba-diving equipment. (purpose)

*Examples adapted from "Undersea Museums," pp. 113–114.

In a s–v sentence pattern, adverbials of place generally stand at the end of the sentence: s–v–ADV. However, this sentence pattern may be inverted as ADV–v–s to place the emphasis on the subject.

A dark shadow lay *on the floor.* S-V-ADV
On the floor lay a dark shadow. ADV-V-S (The emphasis is on the dark shadow.)

3. before the verb
    Two kinds of adverbs are placed before the verb:
    A. Common single-word adverbs of time such as *then, now, soon, always, often, seldom, sometimes, usually, just, almost, ever,* and *never.* Most of these indicate indefinite time. *Now, then,* and *soon* commonly appear at the end of the sentence also.
        When a verb is preceded by an auxiliary, these adverbs generally stand before the main verb after the auxiliary.

        People can *now* visit underwater museums.
        I have *never* visited an underwater museum.

        Note that with the perfect forms of the verb, the adverb goes before the participle. With the perfect continuous forms, the adverb follows *have.*

        The professor has *sometimes* been giving us short tests.

    B. Most adverbs of manner end in *-ly.* These adverbs may stand at the beginning or the end of the sentence or (most commonly) before the verb.

        Hastily the thief destroyed the evidence.
        The thief destroyed the evidence *hastily.*
        The thief *hastily* destroyed the evidence.

H22. ADVERBS IN TWO-WORD VERBS

A number of verbs are regularly followed by adverbs that modify or change their meaning. These are called two-word verbs. When the object of such a verb is a noun, the adverb may stand next to the verb or at the end of the sentence.

Doris *brought back* the book.
Doris *brought* the book *back.*

When the object is a pronoun, the adverb part of the two-word verb stands at the end.

Doris *brought* it *back.*

Common adverb participles in the two-word verb pattern are *back, up, out, down, over, away.*

H23. ADVERBIAL CLAUSES: USES OF SUBORDINATORS

Adverbial (subordinate) clauses may modify verbs or the entire sentence.

We will leave *when you are ready.* (modifier of the verb)
After our talk my friend and I parted. (modifier of the sentence)
Unless I am very much mistaken, it is going to rain this afternoon.

Adverbial clauses at the beginning of a sentence are often separated by a comma unless they are very short. (See section A2b for other examples.)

Below are subordinate-clause indicators.

Time	Place	Condition	Cause
after	where	although	as
as	wheresoever	except that	because
as soon as	wherever	if	for
before		in case	lest
now that		only	in that
once	*Contrast*	provided that	why
since	whereas	unless	since
until (till)		whether	
when			*Purpose*
whenever	*Comparison*	*Manner*	so that
while	as though	how	
	than		

H24. INFINITIVES FOR PURPOSE

Infinitives (*to* + verb) may be used to express purpose.

I went to New York *to see a play.*
You should study hard *to pass the examination.*

Sometimes *in order to* is used.

You should study hard *in order to* pass the examination.

I. Prepositions

I25. BASIC USES OF PREPOSITIONS

Phrases introduced by prepositions may modify verbs or nouns.

They left *at ten o'clock.* (modifier of verb)
The chair *in the corner* is broken. (modifier of noun)

Prepositions do not translate easily from language to language. Below are some of the basic uses of prepositions in English.

Time

in: in the evening (morning)
    in the fall (season)
    in August (month)
    in 1952 (year)
    in two months (meaning
      at the end of)
    in time (idiom meaning
      early enough)
for: I skied for an hour.
from: from Friday till
    Monday,
      from that moment
to: George left at ten
    minutes to two.

on: on August 12
    (definite date)
    on Friday (day of
      the week)
    on Christmas (holiday)
    on your birthday
      (definite day)
    on time (idiom meaning
      punctual)
by: by eight o'clock (not
    later than)
    They worked by the
    hour. (were paid
    hourly wages)
with: With the approach of
    fall, the air gets
    cooler.

Place or direction

at: He is at the dentist's.
    She looked at me.
of: It lies south of the
    border.
on: She wanted a house on
    the coast (river bank,
    and so on).
from: They live miles from
here
    We went from
    laughter to tears.

to: The temperature
    dropped to zero.
    He went to the river.
    She contributed to the
    Red Cross.
    This procedure is to
    your advantage. (idio-
    matic expression)
with: He lived with the
    Johnsons.
    The outcome rests
    with you.

in: She lives in an apartment.
He lives in a dream.

into: I put it into a box.
onto: I jumped onto the bed.

Means or agent

by: The boat was built by
an Italian.
They came by plane.
I did it by myself. (without help)
It arrived by airmail.
By wrapping it yourself,
you save money.

on: We saw it on television.
He is going on foot.
They live on meat.
from: Her honors come from
hard work.
She is burned from
sunbathing.
with: He opened it with a
knife.

Manner

in: In my estimation the
act was noble.
Her joy is in helping
others.
He left in anger.
She was dressed in
blue.
It appealed to us in
several ways.

like: The baby looks like me.
on: I swear this on my
honor.
with: He said it with a smile.
by: They work by the week.

State or condition

at: The nurses are at work.
The nations are at
peace.
The soldiers stood at
ease.
We are at your mercy.
She smiled at the
thought.

by: We were all by
ourselves last night.
(without company)
on: The pharmacist is on
call all night.
in: He was in a hurry.

Quantity

for: We drove for 50 miles.
The suit sold for $50.
to: The odds were 4 to 1
on that horse.
Our team won the football game 14 to 7.

by: The mosquitoes arrived
by the thousands.
The garden was 30 by
60 feet.
They are sold by the
pair.

Purpose

for: He went for an education.
　　 He came for a rest.
　　 She was hired for her creativity.
　　 She asked for a vacation.
　　 This gift is for you.

Association or possession

to: It belongs to John.
　 He is faithful to his beliefs.

Miscellaneous

for: She was named for　　from: You cannot
　　　her aunt.　　　　　　　 distinguish John
　　 He is small for his age.　　 from Jim.

I26. USES OF PREPOSITIONS AFTER CERTAIN VERBS

account for
agree on (something)
agree with (someone)
apologize to
approve of
argue with (someone)
ask for
believe in
belong to
blame (someone) for (something)
blame (something) on (someone)
borrow from
call on
care for
compliment (someone) on
consent to
consist of
convince (someone) of (something)
decide on
depend on
get rid of
hear about
hear from

hear of
insist on
invite (someone) to
laugh at
listen for
listen to
look at
look for
look forward to
object to
plan on
provide for
provide with
recover from
remind (someone) of
see about
substitute for
talk about
talk of
think about
think of
wait for
wait on (meaning *serve*)

I27. USES OF PREPOSITIONS WITH CERTAIN ADJECTIVES AND IN IDIOMATIC EXPRESSIONS

in accordance with	due to
according to	followed by
accustomed to	fond of
angry about (something)	independent of
angry at (someone); angry	interested in
with (someone)	limited to
based on	married to
capable of	proud of
composed of	in regard to
content with	have respect for
different from	similar to
disappointed in	tired of

I28. PREPOSITIONS VERSUS SUBORDINATORS

Some subordinators may also be prepositions. Compare:

They went home *because it was raining.* (subordinator)
They went home *because of* the rain. (preposition)
We left *after the performance was over.* (subordinator)
We left *after the performance.* (preposition)

Other subordinators that may also be prepositions are *before, until, since.*
Sometimes clauses are reduced after subordinators.

Before *going to England,* I need to renew my passport.
While *waiting in the airport,* I saw a friend.
Rather than *waiting until* two o'clock, let's go now. (*Rather than* cannot be followed by a clause.)

J. Modification of Nouns

J29. SUMMARY OF TYPES OF MODIFIERS OF NOUNS

Single-word adjectives:	the *long* road
Single-word nouns:	the *Boston* marathon
Relative clauses:	the book *you gave me*
Appositives:	Flora, *a professor of history,* . . .
Present participles:	the *running* water

Past participles:	the *finished* product
Participial phrases:	the water *running in the streets*
	the product *finished yesterday*
Infinitives:	a book *to read*
Adverbs:	the book *here*
Prepositional phrases:	the book *on the table*

J30. POSITIONS OF MODIFIERS OF NOUNS

Single-word modifiers generally precede the noun. An exception is the adverb used as a modifier (the book *here*). A pair of adjectives, like other phrases, may come after the noun for special emphasis. Such an adjectival is generally separated from the rest of the sentence by commas.

In the oases [of the Arab world], large and small, . . .

No final rule for the order in a series of adjectives can be set forth. The order depends in part on the relationship of the ideas expressed by the modifiers of the noun. Adjectives expressing nationality and nouns modifying nouns generally come last in a series of one-word modifiers.

expensive little French hat
good German cooking
a small yellow toothbrush

J31. RELATIVE CLAUSES, USES OF RELATIVE PRONOUNS

For formation of relative clauses, see A2c, "Combining Sentences with Relative Clauses."

The relative pronouns are *who, whom, whose,* referring to persons, and *that* and *which,* referring to things. *Where* is sometimes used as a relative pronoun.

Who is used as the subject of a clause. *Whom* is used as the object or after a preposition.

The person *who* gets the highest score will win the prize. (subject)
The person *whom* I named will win the prize. (object)
The person *to whom* we give the prize must make a speech. (object of preposition)

In informal speech and writing, *that* may be substituted for *who* or *whom.*

The person *that* gets the highest score will win the prize. (subject)
The person *that* I named will win the prize. (object)

Whose is a possessive.

The person *whose* name was called won the prize.

That is used as the subject or object of a clause referring to things. (See above also.)

The book *that* was lost belongs to me. (subject)
I found the book *that* I lost. (object)

Which is used as the subject or object in nonrestrictive clauses (clauses giving additional information after a person or thing has been identified. See section A2e.).

The house, *which* hadn't been lived in for a year, looked deserted.
  (subject)
The book, *which* none of us had read, did not seem interesting.
  (object)

Which is also used as the object of the preposition or in possessives referring to things.

The chair on *which* you are sitting is an antique.

Generally the possessive of inanimate things is avoided.

The chair *with the broken leg* needs repair.

Where is sometimes used to replace *at which, in which, to which.*

The place *where* they met was far from here. (at which)
The room where the class is held is in another building. (in which)
The place *where* we are going is cool. (to which)

K. Forms and Qualifiers of Adjectives

Adjectives in English may change form only to show degree.

long   longer   longest
good   better   best

Adjectives of more than one syllable generally do not change form to show degree, but they are qualified or intensified, often by *more* or *most.*

expensive   more expensive   most expensive

Other common qualifiers of adjectives follow, arranged roughly so that those indicating a lesser degree of qualification are at the left and those indicating a greater degree of qualification are at the right:

a bit	enough	awfully	least
a little	less	indeed	most
just	more	pretty	so
more or less		quite	too
rather		really	very
somewhat			

Enough is generally placed after the adjective, unless the comparative form of the adjective is being used.

It is *good enough* to be worth the money.

but:

If it is *enough cheaper*, I'll buy it.

K32. EXPRESSIONS OF COMPARISON

Note the qualifying words used in the following expressions of comparison:

She is *taller than* I am.
He is *so tall that* he can touch the ceiling.
She is *old enough to* know better.
He is *too old to* do something like that.

CONVENTIONS IN THE MECHANICS OF WRITING

A. Punctuation

The general purpose of punctuation is to help make ideas clear to the reader. Use punctuation only when there is good reason for its use. Avoid overpunctuation, particularly the indiscriminate use of commas. Here are the standard rules.

A1. PERIOD (.)

1. A period signals the end of each sentence pattern that expresses a statement or a command. Do not place a period after a group of words, no matter how long, that is not a sentence pattern.
2. A period is used after abbreviations.

   Street: St.   Mister: Mr.   et cetera: etc.
   Doctor: Dr.   January: Jan.   (and so forth)

A2. QUESTION MARK (?)

1. A question mark is used after a question, even though the question may be phrased as a statement.

   How did he do it?
   He did?

2. Do not use a question mark after an indirect question, a request, or an included clause introduced by an interrogative word.

> He asked me how I did it.
> Please give me the book.
> I wonder why she said that.

A3. COMMA (,)

1. A comma is used between two sentence patterns joined by *and, but, or, for, nor,* and *so* unless these patterns are very short.

> I would like to accept your invitation, but I shall be out of town on that date.
> There was nothing more that we could do, so we went home.

2. A comma is used between items in a series. The series may be composed of single words, phrases, or clauses.

> The professor gave a long, dull, but exceedingly learned lecture.
> We looked in the house, in the garden, in the barn, and in the attic, but we could not find the cat.

3. A comma is used after word groups acting as modifiers if these word groups begin a sentence. Long word groups used as modifiers often occur at the beginning of a sentence pattern. Such elements are separated from the rest of the sentence by a comma.

> When we finally got home after our long trip, we felt as though we had never been away.
> Unused to so much excitement, the child fell asleep.

4. A comma is used around interrupting or parenthetical elements in a sentence. Following are common interrupting elements:

A. Nonrestrictive constructions (word groups giving information about a noun that has already been identified).

> This book, which I hope you will read soon, gives a complete account of that important event.
> The soldiers, weary and footsore, straggled up the road.

B. Expressions like *I think.*

This is, I believe, the first time such a thing has ever happened here.

5. A comma is used in the following miscellaneous conventions:

A. in dates

January 17, 1968

B. in addresses

1044 High Street, Albany, New York

C. after the name of a state when a city and state are mentioned together within a sentence

New Orleans, Louisiana, is my hometown.

D. in figures, to separate thousands

1,000 (or 1000)
10,000
15,500,000

E. with nouns in direct address

Look, John!
Yes, Mary, it is.

F. with titles and degrees

Mary Jones, M.D., LL.D.
John Jones, captain of the guard

G. after the salutation in informal letters

Dear Mother,

H. after the complementary close in letters

Sincerely yours,
Yours very truly,

I. with phrases introducing direct quotations

William said, "Come here."
"I don't know," Lee said, "of a better place."

J. to separate the sentence connectors *therefore, consequently, however,* and so on, from the rest of the clause in which they occur

Jim likes Pete; however, I do not care for him.
Jim likes Pete; I, however, do not care for him.
Jim likes Pete; I do not care for him, however.

Note the semicolons to mark the ends of the sentence patterns.

A4. SEMICOLON (;)

1. Use a semicolon between sentence patterns (two main clauses) that are closely connected in idea.

A. When the two patterns are not joined by any connective.

That is a good idea; I think we can use it.

B. When the two patterns are joined by a sentence connector.

The job was difficult; however, she did it well.

C. When the two patterns are joined by a conjunction (*and, but,* and so on), but each sentence pattern contains considerable internal punctuation.

I have not forgotten Washington, New York, San Francisco, and Las Vegas; nor have I forgotten my trips to Chicago, Los Angeles, and Spokane.

2. Use a semicolon to separate word groups that contain commas within them.

For officers we elected Rita Brown, the banker, as president; Cliff Burns, superintendent of schools, as vice-president; Mark Harmon, the well-known lawyer, as secretary; and Sy Granger, an officer of the milling company, as treasurer.

A5. COLON (:)

Whereas a semicolon separates, a colon introduces or directs attention to what is to follow.

1. A colon is used between two sentence patterns when the second pattern explains, restates, or amplifies the first.

They raised the tuition for one reason only: they could not operate on the current revenue.

2. A colon is used after a sentence pattern when an enumeration or an explanation is to follow.

   There are three ways to get there: by car, by bus, or by plane.

3. A colon is used in certain miscellaneous conventions:

   A. after the salutation in a formal letter

   Dear Mr. Jackson:

   B. between hours and minutes expressed in figures

   12:00
   2:45

   C. preceding long quoted passages

A6. DASH (—)

1. A dash marks a more abrupt break in thought than a comma. It is used to indicate an abrupt turn of idea and, often, parenthetical material.

   The students at this university—at least the ones that I have talked to—seem to have a sound knowledge of the subject.

2. A dash is used to emphasize a phrase or to make it dramatic.

   There is only one way to describe it—terrible!

A7. EXCLAMATION POINT (!)

An exclamation point is used after a forceful or emotional statement, whether it is a complete sentence pattern or not.

   Look out!
   How wonderful!

A8. QUOTATION MARKS (". . .") or ('. . .')

Quotation marks are always used in pairs. Both elements in the pair are placed above the line, as illustrated.

1. Double quotation marks are used to enclose direct quotations— the actual words of a speaker or writer.

   She said, "I believe this is a good solution to the problem."

2. Double quotation marks are used for short quotations from writers. However, long quotations are generally indented and single-spaced on the typewriter, but not enclosed in quotation marks.

3. Single quotation marks are used to mark a quotation within a quotation.

   The boy replied, "My father always told me, 'John, don't do anything hastily.' "

4. Double quotation marks are used within sentences to indicate the titles of works of art, short musical compositions and short poems, the chapters of a book, and so on.

   Leonardo da Vinci's "Mona Lisa"
   Edvard Grieg's "Piano Concerto in A Minor"

5. Double quotation marks are used to indicate a word used as an example in a sentence rather than for its meaning. Some writers prefer underscoring or italicizing such words.

   "Warbling" is a musical word.
   Look up the meaning of *isotope.*

6. Double quotation marks are used to indicate that a term is used by a particular person or group for a particular purpose. The writer may not agree with this use of the term, and shows it by his use of quotation marks.

   My "mechanical invention," like most of my other bright ideas, did not work.

A9. PARENTHESES ( )

1. Parentheses are used for explanatory remarks.
2. Parentheses are used around figures and letters to enumerate points in outlines or in a body of written material.

   Metaphors (suggested comparisons) are frequently used in poetry.
   You must try to (1) finish the project and (2) finish it on time.

A10. BRACKETS [ ]

Brackets are used to enclose explanations in material quoted from other writers. The words within brackets are clearly not those of the quoted writer.

"He [the American Indian] has left his stamp upon America."

A11. ELLIPSIS (. . .)

Three spaced periods indicate that one or more words have been omitted from quoted material. If the omission occurs at the end of a sentence, use three spaced periods to indicate the omission and follow them by another period to end the sentence.

A12. APOSTROPHE (')

1. An apostrophe is used in contractions. (Contractions are not generally favored in formal writing.)

   hasn't   didn't   o'clock   it's (it is)

2. An apostrophe is used in plurals of letters and figures.

   to's   i's   the 1400's (also the 1400s)

3. An apostrophe is used to indicate possession. In a plural word, and in a singular word of two or more syllables ending in -s, no extra s is added.

   Susan's coat   the children's coats
   the boy's coat   the boys' coats
   James's hat   Diogenes' lantern

4. An apostrophe is not used with *its, my, his,* and other possessive forms of pronouns.

A13. UNDERLINING

Underlining in typewriting or handwriting serves the same purpose as italics in printed material. Following are the uses of underlining.

1. Underline titles of books, plays, magazines, newspapers, long musical scores, and so on.

   Why We Behave Like Americans   *My Fair Lady*
   Harper's Magazine   Beethoven's *Ninth Symphony*
   The *New York Times*

2. Underline words used as words.

   Say *and* with emphasis.

3. Underline words from foreign languages when used in English sentences.

ad hoc
sine qua non
persona non grata

4. Underline words for emphasis. Reserve this for rare occasions, however.

B. Capitalization

1. The first word of a sentence should be capitalized. The first word of a direct quotation within a sentence is capitalized if the quotation is itself a complete sentence.
2. Capitalize proper names.

A. people—their names and titles (see G, which follows).
B. geographical places and the names of the people who live in these places

London, Londoners   India, Indians

C. languages and the names of school subjects deriving from languages

Italian   German   Portuguese   Japanese

D. days of the week, months of the year, and holidays, but not generally the names of centuries and not the names of the seasons

Sunday   Christmas   the fifteenth century
January   summer

E. names of structures, bridges, highways, and ships

the Montauk Highway   Rockefeller Center
Brooklyn Bridge   the S.S. *Queen Mary*

F. titles of school courses, but not the simple identification of a course

Speech 495   speech
Biology 111   biology
Survey of English Literature   literature

G. titles and words showing family relationships when with proper names, in direct address, and in direct reference without a noun marker

President Roosevelt   Doctor Jones   Aunt Mary
Good morning, Grandfather.
I received a letter from Mother.

but:

I visited the doctor today.
Which professor teaches English?
She received a letter from her mother.

H. important words (usually, all words except *a, the,* conjunctions, and prepositions of four letters or fewer when not at the beginning) in titles of books, magazines, newspapers, plays, and so on

The Second Tree from the Corner
Art and Literary Digest
Training in Business and Industry

I. racial, religious, and political groups

Negroes   Methodists   Democrats   Caucasians
(Note: *blacks* and *whites* are not capitalized.)

J. names of historical events and documents

the French Revolution   the Constitution

K. names of organizations

the Red Cross   Delta Tau Delta

L. words that refer to the deity

Jehovah   Him   His name
God   Who   Christ

M. the pronoun *I*

N. words that refer to the whole or parts of a body of land or water

the Western Hemisphere   the Grand Banks
the Indian Ocean   the South Pacific
the South (of the U.S.)   Western Europe

C. Acknowledging Borrowed Material and Ideas

C1. FOOTNOTES

In footnotes give the author's name, the title of the book or article, the edition, the place of publication, the publisher, the date of publication, and the page number of the material referred to. Use the following examples as models for punctuation, and punctuate consistently and exactly.

[1]Alfred Korzybski, *Science and Sanity*, 4th ed. (Clinton, Mass.: Colonial Press, 1973), 35.

[2]Muriel Sibell Wolle, *Stampede to Timberline*, rev. ed. (Chicago: Swallow Press, 1974), 21.

[3]Octavio Paz, *Conjunctions and Disjunctions*, trans. Helen R. Lane (New York: Viking, 1974), 14.

[4]Harold Goodglass and Sheila Blumstein, *Psycholinguistics and Aphasia* (Baltimore: Johns Hopkins University Press, 1973), 167.

[5]W. Ashton Ellis, *Correspondence of Wagner and Liszt*, vol. 1, 2d rev. ed., trans. Francis Hueffer (New York: Vienna House, 1973), 253.

[6]"Cities Where Business Is Best," *U.S. News & World Report* 77 (October 7, 1974): 78–81.

[7]*Encyclopaedia Britannica*, 11th ed., S.V., "airship."

C2. BIBLIOGRAPHY

List bibliographical items in alphabetical order by the author's last name, or by the first important word of the title if no author is given (*A* and *The* are not counted).

Fries, Charles C. *The Structure of English*. New York: Harcourt Brace Jovanovich, 1952, 240–255.

Information Please Almanac, 1947–1958. 2 vols. Garden City, N.Y.: Doubleday, 1947.

Leonard, George B. "Language and Reality," *Harper's Magazine* 249, (November 1974): 46–52.

Vidal, Gore. *Burr*. New York: Random House, 1973, 285–359.

D. Abbreviations

Here are common abbreviations used in writing, with an explanation of their meaning and suggestions for their use. Note that some abbreviations derived from Latin terms are not set in italics.

- ed.—edition, editor, edited by
- e.g. *(exempli gratia)*—"for example"
- ibid. *(ibidem)*—"in the same place" as the immediately preceding reference. If the page reference is not the same, then use: Ibid., 25.
- i.e. *(id est)*—"that is"
- loc. cit. *(loco citato)*—"in the place cited." Suppose reference has been made to the book *Excellence* by John Gardner. Then reference is made to works by Smith, Eiseley, and Jones. Following this is a reference to the work already referred to by Gardner. The reference would look like this: Gardner, loc. cit.
- op. cit. *(opere citato)*—"in the work cited." Suppose a reference has been made to something on page 12 of Gardner's *Excellence* and then one or more references are made to other works. Later you wish to refer to another passage in Gardner's book. The entry might look like this: Gardner, op. cit., 56.
- p.—page
- passim—"here and there"
- pp.—pages
- rev. ed.—revised edition
- s.v. *(sub. verbs)*—under the word
- tr., trans.—translator, translated by
- vol. (vols.)—volume (volumes)

WRITING FOR SPECIAL ASSIGNMENTS

A. The Evaluative Essay

In college courses you may be called upon to write evaluative essays expressing your opinion about what someone else has written or about a speech someone has given. You may have to evaluate a piece of research or an experiment in a scientific field, or an essay or speech explaining or offering a solution to a social or political problem. You may have to analyze a piece of literature or judge another writer's analysis.

Many of the techniques are the same as those for writing any other essay. Below are some that apply particularly to the evaluative essay. Since you will be expressing an opinion, know your overall impression before you write. Nothing is either totally good or totally bad, but generally a critic thinks that it was nearer good than bad or nearer bad than good.

A1. INTRODUCING THE SUBJECT

About one-fourth of your paper should be devoted to telling your reader about the work you are evaluating. In this part of the essay do these things:

1. Give introductory facts about the work.

   A. Is it a speech, an essay, a painting, a play?
   B. Does it deal with scientific research, politics, literature?
   C. Who is the author or speaker, or who did the research?

    D. Where is it reported or published or, if a speech, where was it given?

    E. Who are the intended readers or audience?

2. Acquaint the reader with the subject. State the point of view of the writer or the purpose he or she is trying to fulfill, and briefly summarize the main points.

A2. EVALUATING ASPECTS OF THE SUBJECT AGAINST A STANDARD

About three-fourths of the paper should be devoted to the evaluation. The aspects you will discuss vary with the type of work you are evaluating. Here are some common aspects that critics consider.

1. Scientific research

    A. Was the research on a significant subject? Was it timely? Needed?

    B. Was it the result of a justifiable hypothesis?

    C. Did the project require controlled conditions? If so, were these maintained?

    D. Are the results recorded and interpreted correctly, and are the conclusions justified?

2. Essay on a social or political problem

    A. Is the writer's main point clearly stated?

    B. Does the writer give adequate support for his or her generalizations and assertions?

    C. Is the reasoning sound? If it is deductive, is the major premise— the generalization on which the writer bases the conclusion— one that the reader will accept? Does the conclusion follow logically from the premises? If the order is cause and effect, is there evidence that the situation described is really produced by the causes given? If the essay contains reasoning by analogy, are the two situations really similar?

    D. Are the facts, figures, and examples verifiable? Are they representative of other similar situations?

3. A literary work

    A. Is the dominating impression of interest and value?

    B. How well does the form or structure contribute to the total effect?

C. If the work is a narrative, how do plot, setting, and character help develop the theme?

D. How skillfully does the author use special techniques to achieve his purpose?

If the work is presented orally rather than in writing, here are additional points to consider:

1. A speech

A. Was the subject worth talking about? Did the speaker make her subject clear? Was the speaker qualified to speak on her subject?

B. Was the speech organized so that the thought could be followed easily?

C. Did the speaker develop his ideas with enough concrete material to make them clear and convincing and to hold your interest?

D. Was the speech delivered with voice and action that made the ideas clearer and more impressive?

2. A play

A. Was the characterization convincingly conceived by the playwright? Convincingly executed by the actors?

B. Did the plot contribute to the playwright's purpose?

C. Did the lighting effects, the scenery, the costuming, and the pace contribute to the playwright's purpose?

A3. SUPPORTING YOUR OPINIONS

Use the forms of support you have studied—facts, a line of reasoning, quotation from authority, figures, and so on—to convince your reader of the soundness of your evaluation.

B. The Essay Examination

Many students write an answer to an essay examination like a jackrabbit startled by a hunter. They begin putting words down on paper before they have collected their wits, before they have planned what they want to say. Here are some suggestions for applying what you have learned in this composition class to the writing of essay examination answers. We must assume, of course, that you know the subject matter.

1. When you receive the examination questions, read all of them before you start to write. Pay special attention to the directions.

   A. Discover whether you are asked to answer all the questions, to answer a certain number of them, or to choose alternatives.

   B. If you have a choice of questions, decide at once which ones you feel best qualified to answer. Cross out the numbers of the questions you will omit, so that you will not inadvertently spend time on one you did not intend to answer.

   C. Figure out at this point how much time you have to answer each question. Then as you write, allow yourself equal time for each question. Leave a little space at the end of each answer so that if you finish easy questions in less than the allotted time you can go back and spend the extra time on a difficult question.

2. Before you start to answer a question, read the question carefully to discover exactly what information the instructor is asking for. Look for *key words,* such as the ones explained here:

   • Compare: Emphasize similarities. But in case the instructor is using the word in a general sense, you might mention differences too.

   • Contrast: Stress differences in things, events, problems.

   • Criticize or evaluate: In criticizing, express your own judgment—for and against. In evaluating, give the judgment of authorities as well as your own.

   • Define: Be clear, brief, accurate. Give the limits of the definition. Show how the thing you are defining differs from others in its class.

   • Describe: Often this means to tell or recount in sequence or story form. Or it may mean to give a description.

   • Diagram: Give a drawing. Label the parts, with perhaps a brief description.

   • Discuss: Examine carefully; give reasons for and against in discussion form.

   • Enumerate (list): These words mean the same thing. Present the points briefly in a list.

- Explain: Make clear what is meant. You may want to give reasons for differences in results or opinions.
- Justify: Give reasons for conclusions or decisions. Try to convince the reader.
- Outline: Organize in outline form with main points and subpoints. The main point here is to classify things in brief form.
- Prove: Give logical reasons or evidence that a thing is true.
- Relate: Show the connection between two things.
- Review (state, summarize): These terms mean much the same thing—to give main points, usually omitting details. A *review* may imply examining a subject critically.
- Trace: Describe the development or progress of events from some point in the past; that is, put into chronological order.

3. Plan your answer before you start to write. Rephrase the question in statement form. This statement becomes your topic sentence. On the back of your examination paper jot down key words that remind you of the main points you should discuss.
4. Now you are ready to write. Here are some things to remember:

   A. Include only material that is relevant. Do not waste time telling your instructor things he did not ask for.
   B. Make your ideas clear by supporting your generalizations and assertions with details that develop or support them. If possible, cite references (authorities or texts) to support what you say.
   C. Avoid one-sentence answers. An essay-type question requires an essay-type answer.

5. Reread your answers at the end of the examination period. Check to see if you have said what you intended to say. You may think of an example or have some important comment that you can insert in the margin or between the lines.
6. Make your paper as readable as possible. Write as legibly as you can. Preferably use a pen, but if you have to use a pencil, make sure it has a soft enough lead to make the writing easy to see. Provide enough equipment so that you do not have to spend examination time in borrowing something to write with.

C. The Business Letter

People who receive business letters find it much easier to understand the letters quickly and to file them for future reference if the writer follows certain conventions.

1. Rhetorical conventions

   A. State the reason for the letter in the first sentence.
   B. Briefly explain necessary matters.
   C. In all you say, be courteous. This courtesy should be apparent throughout the letter, but especially in the last sentence.

2. Conventions concerning stationery and form

   A. Write on 8½-by-11 inch, white, unlined paper.
   B. Write in ink or, preferably, on the typewriter.
   C. Space the letter neatly on the page.
   D. In the sample letter that follows this section, note the necessary information at the beginning regarding the writer and the person to whom the letter is addressed. Use block form for giving this information, and sequence the information as illustrated.

3. Conventions of punctuation and capitalization

   A. Do not put any kind of punctuation at the ends of lines except after abbreviated words such as *company* (Co.), *incorporated* (Inc.), *street* (St.), or *avenue* (Ave.).
   B. Here are conventions for salutations:

   Dear Mr. White:
   Dear Ms. Adams: (for either a married or an unmarried woman)
   Dear Sir:
   Gentlemen:

   C. Conventions for the complimentary close (immediately preceding the writer's signature) are as follows:

   Yours truly, (very formal)
   Very truly yours, (very formal)
   Sincerely yours, (the most commonly used)
   Cordially yours, (for business acquaintances you know very well)

Sign a business letter in handwriting, but type or print the name below the signature so that a reply can be correctly addressed.

D. Conventions for signing the letter are

Craig R. Conway (a man)
Ellen R. Wallis (an unmarried woman)
Sara Conway Marshall (the middle name is the woman's family name)
Sara C. Marshall (Mrs. Carl G.) (a married woman identifying herself by giving her husband's name)

Sample business letter

913 Columbus Avenue
Chicago, Illinois 50601
October 15, 1983

Mr. Roderick Blair
President
Blair Furniture Co., Inc.
1605 West 77th Street
New York City, N. Y. 10022

Dear Mr. Blair:

On March 13 I ordered from your firm an upholstered recliner chair, which the salesman, Mr. Anthony Reed, promised to deliver by August 9. I have waited for two months past the promised delivery date, and the chair is still not here. Since I have neither heard from your firm nor received the chair, I ask you to look into the matter and send me word. I do thank you for this courtesy.

Sincerely yours,

John L. Mitchell

D. The Library Research Paper

Often you will be asked to write a paper in which you present the results of your reading about a topic. Your paper may be a summary of information about a subject gained entirely from reading, or you may use facts from your reading to supplement what you already know or to develop or support your own point of view on a topic. Many of the problems in writing such a paper—selecting a topic, narrowing it to suit the scope of your paper, stating the thesis or purpose clearly, organizing the material, and developing points adequately—are identical with those that have been discussed so far. There are particular problems, however, that result from the use of library material.

D1. LOCATING SOURCES OF INFORMATION

Following is a list of suggested sources of material in American libraries:

1. *Encyclopedias.* Encyclopedia articles are often valuable for an overview of the entire subject. These articles are extremely condensed and cover a wide area without going into great detail. Thus a paper in which you present a limited area or a particular point of view in some detail can rarely be based solely on an article in an encyclopedia.

2. Readers' Guide, *or other periodical indexes, or indexes in special subject-matter fields.* The *Readers' Guide* indexes articles from periodicals covering a wide variety of fields. It is brought up to date semimonthly. Articles are listed by author, title, and subject. The subject entries may be most useful. You may want to consult the reference librarian for special indexes in the field you are researching.

3. *Card catalog.* The card catalog indexes books by author, title, and subject. Usually the best way to begin is by looking under the general subject you are writing on. The cards in the catalog genrally give the table of contents of books. This may help you determine whether the book will be of use to you. Generally, though, if an entire book has been written on the aspect of the subject you are going to write about, the subject is too large for your paper.

4. *File of pamphlets and clippings.* Often the reference librarian can direct you to a file of clippings and other miscellaneous items that do not appear in the card catalog. This file is also usually in alphabetical order by subject.

5. *Microfilm or microfiche duplications* of articles in various fields. These need to be read in a microfilm reader. Your librarian can tell you where these are located.

6. *Bibliographical lists in books and articles.* An often overlooked source of further material on your subject is the bibliography that often appears at the end of an article or at the end of a chapter of a book.

When using these sources to find material, record the *author, title, publisher,* and *date of publication* of any reference you think you may use. You will need the information later in making a bibliography and giving credit for material that you used in your paper.

D2. LOCATING PERTINENT MATERIAL IN THE SOURCES

When you have collected a preliminary bibliography of material on your subject, you must next determine what you need to read carefully and possibly take notes on and what you can reject. From the card catalog you may have found chapters of books that you can go to directly. The entire chapter may not serve your purpose, however. Look at the subdivisions of the chapters if they are indicated; then read the opening and summary paragraphs. This procedure will also save you time in reading material from periodicals.

D3. EXTRACTING INFORMATION AND TAKING NOTES

Three major points to remember when note-taking are: (1) Do not take too many notes. (2) Sort out separate pieces of information that may go into different parts of your paper. (3) Take notes in your own words. This last point is the most important. If you take notes in the words of the author, these words tend to be transferred to the finished paper. The paper, then, is not wholly your own. The following suggestions may aid you:

1. Read the sections of your source books and articles that you have decided may be pertinent to your purpose. Then *take notes after you finish reading.* If you take notes as you read the first time, you may not be selective about what you take notes on, and you waste time copying down material you may never use.
2. *Take notes in brief form.* You may want to outline a passage, following the author's line of thinking, or summarize an example or illustration. Summarizing is essentially a matter of removing redundancies.

3. Take your notes on cards, or small sheets of paper, putting *one fact, one quotation,* or *summary of one point* on a card. Later as you organize your paper, you can arrange your notes according to the section of the paper where you can best use the material.

4. Your *organizational pattern* may be clear in your mind before you gather your material, or it may become clear as you find material related to your subject and decide how it can best be put together. As you work out your pattern, sort your notes and *label each card* or slip of paper *according to the section of the paper where the material* on it *best fits.*

5. On each note card *make a notation indicating the source* of the material. This is particularly important, as you will want to footnote much of the material gained from your reading, and you will need all information, including page numbers, in the source. You may want to make the reference on the note card brief, if the complete reference is indicated in your bibliography and may be referred to for footnoting.

6. If you are copying a passage that you expect to quote, write down the material *exactly* as the author wrote it, and *put quotation marks around it.*

D4. INTEGRATING THE MATERIAL INTO A COMPOSITION

Integrating material that you have read into a composition you write is one of the most difficult problems in writing a library research paper, especially for students who do not feel completely at home in the language in which they are writing. The tendency is to copy large pieces of material word for word from the source; the reasoning is that since a native speaker of English presumably wrote it, the English must be correct. If you do this, however, *you* have not written the essay; the author of your source has written part of it for you. Moreover, you may be guilty of plagiarism—that is, presenting the work of someone else as though it were your own. Any extensive amount of plagiarism is an offense punishable by law. Many college professors watch for plagiarism, and they will give a failing grade to the writer of a paper containing large portions of material that the student has not formulated himself or put in the form of quotations with credit to the sources.

How, then, can you use facts, figures, explanations, summaries, examples, and illustrations from your reading in a legitimate way, integrating them into a composition that you can present as your own? Here are some guiding principles:

1. Your paper should be your own in its *purpose,* its *organization,* and the *collection of material* it presents.

   A. Your *purpose* should be your own. You have taken a point of view toward your subject, either before you begin to look for material or in the process of gathering it. It reflects what *you,* not the author of one of your sources, plan to present. A helpful suggestion may be to turn your topic into a question; then read to find the answer. Your paper is your presentation of the answer.

   B. Your *organizational plan* for fulfilling your purpose is your own. Because you are not following exactly what any one person said in any one selection that you have read, your main points will not be exactly the same as those of any other writer on the subject.

   C. Your *material*—facts, figures, illustrations, and so on—will be gathered from various sources, not just from one. If it comes from only one source, you have merely given a summary of what one person said, and this rarely fulfills an assignment to "find out all you can about a subject and report on it," which is what is expected in most term papers. Your *collection of material* and the way in which it is presented must be your own.

2. In using material taken from your reading, *do not use the words of someone else without quoting, do not paraphrase long passages* without indicating clearly that you are doing so, and *do not merely piece together a series of paraphrases* from a number of sources.

   A. It is *legitimate to use the words of another person* if he has said what you want to say better than you can say it or if you want to report his opinion or viewpoint *exactly as he presented it. Use quotation marks* and a *footnote.* Introduce your quotation by words such as "Ross and Doty say, '. . . .' "

   B. There are occasions on which *you may wish to paraphrase*—that is, to report what someone else said but in your own words. If you want to report someone else's ideas or report work someone else has done *to support an idea of* your own, *precede the paraphrase by words indicating what you are doing.* Even more than with quotations, it is important to say in the body of your paper, for instance, "(author) reports that. . . ." or other similar expression, followed by your own words. *Use a footnote* to give the exact source.

C. Since your paper is your own, it should be written in your own words. If you try to put together notes from various sources in words close to those used in the source, the paper will not fit together well. Also, as indicated in the preceding paragraph, credit should be given for paraphrased passages.

3. To have a smoothly written paper that is your own, yet that presents ideas and material taken from other authors, it is often advisable to reread your notes, determine what you want to say, then *write your paper with as little reference as possible to your notes* except to verify a fact or introduce material you wish to quote. You have read on your subject, have mastered it, and are now an "authority" on it in a minor way. You can put together what you have gained from your reading and what you already knew about the subject, possibly from first-hand experience or perhaps from earlier reading. What you have just read and what you already knew become blended.

D5. GIVING PROPER CREDIT TO SOURCES

Giving proper credit to your sources has been discussed in part in the preceding section. In general one should footnote direct quotations, paraphrases, and little-known facts or facts that someone might possibly question. The footnoting of quotations and paraphrases has already been discussed. The footnoting of facts is not quite as clear-cut. Are they relatively unknown? Might the reader want to verify them? Do you want the authority of the source in which you found them to support you in your use of them?

You might study the use of footnoting in this book. Passages for study that have been taken word for word from another source are footnoted. Others might say, "Adapted from (name of author and source)." In writing some of the passages for study in the lessons, the authors in some cases relied on published sources for the facts, but the passages were rewritten to illustrate grammatical principles. When the passage is based on one source, it is footnoted to indicate the source. When a passage is based on general reading or on first-hand observation, no footnoting is used.

Note that in writing a research paper the author of that paper has sole responsibility for the format of the acknowledgments in the footnotes and the bibliography. Since this is so, the format of these acknowledgments should be consistent. The correct form for footnotes and bibliography is indicated on page 292. You may wish to follow, instead, one of the common form sheets, such as the Modern Language Association style sheet. There are variations in recommended forms. The authors of commercial writing, such as textbooks, must follow the format prescribed by the holder of the copyright; therefore, since copyright holders differ in the format they approve, the form of footnotes in such books is often inconsistent.

You may run into other problems in writing term papers and theses. The point in the preparation process at which you can finally limit your topic and state it specifically is difficult to determine because it depends in part on the material that you are able to find. Determining the organizational pattern is also affected by this. The four points covered, however, are those that are peculiar to writing papers based on reading and that seem to cause the greatest problems for native users of the language—and perhaps even greater ones for those studying English as a foreign language.

A final word: Do not quote and do not paraphrase unless you give your source. An entire paper should not be made of paraphrases and quotations.

Index

Note: The page numbers in italic refer to the pages on which exercises appear.